SEXUAL ETHICS AND THE NEW TESTAMENT

COMPANIONS TO THE NEW TESTAMENT

SEXUAL ETHICS
AND THE
NEW TESTAMENT

Behavior and Belief

RAYMOND F. COLLINS

A Herder and Herder Book
The Crossroad Publishing Company
New York

For Mary and Marie,
Beacons of Humanity
in a Hostile Environment

The Crossroad Publishing Company
370 Lexington Avenue, New York, NY 10017

Printed in the United States of America

Library of Congress Cataloging-in-Publication Data

Collins, Raymond F., 1935
    Sexual ethics and the New Testament : behavior and belief / Raymond
F. Collins.
        p.   cm.   (Companions to the New Testament)
    Includes bibliographical references and index.
    ISBN 0-8245-1801-2
    1. Sex Biblical teaching.   2. Sexual ethics Biblical teaching.
3. Christian life Catholic authors.   4. Bible. N.T. Criticism,
interpretation, etc.   I. Title.   II. Series.

BS 2545.S36 C65 2000
241'.66 dc21
                                                        99-053598

1   2   3   4   5   6   7   8   9   10   04   03   02   01   00

Contents

Preface to the Series

THE COMPANIONS TO THE NEW TESTAMENT SERIES aims to unite New Testament study with theological concerns in a clear and concise manner. Each volume:

- engages the New Testament text directly
- focuses on the religious (theological/ethical) content of the New Testament
- is written out of respect for the integrity of the religious tradition being studied. This means that the New Testament is studied in terms of its own time and place. It is allowed to speak in its own terms, out of its own assumptions, espousing its own values.
- involves cutting-edge research, bringing the results of scholarly discussions to the general reader
- provides resources for the reader who wishes to enter more deeply into the scholarly discussion.

The contributors to the series are established scholars who have studied and taught the New Testament for many years and who can now reap a wide-ranging harvest from the fruits of their labors. Multiple theological perspectives and denominational identities are represented. Each author is free to address the issues from his or her own social and religious location, within the parameters set for the series.

It is our hope that these small volumes will make some contribution to the recovery of the vision of the New Testament world for our time.

Charles H. Talbert
Baylor University

Preface

HUMAN SEXUALITY IS A COMPLEX REALITY that permeates any person's entire human existence. There exists no single prism from which to look at human sexuality. It can be studied from the anatomical, biological, economic, ethical, physiological, psychological, relational, and sociological points of view, to mention but a few vantage points from which one might choose to examine the mysterious reality that is human sexuality.

Looking at human sexuality through the lenses provided by the authors of the New Testament, a reader obtains some insight as to how the disciple of Jesus is called to live out his or her existence as a sexual being and as a disciple of Jesus, but there is no easy answer as to how sexuality and discipleship relate to one another. As a sexual being, the Christian is called to be a disciple. As a disciple, the Christian is called to live a sexual existence.

The study that is offered in these pages makes no claim to be a systematic presentation of Christian sexual ethics. Rather it seeks to allow the texts of the New Testament themselves to speak their piece and provide the insights on the basis of which a Christian sexual ethics might be developed. This book is a study of the pertinent texts. Using a historical-critical method of exegesis, it looks to the meaning of the relevant New Testament texts in their own historical and literary contexts.

Each of those contexts is exceedingly complex. The texts of the New Testament were written during a period of time that was almost a full century long. The texts echo traditions and stories that go back to Jesus

himself and beyond him to the people whose life he shared as one committed to the God of Abraham, Isaac, and Jacob. For the most part, the
texts were written for Christians living in the Hellenistic culture of
the Greco-Roman world. The message that they imparted was deeply
embedded within that world. Religiously informed but culturally produced, the New Testament texts that deal with sexuality sometimes
embrace the sexual stereotypes and biases of the cultures within which
they were produced. At other times they confront the mores of the
times and the standards of the day. The Christian communities within
which the New Testament authors lived were communities that lived
in time and space. Each of the communities was different from the others. Each had its own problems within and its pressures from without.
Some of the earliest texts produced by the New Testament authors
were written at a time when the disciples of Jesus were expecting an
imminent parousia. Others were written as the frontiers of the gospel
moved into the strange world of Hellenism. Some of the later texts
were written at a time when the Christian churches were beginning to
redefine themselves for the long haul of history, now some two mil-
lennia long. Some of them sought to accommodate the tradition to the
ethos of a Hellenistic world that had long since captured the day.

Were the history within which the various texts of the New Testament a simple one, this study would be somewhat less complex than
it is. Yet even if that were the case, the study of the texts could hardly
be simple and systematic. Each of the twenty-seven books of the New
Testament has its own identity and its own point of view. None of the
books has a treatise on sexual ethics as such. Perhaps 1 Corinthians
5–7 comes closest to being such a treatise. Paul's words of advice on sex
cover a fairly broad range of related issues and are culturally conditioned. To a large extent they respond to specific sexual problems
about which the apostle had been informed (1 Cor. 5:1; 7:1).

For the most part what the New Testament has to say about sexual
ethics is to be found in texts with several different literary genres.
There are stories about Jesus and there are letters. There is catechetical material and there are conflict stories. There are lists of virtues and
lists of vices. There is parenesis and there are midrashic explanations
of biblical traditions. There are bits of practical advice and words that
speak of the qualities that one would expect to find in a member of the
Christian household. Each of the literary genres within which ethical
material is contained carries with it its own hermeneutical challenge.

To read the pertinent texts within their own historical and literary contexts is to read them in the language in which they were written. For most of us that is a nearly impossible task. Even those who can read the Greek of a Mark or a Paul are hard pressed to capture the precise nuance of the author's words. Most of us must approach the texts of the New Testament with the help of a translation. This study approaches the texts with the help of the New Revised Standard Version of the New Testament. It is the version of the New Testament that the author of the study finds to be of the greatest help in bringing understanding to the ancient texts. This valuable tool is, however, but a translation. Its rendering of the meaning of the texts is not always quite as nuanced as a detailed study of the sexual ethics of the New Testament requires. Reference to the Greek language of the New Testament texts is intended to help the reader remember that the focus of this study is the meaning of the New Testament texts themselves.

No scholar can afford to live in an ivory tower. Neither Jesus nor the rabbis of old lived in isolation when they taught about human sexuality. Neither Paul nor the disciples who produced the Pauline pseudepigrapha worked in a vacuum. No more than Jesus and the rabbis or Paul and his disciples was the author of this study able to work in isolation. Nor did he want to.

Beyond my gratitude to the editors of the New Revised Standard Version of the Bible who have provided the biblical text used in this book, I am most grateful to James N. Rhodes, my graduate assistant, who did so much legwork and who deleted from the work the errors of wandering eyes and arthritic fingers. I am likewise grateful to Ms. Joan Fricot, a lecturer at Johnson & Wales University, who ferreted out the grammatical errors and the stylistic inconsistencies. I am grateful to Dr. Charles Talbert of Baylor University, the general editor of the series, not only for the invitation to do the study but also for seeing it through to publication. Finally, I am most grateful to Ms. Mary Dancy and Mrs. Marie Vignali, my assistants during a six-year tenure as dean of the School of Religious Studies at The Catholic University of America, who supported me in my multiple activities as scholar, professor, and dean. This study is but a token of my gratitude to them.

Abbreviations

Pseudepigrapha

Apoc. Abr.	*Apocalypse of Abraham*
3 Apoc. Bar.	*Apocalypse of Baruch,* Greek
1–2 Enoch	*Ethiopic, Slavonic Enoch*
Ep. Arist.	*Epistle of Aristeas*
Jub.	*Jubilees*
Pss. Sol.	*Psalms of Solomon*
Sib. Or.	*Sibylline Oracles*
T. Benj.	*Testament of Benjamin*
T. Dan.	*Testament of Dan*
T. Gad	*Testament of Gad*
T. Iss.	*Testament of Issachar*
T. Jos.	*Testament of Joseph*
T. Jud.	*Testament of Judah*
T. Levi	*Testament of Levi*
T. Naph.	*Testament of Naphtali*
T. Reub.	*Testament of Reuben*
T. Sim.	*Testament of Simeon*

Mishnaic and Rabbinic Literature

1. Names of tractates (preceded by *m.* [= Mishnah], *b.* [= Babylonian Talmud], *y.* [= Jerusalem Talmud], or *t.* [= Tosefta]

ʿ*Abod. Zar.*	*Aboda Zara*	*Ber.*	*Berakot*
ʾ*Abot*	ʾ*Abot*	*B. Meṣ.*	*Baba Meṣiʿa*

Giṭ.	_Giṭṭin_	Qidd.	_Qiddušin_
Ḥal.	_Ḥalla_	Sanh.	_Sanhedrin_
Ker.	_Keritot_	Shab.	_Shabbat_
Ketub.	_Ketubim_	Soṭa	_Soṭa_
Meg.	_Megillot_	Tamid	_Tamid_
Ned.	_Nedarim_	Yebam.	_Yebamot_
Nid.	_Niddah_	Yoma	_Yoma_
Pes.	_Pesaḥim_		

2. Other Rabbinic Writings

Deut. Rab.	_Deuteronomy Rabbah_
Exod. Rab.	_Exodus Rabbah_
Lev. Rab.	_Leviticus Rabbah_
Mek.	_Mekilta_
Num. Rab.	_Numbers Rabbah_
Pesiq. R.	_Pesiqta Rabbati_
Sipra Lev.	_Sipra Leviticus_
Sipre Deut.	_Sipre Deuteronomy_
Sipre Lev.	_Sipre Leviticus_

Other Jewish Literature

CD	Cairo (Genizah text of the) _Damascus Document_
1QS	(Qumran) _Manual of Discipline_

Early Patristic Literature

Barn.	_Barnabas_
2 Clem.	_2 Clement_
Did.	_Didache_
Herm. Man.	_Hermas, Mandates_
Herm. Sim.	_Hermas, Similitudes_
Ign. Eph.	Ignatius, _Letter to the Ephesians_
Ign. Magn.	Ignatius, _Letter to the Magnesians_

Periodicals, Reference Works, and Serials

AB	Anchor Bible
ABD	_Anchor Bible Dictionary_
ABRL	Anchor Bible Reference Library
ACNT	Augsburg Commentary on the New Testament
AGJU	Arbeiten zur Geschichte des antiken Judentums und des Urchristentums

ANET	*Ancient Near Eastern Texts,* ed. James Pritchard
ANTC	Abingdon New Testament Commentary
AusBR	*Australian Biblical Review*
AV	Authorized Version
BETL	Bibliotheca Ephemeridum theologicarum Lovaniensium
Bib	*Biblica*
BibSac	*Bibliotheca Sacra*
BT	*Bible Translator*
BTB	*Biblical Theology Bulletin*
BZ	*Biblische Zeitschrift*
CBQ	*Catholic Biblical Quarterly*
CEV	Contemporary English Version
CRINT	Compendia rerum iudaicarum ad Novum Testamentum
CSCO	Corpus scriptorum christianorum orientalium
DR	*Downside Review*
EBib	Études bibliques
EDNT	*Exegetical Dictionary of the New Testament,* ed. Horst Balz and Gerhard Schneider
EncJud	*Encyclopedia Judaica*
ETL	*Ephemerides theologicae Lovanienses*
EvT	*Evangelische Theologie*
FNT	*Filología Neotestamentaria*
GNS	Good News Studies
HBT	*Horizons in Biblical Theology*
HNTC	Harper's New Testament Commentary
HTCNT	Herder's Theological Commentary on the New Testament
HTKNT	Herders theologischer Kommentar zum Neuen Testament
HTR	*Harvard Theological Review*
HUCA	*Hebrew Union College Annual*
ICC	International Critical Commentary
JB	Jerusalem Bible
JETS	*Journal of the Evangelical Theological Society*
JSNT	*Journal for the Study of the New Testament*
JSOT	*Journal for the Study of the Old Testament*
LCL	Loeb Classical Library
LS	*Louvain Studies*
LTPM	Louvain Theological and Pastoral Monographs
LXX	The Greek Bible (the Septuagint)
MAL	Middle Assyrian Laws
MM	*The Vocabulary of the Greek Testament,* by James H. Moulton and George Milligan
MT	Masoretic Text
NAB	New American Bible
NCB	New Century Bible

NEB	New English Bible
NIBC	New International Bible Commentary
NIGTC	New International Greek Testament Commentary
NIV	New International Version
NKJV	New King James Version
NovTSup	Supplements to *Novum Testamentum*
NRSV	New Revised Standard Version
NTD	Das Neue Testament Deutsch
NTS	*New Testament Studies*
PG	*Patrologia graeca*, ed. J.-P. Migne
PL	*Patrologia latina*, ed. J.-P. Migne
QD	Quaestiones disputatae
REB	Revised English Bible
RivB	*Rivista Biblica*
RSV	Revised Standard Version
SacPag	Sacra Pagina
SB	*Sources bibliques*
SBLDS	Society of Biblical Literature Dissertation Series
SCHNT	Studia ad corpus hellenisticum Novi Testamenti
SNTSMS	Society for New Testament Studies Monograph Series
SNTSU	Studien zum Neuen Testament und seiner Umwelt
SR	*Studies in Religion/Sciences religieuses*
Str-B	Hermann Strack and Paul Billerbeck, *Kommentar zum Neuen Testament aus Talmud und Midrasch*
SUNT	Studien zur Umwelt des neuen Testaments
SVF	*Stoicorum Veterum Fragmenta*, ed. Hans Friedrich August von Arnim
TD	*Theology Digest*
TDNT	*Theological Dictionary of the New Testament*, ed. Gerhard Kittel and Gerhard Friedrich
THKNT	Theologischer Handkommentar zum Neuen Testament
TLNT	Ceslas Spicq, *Theological Lexicon of the New Testament*
TPIC	Trinity Press International Commentary
TPINTC	Trinity Press International New Testament Commentary
USQR	*Union Seminary Quarterly Review*
VC	*Vigiliae Christianae*
WBC	Word Biblical Commentary
ZAW	*Zeitschrift für die alttestamentliche Wissenschaft*
ZNW	*Zeitschrift für die neutestamentliche Wissenschaft*

1

Stories about Jesus

HE MOST RECENT OF THE CANONICAL GOSPELS, the Gospel according to John, tells a marvelous little story (John 7:53–8:11) that illustrates very well Jesus' attitude toward sex and ethics.[1] The story is the tale of the woman caught in adultery. As the storyteller begins to narrate the tale, he says that the crowds who had observed Jesus' confrontation with the representatives of the Pharisees on the previous day had returned to their homes (7:53). Jesus repaired to the Mount of Olives for reasons unstated but presumably to pray. At daybreak Jesus returns to the temple mount. All the people come to Jesus. He sits down and proceeds to teach them.

A CASE STUDY

What the narrator is about to present is a case study in sexual ethics. The setting of the scene is carefully structured. The scene is the temple mount. The audience is "all the people." Jesus sits down to teach them. This is the first time that "the people" (*ho laos*) appear in the Fourth Gospel. It is the only time that "all the people" (*pas ho laos*) appear and the only time that Jesus assumes the rabbinic posture of sitting down to teach.[2] These three factors—the place, the audience, and the formal posture of the teacher—accentuate the lesson that is about to be taught. It is presented in the form of a case study.

The scribes and the Pharisees bring to Jesus a woman discovered in the very act of adultery. Caught *in flagrante delicto*, the woman is

1

brought to Jesus and made to stand in front of the crowd. Because Jesus is presented as being on the temple mount, one might expect the presence of some Sadducees. It is, however, the Pharisees and scribes who bring the woman to Jesus. The Pharisees are that group of first-century C.E. Jews who were noted for their attention to the observance of the law. The scribes were their legal experts, particularly trained in the interpretation of the Torah.

The Pharisees and their scholars address Jesus as "Teacher" (*didaskale*). This form of address, used in the narrative setting that has been developed for the story, presents a scenario in which the teacher is expected to give his teaching. As formulated by the scribes and Pharisees, the case is that of "a woman who had been caught in the very act of adultery" (John 8:4). With regard to such a case, the law is clear: "Moses commanded us to stone such women." Jesus is asked to adjudicate the case: "Now what do you say?"

Even without reading the narrator's observation that they had said this to test him (John 8:6), the reader of the narrative is well aware that this is really a test case. The teacher himself is under scrutiny. How is he to judge a case in which the law is so clear? And clear it was. Not only did the Decalogue[3] prohibit adultery (Exod. 20:14; Deut. 5:18); punishment for the crime was also stipulated in the law. Adultery was a capital crime for which the death penalty was mandated.[4] The law says, "if a man commits adultery with the wife of his neighbor, both the adulterer and the adulteress shall be put to death" (Lev. 20:10).[5] A later collection of Israelite law was equally specific in this regard: "If a man is caught lying with the wife of another man, both of them shall die, both the man who lay with the woman as well as the woman. So you shall purge the evil from Israel" (Deut. 22:22).[6]

These provisions of the law of Moses were consistent with those codes of ancient Near Eastern law which considered adultery to be a "great crime."[7] It was commonly stipulated that both the adulterer and his consort were to be put to death. The Code of Hammurabi[8] and Assyrian laws[9] set out the death penalty as the punishment for adultery but leave some discretion to the aggrieved husband in this regard. Deuteronomy's codicil, "so you shall purge the evil from Israel," indicates that a similar discipline was to be enforced in the land of God's people. The death penalty was to be enforced so that the land of Israel might be holy unto the Lord. This codicil implies that responsibility for the punishment of adultery lay within the public domain.

Neither the prescription in Leviticus nor that in Deuteronomy stipulates the form of death. In Deut. 22:23–24 sexual intercourse between a man and another man's betrothed is identified as a form of adultery[10] for which death by stoning is the appropriate punishment. The adulterous woman may have been stripped naked before being stoned. Thus shamed, she may have had stones thrown at her; alternatively she may have been thrown into a rocky ravine.[11] Genesis 38:24, however, indicates that burning was the punishment that was to have been inflicted on Tamar, who was considered to be a married woman since she had been promised to Shelah (Gen. 38:11).

On the other hand, two prophetic texts suggest that the real punishment meted out to an adulteress was that she was to be divorced by her husband (see Hos. 2:2 [= 2:4 MT]; Jer. 3:8).[12] In the prophetic literature, where the adulteress is a symbol for unfaithful Israel,[13] stripping is frequently mentioned as a punishment for an adulterous wife. The practice was common in the ancient Near East. Since it was a husband's responsibility to provide clothing for his wife (Exod. 21:10), some commentators suggest that, in addition to inflicting public shame, stripping an adulterous woman expresses the idea that she is being divested of the clothes provided for her by her husband.[14]

The apparent discrepancy between the prophetic texts that speak of stripping and of divorce as the punishment for adultery and the legal texts of Leviticus and Deuteronomy[15] that mandate the death penalty creates two possibilities for interpretation. The discrepancy might imply that the texts that make adultery a capital crime were intended to impose stricter penalties at a time when the prevailing practice was that the aggrieved husband divorce his adulterous wife. On the other hand, it is possible—and this is more likely—that the prophetic texts attest that in actual practice the punishment inflicted on an adulterous woman was that she was divorced by her husband,[16] despite the greater severity of the provisions of the law in this regard. It has also been suggested that in postexilic times excommunication from the cult community replaced death as the punishment for adultery.[17] The codicil of Deut. 22:22b, "so you shall purge the evil from your midst," can, in fact, be interpreted as an excommunication formula. The codicil proclaimed that adultery was to be considered not only an offense of a woman against her husband, nor merely a civil tort, but also a sacral offense against God and his people.

In Israel adultery was committed only when a man had sexual relations with a woman who was married to someone else. The man's adultery was not a violation of his own marriage covenant; it was a vio-

lation of the sexual and familial rights of his neighbor. Adultery was a
form of treachery, an assault on the family, whose sanctity was so
important to Israel's national interest. Adultery was prohibited in
order to protect the legitimacy of the married man's children.[18] This
was extremely important in a society that did not have a belief in life
after death.[19] People's hope for the future lay in their hope for their
own children. The punishment for adultery served to protect the rights
of an aggrieved husband. Progeny and property were the rights of the
free Israelite male. When a married woman committed adultery, the
alienation of some of her husband's property was always a danger,[20]
especially were she to become pregnant as a consequence of the illicit
sexual union.[21]

In the ancient Near East, the punishment of the adulterer was con-
tingent upon the punishment of the adulteress.[22] Even when allowing
some discretion to a cuckolded husband, ancient legal texts do not
allow the aggrieved husband to demand punishment for his wife's
lover if he intended to pardon her. Were a man to kill his wife and her
lover caught *in flagrante delicto,* he would not be considered to have
committed homicide provided that he killed both his wife and her
lover.

THE DRAMA

All things considered, there is something quite academic about the
scenario presented in the Fourth Gospel's story about the woman
caught in adultery. The story seems to be more a kind of classroom tale
than a description of an incident that had actually taken place during
Jesus' historical lifetime. One amazing feature of the narrative is that
neither of the two men involved in the case appears in the story. The
aggrieved husband is nowhere mentioned, nor is there any mention of
the man who was caught in adultery. If the woman was caught *in flagrante delicto,* so too was her lover. Customary law demanded that he
be punished as well as she, but the case given to Jesus is one in which
the adulterer is strangely absent from the docket and from the legal
discourse in which the case is presented. Moreover, even if death had
been the penalty actually inflicted on an adulteress and her paramour
in ancient Israel, it is most unlikely that the death penalty could have
been administered during the Roman occupation of Palestine, let alone
by a group of scribes and Pharisees who had not convened as a formal

court.[23] Roman jurisprudence often allowed local authorities to administer some forms of justice; judgment on capital offenses was generally reserved to imperial authorities.

As the Gospel story unfolds, Jesus responds to the provocative question, "Now what do you say?" (John 8:5) with a deafening silence (cf. John 19:9). Instead of rising verbally to the interlocutors' challenge, Jesus bends over and writes on the ground with his finger. This is the first and, apart from John 8:6, the only mention of Jesus' writing in the entire New Testament. Scholars and those who are otherwise intrigued about the life of Jesus have long speculated about what it was that Jesus wrote.[24] It may be that Jesus wrote nothing at all. He may simply have been drawing lines or doodling on the ground while concealing his own emotions[25] and waiting for the interlocutors to perceive the folly of their approach. That he wrote with his finger (8:6) is a graphic detail that serves to focus the reader's imagination on the figure of Jesus. As the reader is captivated by the gesture of the virtually solitary figure amid the crowd, so too were the scribes and the Pharisees. Attention is drawn away from the woman standing before the crowd to the solitary figure of a man who had stooped over and was writing with his finger on the ground.

Impatient with Jesus' scratching in the dirt, the scribes and Pharisees continue to press for a judgment on the case (8:7a; cf. 8:5). Rather than judge the accused woman, Jesus rises and passes tacit judgment on the prosecutors. "Let anyone among you who is without sin be the first to throw a stone at her," he says (8:7), turning the tables on those who were so zealous to ensure that traditional standards of sexual morality be upheld to the letter of the law.

Having rendered his judgment, Jesus returns to his self-appointed task of writing on the ground. By omitting the narrative detail of Jesus' using his finger as a writing instrument, the Johannine narrator allows the reader's imagination to drift away from the figure of a seemingly disinterested Jesus hunched over the ground. Jesus has virtually departed from the scene as his interlocutors are left to ponder his judgment. That they do. The narrator reminds the reader that the interlocutors heard what Jesus had to say (v. 9). In response, they began to move away, almost in procession, the seniors among them leading, until there was finally no one left. As each one of the accusers brought judgment to bear upon himself, each had to admit that he was not without sin. None of the righteous accusers was without sin.[26]

Then the scene shifts. Only two characters occupy the narrator's

stage, a bent Jesus and a standing woman. Rising, Jesus speaks to the
woman for the first time. Addressing her as "woman," Jesus asks,
"Where are they?" She does not know the answer. "They" have gone
and she is alone with the teacher. A second question follows, "Has no
one condemned you?" "No one," she replies and there was to be no
one. Jesus himself[27] was to render a judgment of noncondemnation.
The story comes to its end with the dismissal of the woman who had
been accused. As a parting exhortation, Jesus tells her to sin no more.

This dramatic narrative is well written, consisting of the presentation of a dramatic scenario (8:2–6a), followed by two surprising judicial
scenes (8:6b–9a, 9b–11). As the scene is set, the Pharisees and their
legal experts bring a flagrant adulteress to Jesus, teacher and judge,
within the very precincts of the temple itself. In the presence of a
crowd, they demand Jesus' opinion. The facts of the case are obvious;
the woman was apprehended in the very act of adultery. The penalty
for such a violation of the law was clear: death by stoning was the
mandatory sentence. Put to the test, Jesus was asked to adjudicate the
case.

The two judicial scenes that follow upon the presentation of the
case are parallel. A nonchalant and virtually disinterested Jesus stoops
down and doodles on the ground. Rising, he speaks to his audience.
Jesus challenges each audience with an appropriate exhortation. In
each case, the audience departs the scene after the exhortation.[28]

THE STORY BEHIND THE STORY

The dramatic tale of the woman caught in adultery is set off as a literary unit within the Fourth Gospel by the comings and the goings of the
characters in the scene. The verb "to go" (*poreuō*) in 7:53 and 8:11 sets
the scene apart from the encompassing narrative units. The presence
of the crowds, the presence of the Pharisees, and the discussion of the
interpretation of the law and its casuistic judgment make the story of
the woman caught in adultery a fitting sequel to the narrative aside
contained in 7:45–52. The lesson to be drawn from the narrative,
namely, that sinners should not be overly eager to pass judgment on
others, is conveniently located after two tabernacle scenes that respectively feature a saying of Jesus on not judging by appearances (7:24) and
Nicodemus's discussion with the Pharisees about not judging without
a proper hearing. At the end of the story about the adulteress, a

resumptive "again" (*palin*) in 8:12 points to the beginning of a new scene in the narrative sequence.

Although the tale of the woman caught in adultery is well situated within the Johannine narrative, scholars have long wondered whether the story was actually part of the Fourth Gospel when that Gospel was finally edited within the community of the Beloved Disciple toward the end of the first century C.E.[29] The story is not found in a wide variety of the oldest and best Greek manuscripts of the Fourth Gospel, including two third-century papyri (P[66], P[75]) and the two fourth-century codices generally considered to be the best of the ancient witnesses to the text of the Fourth Gospel.[30] The story is also absent from some of the oldest Eastern translations of the Gospel, including various Syriac, Coptic, Armenian, and Georgian versions, as well as a few old Western translations of the Gospel. None of the Greek fathers of the church comments on the story until Euthymius Zigabenus does so in the twelfth century C.E.

Not only is the story of the adulteress absent from a wide variety of ancient Greek manuscripts and some of the older translations of the New Testament,[31] but the history of the story indicates that the narrative has wandered within the textual tradition. Some of the manuscripts of the Fourth Gospel that have the story place it after the first scene of Jesus present in Jerusalem during the Feast of Tabernacles (7:14–36),[32] or in the middle of the second Tabernacles scene (right after 7:44).[33] Other manuscripts append the story to the Fourth Gospel, that is, immediately after the Gospel's formal conclusion in 21:25.[34] Still other manuscripts locate the story within the Gospel according to Luke, where it is found as the final scene in the temple section (Luke 19:47–21:38).[35]

It is not only the textual history of the passage that gives rise to questions about the origin of the story. The style and tenor of the story suggest that it was not originally composed within the Johannine community. In this relatively short story there are seventeen expressions that are not otherwise found in the Fourth Gospel, including such phrases as "the Mount of Olives," "early in the morning," "scribes and Pharisees," "adultery" and "committing adultery," "bent down" and "straightened up," "elders," "condemn," and "from now on."[36] Other expressions found in the story about the woman caught in adultery do appear elsewhere in the Fourth Gospel, but in these instances they are used in a way that is quite different from the way they are used in the story about the woman caught in adultery. Among these expressions are "people," "sat down," "teacher," "commanded," "stone" (both as a verb and as a noun), "test," "finger," "ground," and "woman."[37] These are the very words and expressions that make the story the fascinating and provocative tale that it is.

Finally, the tenor of the story is so unlike what is found in the rest of the Fourth Gospel. Although it is told in a more dramatic and solemn manner, it is rather similar to the controversy stories found in the Synoptic Gospels, none of which, however, concerns adultery. Its dialogic character is consistent with the style in which the Fourth Gospel has been written, but its manifest duality[38] and its literary genre as a conflict story attest to its similarity to the type of stories found in Matthew, Mark, and Luke. The portrayal of Jesus as a teacher[39] and the presence of the scribes and Pharisees with their attempt to test Jesus are features of the story that remind the reader of any number of similar narratives in the Synoptic Gospels. The total weight of this external and internal evidence has led to the consensus judgment among scholars that the story of the woman caught in adultery was not part of the Fourth Gospel such as it was finally edited within the Johannine community at the end of the first century C.E.

Other evidence suggests, however, that various forms of the story were being told in Christian churches from the second century onward.[40] Of Papias, an early-second-century bishop of Hierapolis, it is said that "he also gives another history of a woman, who had been accused of many sins before the Lord, which is also contained in the gospel according to the Hebrews."[41] None of the extant fragments of the Gospel according to the Hebrews, however, contains the story of the woman caught in adultery. Neither do the extant works of Origen, who reputedly used the Gospel according to the Hebrews with some frequency,[42] contain any allusion to the story of the adulterous woman. In any case Eusebius's report about Papias speaks about a story that had been told about a sinful woman who had been brought to Jesus, but it does not mention a story about an adulteress as such.

Another story about Jesus and a sinful woman is reported by an anonymous third-century author:

> But if you do not receive him who repents, because you are without mercy, you shall sin against the Lord God. For you do not obey our Savior and our God, to do as even he did with her who had sinned, whom the elders placed before Him, leaving the judgment in His hands, and departed. But He, the searcher of hearts, asked her and said to her, "Have the elders condemned you, my daughter?" She said to him, "Nay, Lord."

And he said unto her, "Go, neither do I condemn you." (*Didascalia Apostolorum* 8.2.4)[43]

The tradition to which this anonymous author refers in advising church leaders how they should act in reconciling sinners to the church is obviously based on a story similar to that found in John 7:53– 8:11. As is the case with the tradition attributed to Papias, this particular tradition does not specify that the sin of the woman was adultery.

In the fourth century, Didymus the Blind provides yet another patristic witness to the story about the woman caught in adultery. In his commentary on Qoh. 7:21–22a, Didymus writes:

> We find, therefore, in certain gospels: A woman, it says, was condemned by the Jews for a sin and was being sent to be stoned in the place where that was customary to happen. The savior, it says, when he saw her and observed that they were ready to stone her, said to those who were about to cast stones, "he who has not sinned, let him take a stone and cast it. If anyone is conscious in himself not to have sinned, let him take up a stone and smite her." And no one dared. Since they knew in themselves and perceived that they themselves were guilty in some things, they did not dare to strike her. (*EcclT* 223.6b–13a)[44]

This text, written in Greek, was discovered in 1941 near Toura, in Egypt, by a group of soldiers who were digging out a grotto for use as a munitions dump. Obviously similar to the story found in John 7:53– 8:11, Didymus's commentary provides us with the oldest extant text of the story. Like other patristic evidence, this commentary does not specify that the woman who was about to be stoned had been caught in the very act of adultery. Nor does it tell us that the scene was set up by a group of scribes and Pharisees to entrap Jesus. Rather, Didymus tells the story of the merciful Jesus' intervention in a case of capital punishment.

These patristic texts show that a story similar to the story of the woman caught in adultery circulated among the churches of early Christianity. Didymus provides us with evidence that a written version of the story existed as early as the fourth century, that is, a century before any attestation of John 7:53–8:11 in extant manuscripts of the New Testament.

THE CASE OF ADULTERY

The story of the woman caught in adultery, while not written by the Johannine evangelist, is a very old tale whose roots may lie in an oral tradition about Jesus that derives from the early church itself. The Johannine story is unique. There is no mention of the woman's paramour, for whom a similar penalty—death, according to the scenario of John 7:53–8:11—should have been meted out according to the provisions of biblical and ancient Near Eastern law.[45] Nor is there any mention of the cuckolded husband, the aggrieved person whom one might have expected the storyteller to identify as one of those who brought charges against the woman. Feminist critics of the Johannine tale are surely justified in their observations that the story unjustly points to the woman as being the especially guilty party in an adulterous liaison.

Notwithstanding the somewhat artificial, though artful, construction of the tale, the Johannine story has been told to help the reader understand something about Jesus the teacher. In the first scene of judgment, Jesus' judicial challenge (8:7) implies not only that one ought not to be overly anxious to judge others but also that the crime of adultery is to be seen as no more serious than other sins. In the second scene of judgment, when Jesus is alone with the sinful woman, the reader is confronted with a teacher who has become a compassionate and merciful judge. The forceful "I" of the apothegm (8:11) presents Jesus as the agent of God in offering a judgment of noncondemnation on the woman. Before the judgment seat of God, her adultery does not give rise to condemnation. What comes from the lips of Jesus is an exhortation to sin no more.

The Johannine narrative clearly describes adultery as sinful, but it is not the ultimate sin. It is no more condemnable than other sins. Those who have encountered Jesus and his mercy are, nonetheless, to avoid adultery. The sin of adultery is incompatible with an integrated experience of Jesus' mercy. When, however, adultery does take place, it can be forgiven by the merciful Jesus. The adulteress is no more guilty than her paramour, nor is she more guilty than those who would stand in ready judgment on her.

JESUS AND ANOTHER WOMAN
(LUKE 7:36–50)

Some similarity exists between the Fourth Gospel's singular tale of the woman caught in adultery and other New Testament stories that describe encounters between Jesus and women presumed to be sinful. One of these is Luke's poignant story about a sinful woman who bathed Jesus' feet with her tears, dried them with her hair, kissed them, and then anointed them with an ointment that she had brought with her in an alabaster jar. The scene is the home of "one of the Pharisees."[46] As the story unfolds the host is identified as a man named Simon (7:40–44). Jesus is seated at table when an unidentified woman, having learned that Jesus was dining in Simon's home, went to the house. On entering, she stood behind Jesus. Undoubtedly the evangelist expects his readers to think of a scene in which Jesus is reclining at table, as was customary at the time, during a late-afternoon dinner. A weeping woman is standing behind him, her tears falling on his feet. Bending down, she dries the feet with her hair, kisses them, and then anoints them with the ointment that she had brought with her.

Anointing Jesus' feet was something that the woman had intended to do. She had brought the alabaster jar with her (7:37). The woman was able to approach Jesus since it was a Palestinian custom to allow passersby to come into a public dinner.[47] What was shocking about the woman's presence and the intimacy of her gesture was the fact that she was a "sinful" woman. The evangelist draws attention to her sin in Simon's soliloquy, "If this man were a prophet, he would have known who and what kind of woman this is who is touching him—that she is a sinner" (7:39). Simon's words enable the evangelist to underscore Jesus' prophetic insight. With this narrative touch the evangelist enhances his portrayal of Jesus as a prophet.[48]

Commentators often infer from Simon's soliloquy that the woman who anointed Jesus' feet was publicly known to have committed some form of sexual transgression. Many suggest that she was probably a public prostitute, whose profession involved her in a life of habitual unchastity.[49] Others argue that the unidentified woman is simply presented as someone who was known to have committed adultery.[50] Readers tend to think that the woman in the scene was the town harlot.[51]

Luke, however, does not specify that she was guilty of any sexual transgression.[52] The evangelist could have identified the woman as a prostitute (*pornē*), but he does not do so.[53] He assiduously avoids telling his readers what kind of sins the woman might have committed.[54] Luke simply underscores the magnitude of her sins (7:39, 47) so as to highlight the quality of God's mercy extended to her and her response to the gift of forgiveness.[55] The latter is, of course, the point of the story. God's mercy extended to sinners and outcasts and Jesus' ministry to the despised and the marginalized are thematic features of

Luke's Gospel. The Lukan Jesus befriends sinners and freely associates with them.[56] The presence of women in Jesus' life and ministry is a characteristic trait of the third Gospel.[57]

The story of Jesus being anointed by a sinful woman gives ample evidence of the evangelist's theological interests and redactional techniques.[58] Not the least of the latter is the use of the Hellenistic symposium motif. Jesus' speech on the occasion of a dinner is an important feature of Luke's story about Jesus.[59] Luke 7:37 is the first of three times in his Gospel in which the evangelist portrays Jesus at dinner in the home of a Pharisee (see also Luke 11:37; 14:1). In his story Jesus seizes the occasion to speak about hospitality and forgiveness (7:44–47), but he gives no indication whatsoever that the woman whose presence behind him occasioned his speech was guilty of adultery or any sexual sin. The point of his story is that a person who has been forgiven responds with an outpouring of love.

MARY OF BETHANY

Luke's story of the nameless woman who anointed Jesus' feet is often compared with the Johannine story of Jesus' feet being anointed by Mary of Bethany (John 12:1–8).[60] Mary was the sister of Lazarus, whom Jesus had raised from the dead. During a kind of celebratory dinner that followed Jesus' raising of Lazarus from the dead,[61] Mary anointed Jesus' feet with a pound of costly perfume made of pure nard. The account in the Fourth Gospel focuses particular concern on the extravagance of Mary's gesture. The author observes that the ointment was worth an entire year's wages for the ordinary laborer, three hundred denarii.[62] So expensive was the ointment that Mary's use of it to anoint Jesus' feet led to a dispute between Judas Iscariot and Jesus. With the dispute the evangelist's lengthy story about the raising of Lazarus from the dead (John 11:1–12:8) comes to an end.

The story about Lazarus's death and resurrection—in fact resuscitation rather than resurrection—sheds light on the death and resurrection of Jesus. The episode of Mary anointing Jesus' feet brings the story to closure. The evangelist observes that the anointing took place against the horizon of Jesus' burial (John 12:7) and characterizes Judas as an evil person who did accept the mission of Jesus. In composing his closing scene, the evangelist has drawn attention to the dramatic opposition between Jesus' death and resurrection and has heightened the christological significance of the anointing. He has not, however, identified Mary of Bethany as a sinful woman; still less has he identified her as a woman who was in any way guilty of sexual transgression.

THE SAMARITAN WOMAN

Another story that might be brought into consideration in this panorama of New Testament narratives describing encounters between Jesus and women is the Johannine story of Jesus' meeting the Samaritan woman at the well (4:5–42). It was a surprising meeting. Even Jesus' disciples were astonished that he was speaking with a woman (4:27). The woman is portrayed as having had a complex marital history (4:16–18). She had had five husbands,[63] but she was living with a man to whom she was not married at the time that she spoke to Jesus. Jesus' insight into her storied past leads the woman to acknowledge that Jesus is a prophet (4:19). Thereafter she becomes a Johannine witness (4:39) and evangelist. It is clear that the evangelist takes no particular interest in the woman's marital history. He uses that history, of which the woman may well have been ashamed (4:17a), simply to highlight Jesus' prophetic knowledge.[64] "Whoever asserts that Jesus wishes to lay bare her morals," writes Ernst Haenchen, "misunderstands the text."[65]

The story of Jesus' meeting a Samaritan woman by the well and the Lukan story of Jesus' forgiving the sins of the woman who anointed his feet are not stories about sexuality and sexual transgressions. The two narratives are not even stories about forgiveness for sins of a sexual nature. They are, nonetheless, stories about gender. They portray women deemed to be unworthy of contact with Jesus as people for whom he has a particular concern. The stories essentially reveal the prejudice of a judgmental Pharisee as well as the prejudice of Jesus' disciples.[66] These stories, together with the story of the adulteress, reflect the relatively low social status of women because of their sexuality in the sociocultural world in which Jesus lived and in which the Gospels were written.[67]

Apart from the tale of the woman caught in the act of adultery, none of these Gospel stories about Jesus and a woman has anything to say about sexual transgressions. The story of the adulteress says simply that the sin of adultery is not to be repeated, even if it is a sin that Jesus willingly forgives.

NOTES

1. In the Roman Catholic liturgy the story is used as a Sunday Gospel lection on the fifth Sunday of Lent in Cycle C. It is also used as the Gospel reading for the fifth Monday of Lent, when the first reading is the story of Susanna (Daniel 13). Despite this liturgical usage, contemporary critical scholarship generally judges that the story was not part of the original text of the Fourth Gospel. See below, pp. 7–8. In most modern editions of the Gospel, the disputed passage appears in brackets or with some other indication of its disputed status. A note in *The New Scofield Reference Bible* indicates, however, that it is to be considered a "genuine part of the Gospel."

2. Cf. Matt. 5:1; 13:1–2; Mark 9:35. Elsewhere in the Fourth Gospel Jesus sits down on only two occasions. One occasion is when he sits on an ass as he enters Jerusalem (12:14). The other time is when he is made to sit on the judgment seat by Pilate (19:13), although this passage may imply that Pilate sat on the judgment seat.

3. Unlike the Synoptics (Matt. 5:17–48; 15:1–9; 19:16–30; Mark 7:1–13; 10:17–31; Luke 18:18–30), the Fourth Gospel (cf. John 7:23) does not contain any explicit discourse on the Ten Commandments.

4. The sayings in Prov. 2:16–19 and 7:25–27 seem to allude to death as punishment for adultery.

5. The text is found in a collection of penal laws in Lev. 20:1–27. The phrase "if a man commits adultery with the wife of his neighbor" in Lev. 20:10 is repeated in the Hebrew Bible, presumably for emphasis.

6. It may be that under Israelite law punishment for adultery could be meted out only if the adulterers were caught *in flagrante delicto*. See Num. 5:13.

7. Gen. 39:9 describes adultery as "great wickedness." In Ugaritic and Egyptian texts it is described as a "great sin."

8. See the Code of Hammurabi 129: "If the wife of a man has been caught having sexual intercourse with another man, they shall bind them and throw them into the water. If the husband of the woman wishes to spare his wife, then the king in turn may spare his subject" (*ANET*, 171).

9. For example, "If the wife of a man has gone out from her house to a man where he lives and he has intercourse with her knowing that she is a man's wife, both the man and the woman shall be killed" (Middle Assyrian Laws, A 13; see *ANET*, 181).

10. Similarly Code of Hammurabi 131.

11. Compare Dan. 13:61–62 [= Susanna 61–62], where the Old Greek translation has, "they bound them, led them out, and threw them into a ravine." This was the form of "stoning" implied by the Mishnah, which lists a man's adultery with a betrothed woman as one of the crimes for which stoning is the appropriate punishment. See *m. Sanh.* 6:4.

12. It is not altogether certain that these two texts actually tell us about punishment for adultery. The setting for the collection of sayings in Hos. 2:2–13 is the legal process (a *rîb*) against an unfaithful wife; Hos. 2:2 actually cites the formula for divorce, but it is Yahweh who is the aggrieved spouse.

What follows, however, seems to speak of withholding punishment (Hos. 2:2b–3. The NRSV's "or" means "or else," "lest") and reconciliation (Hos. 2:7b). Jer. 3:8 uses the metaphor of divorce to refer to the exile of the northern kingdom.

13. See Hos. 2:3, 10 [= 2:5, 12 MT]; Jer. 13:22–26; Ezek. 16:37, 39; 23:26, 29.

14. Thus Robert Gordis, "Hosea's Marriage and Message: A New Approach," *HUCA* 25 (1954): 9–35, esp. 20–21; Hans Walter Wolff, *Hosea: A Commentary on the Book of Hosea*, Hermeneia (Philadelphia: Fortress, 1974), 34; Anthony Phillips, "Another Look at Adultery," *JSOT* 20 (1981): 3–25, esp. 15–16.

Henry McKeating and Cyrus H. Gordon suggest that stripping a woman of her clothing was part of the divorce ritual. See McKeating, "Sanctions against Adultery in Ancient Israelite Society, with Some Reflections on Methodology in the Study of Old Testament Ethics," *JSOT* 11 (1979): 57–72, esp. 61; Gordon, "Hos. 2:4–5 in the Light of New Semitic Inscriptions," *ZAW* 13 (1936): 277–80; Gordis, "Hosea's Marriage," 20–21, esp. n. 30a.

15. See the casuistry and appended codicil of Deut. 22:22.

16. The stripping mentioned in Hos. 2:5 may indicate that there was no question of the woman being executed for adultery at the time of Hosea (see Phillips, "Another Look," 16).

17. See Phillips, "Another Look," 19.

18. Apropos of the law on adultery in Deut. 22:23–27, Phillips has observed that "it is not sexual ethics but paternity which is uppermost in the legislator's mind" ("Another Look," 7; cf. *Ancient Israel's Criminal Law: A New Approach to the Decalogue* [New York: Shocken, 1970], 117).

19. Belief in the resurrection of the dead is a form of theological hope that began to emerge in the second century B.C.E. See Dan. 12:2–3.

20. If a man's wife were to give birth to an illegitimate child, part of his "estate" would pass on to people who were not his descendants. This was particularly important in a culture in which land was passed on from generation to generation within the same family and where goods were considered to exist in a finite quantity.

21. "Adultery," notes Satlow, "is also the 'theft' of a woman's reproductive potential from her husband" (see Michael L. Satlow, *Tasting the Dish: Rabbinic Rhetorics of Sexuality*, Brown Judaic Studies 303 [Atlanta: Scholars Press, 1995], 118).

22. The casuistry of the Middle Assyrian Laws (A 13–16) offers various examples. The principle is that "they shall treat the adulterer as the man orders his wife to be treated" (MAL A 14). These Assyrian laws offer cases in which the death penalty, the penalty of mutilation, or no penalty at all is given to the partners in consensual adultery. Thus, "If a man should seize another man upon his wife and they prove the charges against him and find him guilty, they shall kill both of them; there is no liability for him (i.e., the husband). If he should seize him and bring him either before the king or the judges, and they prove the charges against him and find him guilty—if the woman's husband kills his wife, then he shall also kill the man; if he cuts off his wife's nose, he shall turn the man into a eunuch and they shall lacerate his entire face; but if [he wishes to release] his wife, he shall [release] the man" (MAL A 15, as it

is given in Martha T. Roth, *Law Collections from Mesopotamia and Asia Minor*, Writings from the Ancient World 6 [Atlanta: Scholars Press, 1995], 158). See *ANET*, 181; cf. Hittite Law 198 (*ANET*, 196).

23. In rabbinic literature there are only two reported cases of Jews putting adulterers and adulteresses to death. In both instances the adulteress is the daughter of a priest. See *m. Sanh.* 7:2; *b. Sanh.* 52b.

24. See the summaries in Raymond E. Brown, *The Gospel According to John (I–XII)*, AB 30 (Garden City, N.Y.: Doubleday, 1966), 333–34; and Rudolf Schnackenburg, *The Gospel According to St John*, vol. 2 (New York: Crossroad, 1980), 165–66. In recent years Andrew Nugent, noting that "writing with the finger" occurs in the Bible only in Exod. 31:18 and Deut. 9:10, suggests that the narrative detail of Jesus' gesture was intended to evoke a comparison between what Jesus did in the Temple and what Yahweh did on Sinai ("What Did Jesus Write? [John 7,53–8,11]," *DR* 108 [1990]: 193–98). Paul Minear, in turn, has speculated that Jesus' writing on the ground was a messianic gesture. Jesus asserts his authority over the earth to set the stage for the eschatological act of judgment and forgiveness. The idea that the writing on the ground is a prophetic gesture expressing divine judgment was already found in a trio of Western fathers of the church—Ambrose, Augustine, and Jerome. See P. S. Minear, "Writing on the Ground: The Puzzle in John 8:1–11," *HBT* 13 (1991): 23–37; J. Ian H. McDonald, "The So-Called *Pericopa de adultera*," *NTS* 41 (1995): 415–27, esp. 421–22, 425.

25. See E. Power, "Writing on the Ground (Ioh. 8,6–8)," *Bib* 2 (1921): 54–57. Power suggests that Semites doodled on the ground to conceal the fact that they were distressed.

26. In his commentary on Qoheleth, Didymus the Blind opined that "no one dared" to throw a stone. He explained that, "since they knew in themselves and perceived that they themselves were guilty in some things, they did not dare to strike her" (*EcclT* [= Commentary on Ecclesiastes, according to the Tura papyrus] 223.11b–13a). See Johannes Kramer and Bärbel Krebber, *Didymos der Blinde: Kommentar zum Ecclesiastes*, Papyrologische Texte und Abhandlungen 16 (Bonn: Rudolf Habelt, 1972).

27. Note the emphatic *egō* in 8:11.

28. That the narrative takes place in the presence of the crowds is an integral part of the narrator's scenario (8:2). For the consistency of the narrative, it would appear that they too must depart the scene so that Jesus can be left alone with the woman (8:9). On the other hand, it can be argued that the narrative loses something of its didactic force if there was no one to witness Jesus' dialogue with the woman. If the narrator intended his readers to infer that both judicial scenes were played out in the presence of the crowds, the word "them" (*autois*) in 8:12 could refer to these crowds in the temple precincts. There would remain, however, the difficulty that in the narrative of 7:53–8:11 Jesus seems to speak only to the scribes and Pharisees and to the woman.

29. See the discussions in Ulrich Becker, *Jesus und die Ehebrecherin* (Berlin: Alfred Töpelmann, 1963), 8–74; Kurt Aland, *Studien zur Überlieferung des NT und seines Textes* (Berlin: Walter de Gruyter, 1967), 43–45; Gary M. Burge, "A Specific Problem in the New Testament Text and Canon: The

Woman Caught in Adultery (John 7:53–8:11)," *JETS* 27 (1984): 141–48; Bruce M. Metzger, *A Textual Commentary on the Greek New Testament* (2nd ed.; Stuttgart: United Bible Societies, 1994), 187–89; and G. Colombo, "La critica testuale di fronte alla pericope dell'adultera," *RivB* 42 (1994): 81–102. John P. Heil has attempted to defend the authenticity of the pericope in "The Story of Jesus and the Adulteress (John 7,53–8,11) Reconsidered," *Bib* 72 (1991): 182–91. His arguments have been soundly rebutted by Daniel B. Wallace in "Reconsidering 'The Story of Jesus and the Adulteress Reconsidered,'" *NTS* 39 (1993): 290–96.

30. These are Codex Sinaiticus (ℵ) and Codex Vaticanus (B). The story is also absent from Codex Alexandrinus and Codex Ephraemi Rescriptus (A, C). These two fifth-century codices do not contain this section of the Fourth Gospel. The size of the extant pages of these codices suggests that the codices did not originally contain the story. The story is also absent from a wide variety of ancient manuscripts including Codex Koridethi, Codex Washingtoniensis, and such other majuscules as L, N, T, X, Y, Δ, Ψ, 0141, and 0211. The earliest Alexandrian manuscript in which it appears is the ninth-century minuscule, no. 892. The oldest extant New Testament manuscript that contains the story of the woman caught in adultery is a fifth-century Western codex, Codex Bezae Cantabrigiensis (D).

31. That the manuscript evidence for the story contains more textual variation than any other New Testament text of comparable length adds further complexity in any discussion of the origin of the story. Particularly problematic is 8:6a. Various commentators and text critics consider the reference to Jesus' being tested as a late interpolation under the influence of Matt. 22:15 and Luke 6:7. See Brad H. Young, "'Save the Adulteress!': Ancient Jewish *Responsa* in the Gospels?" *NTS* 41 (1995): 59–70, esp. 59–63.

32. Thus the twelfth-century minuscule, no. 225.

33. Thus some Georgian manuscripts.

34. Thus some Armenian manuscripts, and minuscules nos. 1, 565, 1076, 1570, and 1582.

35. Thus the Farrar family of minuscules (f^{13}, including minuscules nos. 13, 69, 124, 174, 230, 346, 543, 788, 826, 828, 983, 1689, 1709, etc., the oldest of which date to the eleventh century). J. Ruis-Camps considers the tale of the adulteress to have been originally part of Luke's proper material. He suggests that the story was inspired by the Markan story of Jesus' discussion with the Pharisees on the legitimacy of divorce (Mark 10:2–12). See J. Ruis-Camps, "Origen lucano de la pericopa de la mujer adultera (Jn 7,53–8,11)," *FNT* 6 (1993): 149–75. See also the discussion in Becker, *Ehebrecherin,* 43–74, and Michel Gourgues, "'Moi non plus je ne te condamne pas': Les mots et la théologie de Luc en Jean 8,1–11 (la femme adultère)," *SR* 19 (1990): 305–18.

36. The seventeen expressions are "the Mount of Olives" (*to horos tōn elaiōn,* 8:1), "early in the morning" (*orthros,* 8:2), "scribes and Pharisees" (*hoi grammateis kai hoi pharisaioi,* 8:3), "adultery" (*moicheia,* 8:3), "[stand] before" (*en mesō,* 8:3, 9), "in the very act" (*autophōros,* 8:4), "commit adultery" (*moicheuō,* 8:4), "bend down" (*kyptō,* 8:6, 8), "write" (*katagraphō,* 8:6), "keep on" (*epimenō,* 8:7), "straighten up" (*anakyptō,* 8:7, 10), "without sin"

(*anamartētos*, 8:7), "one by one" (*heis kath'eis*, 8:9), "elders" (*presbyteros*, 8:9), "left" (*kataleipō*, 8:9), "condemn" (*katakrinō*, 8:10, 11), and "from now on" (*apo tou nyn*, 8:11). Three of these, "in the very act," "write" (with the compound *katagraphō*), and "without sin," are not used elsewhere in the New Testament.

37. The list includes "people" (*laos*, 8:2; 11:50; 18:14), "sit down" (*kathizō*, 8:2; 12:14; 19:13), "teacher" (*didaskale*, in the vocative, 8:4; 1:38; 20:16), "catch" (*katalambanō*, 1:5; 8:3, 4; 12:35), "in the law" (*en tō nomō*, 8:5, 17; 1:45; 10:34; 15:25), "command" (*entellomai*, 8:5; 14:31; 15:14, 17), "stone" (*lithazō*, [verb], 8:5; 10:31, 32, 33; 11:8), "test" (*peirazō*, 8:6; 6:6); "have some charge" (*katēgoreō*, 8:6; 5:45), "finger" (*daktylos*, 8:6; 20:25, 27), "ground" (*gē*, 8:6, 8; 3:22, 31; 6:21; 12:32; 17:4; 21:8, 9, 11; cf. 12:24), "stone" (*lithos* [noun], 8:7, 59; 10:31; cf. 11:38, 39, 41; 20:1), "begin" (*archō*, 8:9; 13:5), "woman" (*gynai*, in the vocative, 8:10; 2:4; 4:21; 19:26; 20:13, 15), and "sin no more" (*mēketi hamartane*, 8:11; 5:14). Some of these differences are only a matter of nuance; others a matter of a different attribution. For example, in the story of the woman caught in adultery, it is she who is to be stoned and Jesus who is tested. In the Fourth Gospel, it is Jesus who is to be stoned and Jesus who tests.

38. Cf. Frans Neirynck, *Duality in Mark: Contributions to the Study of the Markan Redaction*, BETL 31 (rev. ed.; Louvain: University Press/Peeters, 1988).

39. Compare, for example, 7:53b–8:1 with Matt. 5:1–2 and the use of the vocative "teacher" (8:4) with Matt. 8:19; 12:38; 19:16; 22:16, 24, 36; Mark 4:38; 9:17, 38; 10:17, 20, 35; 12:14, 19, 32; 13:1; Luke 3:12; 7:40; 9:38; 10:25; 11:45; 12:13; 18:18; 19:39; 20:21, 28, 39; 21:7.

40. For a discussion of the patristic evidence, see Bart D. Ehrman, "Jesus and the Adulteress," *NTS* 34 (1988): 24–44; and McDonald, "So-Called *Peri-copa de adultera*."

41. Eusebius of Caesarea, *Ecclesiastical History* 3.39 (*PG* 20:300). The Gospel according to the Hebrews was apparently known to Jerome, who claims to have translated it into Latin and Greek (*Liber de viris illustribis* 2 [*PL* 23:611]). On the Gospel according to the Hebrews, see Philip Vielhauer, "The Gospel of the Hebrews," in Wilhelm Schneemelcher, *New Testament Apocrypha*, vol. 1, ed. Edgar Hennecke (London: SCM, 1963), 158–65; Ron Cameron, "Hebrews, Gospel of the," *ABD* 3:105–6.

42. See Jerome, *Liber de viris illustribis* 2 (*PL* 23:611).

43. The *Didascalia Apostolorum* was originally written in Greek, but no Greek manuscript of the text is extant. What does exist are a poor Syriac version and some Latin fragments. This English translation comes from Arthur Vööbus, *The Didascalia Apostolorum in Syriac*, CSCO, *Scriptores Syri*, 177 (Louvain: Secrétariat du CSCO, 1979).

44. The translation comes from Ehrman, "Jesus and the Adulteress," 25. Cf. above, p. 16 n. 26.

45. Cf. Josephus, *Against Apion* 2.201: "A husband is to lie only with his wife whom he hath married; but to have to do with another man's wife is a wicked thing; which, if anyone venture upon, death is inevitably his punishment."

46. On the Pharisees in the Gospel according to Luke, see Jack Dean Kings-

bury, "The Pharisees in Luke-Acts," in *The Four Gospels 1992: Festschrift Frans Neirynck*, ed. Frans van Segbroeck, Christopher M. Tuckett, Gilbert van Belle, and Josef Verheyden, 3 vols., BETL 100A, B, C (Louvain: University Press, 1992), 2:1497–1512, esp. 1498–1502. In the other Synoptic stories of Jesus' anointing by a woman (Matt. 26:6–13; Mark 14:3–9), Simon is identified as a leper rather than as a Pharisee (Matt. 26:6; Mark 14:3) and the woman is simply identified as a woman (*gynē*) with an alabaster jar of ointment (Matt. 26:7; Mark 14:3).

47. Cf. Luke 14:12–13, 21b–23; Matt. 22:9–11; Str-B, 4.2, 615; Alfred Plummer, *A Critical and Exegetical Commentary on the Gospel According to S. Luke*, ICC (5th ed.; Edinburgh: T. & T. Clark, 1922), 210.

48. See Luke 4:16–30; see also Albert Vanhoye, "L'intérêt de Luc pour la prophétie en Lc 1,76; 4,16–30 et 22,60–65," in *Four Gospels*, ed. van Segbroeck et al., 2:1529–48.

49. Thus Plummer, who comments, "a person of notoriously bad character, and probably a prostitute" (*Luke*, 210). Cf. Karl Heinrich Rengstorf, *Das Evangelium nach Lukas*, NTD 3 (Göttingen: Vandenhoeck & Ruprecht, 1937), 102; E. Earle Ellis, *The Gospel of Luke*, NCB (London: Nelson, 1966), 123–24; Heinz Schürmann, *Das Lukasevangelium*, HTKNT 3.1 (Freiburg/Basel/ Vienna: Herder, 1969), 1:431; and I. Howard Marshall, *The Gospel of Luke: A Commentary on the Greek Text*, NIGTC (Grand Rapids: Eerdmans, 1978), 308, with reference to the work of Joachim Jeremias and J. D. M. Derrett; and Eduard Schweizer, *The Good News According to Luke* (Atlanta: John Knox, 1984), 139.

50. Thus Theodor Zahn, *Das Evangelium des Lucas ausgelegt* (4th ed.; Leipzig: Deichert, 1930), 320–21.

51. Apart from the Pharisee's musing in 7:39, the principal reason for considering the "sinful" woman (*hamartōlos*) to be a prostitute appears to be the Matthean pairing of tax collectors and prostitutes in Matt. 21:31, 32. Elsewhere Matthew pairs tax collectors with sinners (*hamartōloi*). See Matt. 9:10, 11; 11:19; cf. Mark 2:15, 16 [twice]; Luke 5:30; 7:34. The pairing of tax collectors and sinners is found in Mark (Mark 2:15–16; par. Matt. 9:10–11; Luke 5:30) and Q (Luke 7:34 = Matt. 11:19). The pairing of tax collectors and prostitutes comes from Matthew's proper material, if not perhaps from his editorial hand. Matthew's redaction is ultimately irrelevant to the Lukan understanding of "sinner."

52. Still less does Luke identify the sinful woman as Mary Magdalene, as did a much later popular tradition (on the basis of Mark 16:9?) in the Western church, dating back to the sixth century. The tradition has no historical foundation. See R. F. Collins, "Mary Magdalene," *ABD* 4:379–91, esp. 390; A. R. C. Leaney, *The Gospel According to St Luke*, HNTC (2nd ed.; New York: Harper, 1966), 146–47. Surprisingly Leaney makes no comment whatsoever on the nature of the woman's sin.

53. Luke's story of the prodigal son tells how the young man had wasted his father's money on prostitutes (*meta pornōn*, Luke 15:30). Apart from Matt. 21:31–32, Luke 15:30 is the only mention of "prostitutes" in the canonical Gospels.

54. See in this regard the observations of Joseph A. Fitzmyer, *The Gospel*

According to Luke I-IX, AB 28 (Garden City, N.Y.: Doubleday, 1981), 688–89; cf. C. F. Evans, *Saint Luke*, TPIC (London: SCM; Philadelphia: TPI, 1990), 361.

55. Apropos of Luke's use of "sinner" in 7:37, Walter Grundmann observed that she may have been considered a sinner if she were the wife of a man whom the Pharisees considered a sinner because he didn't properly observe the law. See W. Grundmann, *Das Evangelium nach Lukas*, THKNT 3 (Berlin: Evange-lische Verlagsanstalt, 1961), 170; cf. Adolf Schlatter, *Das Evangelium des Lukas: Aus seinen Quellen erklärt* (2nd ed.; Stuttgart: Calwer, 1960), 259; Ellis, *Luke*, 124. The observation may be apposite to the interpretation of "sin-ner" (*hamartōlos*) in 7:37. Such an interpretation would, however, be incon-sistent with 7:47, which attributes personal sin to the woman. On the other hand, the woman would be considered a sinner if she had frequent contact with Gentiles or if she were engaged in an occupation that was considered to incur ritual impurity. Each of these possibilities would entail multiple "sins." Apropos of 7:47, see Joël Delobel, "Lk 7,47 in its Context: An Old Crux Revis-ited," in *Four Gospels*, ed. van Segbroeck et al., 2:1581–90.

56. See Luke 5:8, 30, 32; 7:34; 13:2; 15:1, 2, 7, 10; 18:13; 19:7.

57. Mary, Elizabeth, Anna, Martha and Mary, the Galilean women, Mary Magdalene, Jairus's daughter, the woman with the hemorrhage, and the crip-pled woman whom Jesus healed on a sabbath. The Lukan Jesus also tells sto-ries about various women: the woman who pleaded with the unjust judge, the woman who lost her money, the woman who was seven times a widow, and the widow who gave her all to the temple treasury.

58. See Joël Delobel, "L'onction par la pécheresse: La composition littéraire de *Lc.*, VII,36–50," *ETL* 42 (1966): 415–75.

59. The symposium pattern occurs in 5:29–39; 7:36–50; 14:1–23; 22:14–31. Luke's predilection for the symposium motif is particularly evident when Luke 11:37 is compared with its parallels in Matt. 14:1 and Mark 7:1. In addi-tion to Luke's use of the symposium motif, there are many references to Jesus' eating and drinking throughout his story about Jesus. The three parables on mercy and forgiveness in Luke 15 are also occasioned by Jesus' dining habits (see Luke 15:2–3). See also Luke 19:1–10, where the expressions "to welcome" (*hypedexato*, "to receive hospitably," 9:6) and "to be the guest" (*katalysai*, often with the connotation of being received as an overnight guest) suggest that Zacchaeus provided a meal for Jesus.

60. Cf. Maurits Sabbe, "The Anointing of Jesus in John 12,1–8 and its Syn-optic Parallels," in *Four Gospels*, ed. van Segbroeck et al., 3:2051–82. In its broad outlines the story is similar to the Synoptic stories of Jesus being anointed by an anonymous woman while he was a dinner guest of a man named Simon (Matt. 26:6–13; Mark 14:3–9; Luke 7:36–50). The only two words that occur in all four accounts, however, are "house" (*oikia*) and "ointment" (*myron*). Sabbe claims (p. 2053) that the Fourth Evangelist apparently knew the Lukan narrative and that the Lukan form of the narrative seems to have influ-enced the Johannine redaction (p. 2053).

61. Since dead people do not eat, the dinner would have attested to the real-ity of the resurrection (cf. Mark 5:43; Luke 8:55).

62. The denarius, a large silver coin, was the accepted salary for a day's work by a common laborer. Three hundred denarii would have represented

wages for a full year's work apart from the days of sabbath rest. See John W. Betlyon, "Coinage," *ABD* 1:1076–89, esp. 1086.

63. Jews were allowed but three spouses (see Str-B, 2:437; see, however, Mark 12:18–27 par.), but it is not certain that Samaritans observed the same mores. Rudolf Schnackenburg, however, notes: "with the strict views of Orientals on morality, the Samaritans must also have considered such frequent remarriage as dishonorable and illegitimate" (*The Gospel according to St. John*, vol. 1, HTCNT (New York: Herder & Herder, 1968), 433. The narrative trait of the Samaritan woman's frequent marriages would have been consistent with Jewish opinion about the low morals of Samaritans.

64. See J. Eugene Botha, *Jesus and the Samaritan Woman: A Speech Act Reading of John 4:1–42*, NovTSup 65 (Leiden: Brill, 1991), 154; Francis J. Moloney, *Belief in the Word: Reading John 1–4* (Minneapolis: Fortress, 1993), 148.

65. Ernst Haenchen, *John 1*, Hermeneia (Philadelphia: Fortress, 1984), 221; cf. Jerome H. Neyrey, "What's Wrong with This Picture? John 4, Cultural Stereotypes of Women, and Public and Private Space," *BTB* 24 (1994): 77–91.

66. In the Fourth Gospel the "disciples" are not simply to be equated with "the Twelve." See John 6:66–71; see also R. F. Collins, "The Twelve: Another Perspective: John 6,66–71," *Melita Theologica* 90 (1989): 95–109; reprinted in *These Things Have Been Written: Essays on the Fourth Gospel*, LTPM 2 (Louvain: Peeters, 1990; Grand Rapids: Eerdmans, 1991), 68–86.

67. See D. A. Lee, "Women as 'Sinners': Three Narratives of Salvation in Luke and John," *AusBR* 44 (1996): 1–15.

2

Conflict on Divorce

HE FOURTH GOSPEL'S STORY about the woman caught in adultery is unique. It is the only story in the Fourth Gospel, in fact in the entire New Testament, that presents Jesus as someone who is asked to adjudicate a case of sexual ethics. Apart from this single narrative, what the Fourth Gospel has to contribute to the understanding of sexual ethics is an appreciation of human relationships and the awesome demand to love as Jesus has loved us.[1]

Something similar can be said apropos of the Synoptic Gospels. The stories that Matthew, Mark, and Luke tell about Jesus have much to say about the demands of love, the nature of human relationships, and the demands of discipleship, but they have relatively little to say about sexual ethics as such. There is, nonetheless, one story about Jesus that stands out in this regard. This is the tale of his encounter with some Pharisees on the subject of divorce (Matt. 19:3–12; Mark 10:2–12).[2] Like the later story of Jesus' encounter with scribes and Pharisees on the case of adultery *in flagrante delicto*, the Synoptic story of Jesus' encounter with the Pharisees on the matter of divorce is presented as a test case (cf. Matt. 19:3; Mark 10:2). Like the Johannine story, the Synoptic story of Jesus' encounter on the subject of divorce has the literary form of a conflict story.[3] At issue in each of the stories is a provision of ancient Jewish law: the punishment of adultery in the Johannine story, the tolerance of divorce afforded by Deut. 24:1 in the Synoptic story. In each instance the conflict issues forth in a memorable statement by Jesus.[4]

22

MARK 10:2–12

Most contemporary scholars are of the opinion that Mark's Gospel is the oldest of the New Testament stories about Jesus. The story was written about the year 70 C.E., roughly at the time that the temple of Jerusalem was destroyed and the city was put to the torch. Matthew's Gospel was written some fifteen or so years later, when various Jewish groups, deprived of the unifying effect of worship in the temple, fell to bickering among themselves as to which of them offered the proper interpretation of the law. Which group represented Judaism at its best? Within this context Matthew revised Mark's story about Jesus for the benefit of Christian Jews. It tells the story of Jesus who had come to fulfill the law and the prophets (Matt. 5:17). Mark's story had been written for Gentile Christians. It lacks the focus on the scriptures that is to be found in Matthew. It describes conflicts between Jesus and the Pharisees in Galilee, but it lacks the harshness with which Matthew characterizes the scribes and Pharisees.

Mark's story about the conflict between Jesus and the Pharisees on divorce is found toward the end of Jesus' ministry in Galilee. The conflict begins with the Pharisees' pointed question, "Is it lawful for a man to divorce his wife?" This is a provocative question; Mark's Greek text indicates that the Pharisees asked the question about divorce, "testing him [Jesus]." It is also a legal question. The question means: "Is a man within his rights under the law to divorce his wife?" The question, as posed, arises in a Palestinian context, where men could divorce their wives in accordance with the provisions set down in Deut. 24:1 but where a woman was not allowed to divorce her husband.

In the ensuing discussion Jesus asks the Pharisees what the Mosaic law had to say about the subject. The Pharisees respond with a reference to the certificate of divorce whose conditions were stipulated in Deut. 24:1. The certificate served as a bill of freedom allowing the divorced woman to be remarried. Effectively the Deuteronomic legislation on the certificate of divorce afforded some measure of protection to the woman. The law required that there be some grounds for divorce. The law also required that certain legal formalities be properly attended to. Finally, the certificate meant that the woman was not left alone in a man's world. It was possible for her to be remarried; she was free to do so. In no way did the law make it mandatory for a man to divorce his wife; it simply allowed him to do so if there were sufficient grounds. In this respect the Pharisees were correct when they said to Jesus, "Moses allowed a man to write a certificate of dismissal and to divorce her" (Mark 10:4).

Rather than engaging the Pharisees in legal discussion, Jesus castigated them for their hardness of heart. Thereupon Jesus began to discuss the scripture with them. Mark's narrative has the character of a scholarly dispute. Jesus identified the prescription of Deut. 24:1 as a commandment, a *mitzvah*.[5] The Pharisees made their point with a reference to Deut. 24:1. Jesus made his point with reference to the twofold story of creation in Genesis 1 and 2. From the first creation story, Jesus quoted a scripture that pointed to the coexistence of man and woman in God's work of creation (Gen. 1:27). From the second story, Jesus quoted the scripture that spoke of man's desire for woman and of their union in sexual intercourse (Gen. 2:24). According to the rules of rabbinic debate, Jesus one-upped the Pharisees by referring to a passage that came from an earlier part of the Torah. The story of creation was older than the story of Mosaic legislation. Hence, it ruled the day. Having bested his opponents in a scriptural debate, Jesus was able to draw a compelling inference: "Therefore what God has joined together, let no one separate" (10:9).

Jesus did not respond directly to the Pharisees' question, "Is it lawful for a man [*andri*, the adult male] to divorce his wife?" (10:2). The Pharisees asked about the precepts of the law. While acknowledging that the regulation of divorce was a commandment of the law, Jesus affirmed that the legislation had been enacted because of the hardness of peoples' hearts, their cardiosclerosis. Jesus talked to them about God's plan in creating human beings with male and female gender. Then he uttered an exhortation.[6] In Mark's narrative Jesus did not, however, directly answer the Pharisees' question about the law.

The legal question is answered back "in the house," when the disciples continue to query[7] Jesus about the matter under discussion. In Mark's Gospel the house is a privileged place of Jesus' discourse with his disciples. This reflects the social situation of the early church. The first Christians gathered in homes. There they celebrated Eucharist. There too they discussed the meaning of Jesus' teaching and his ministry. "Back in the house" Jesus responded to the disciples' question about the legality of a man divorcing his wife. "Whoever," said Jesus, "divorces his wife and marries another commits adultery against her" (10:11).

To this Jesus adds, "and if she divorces her husband and marries another, she commits adultery" (10:12). The second part of Jesus' response is somewhat surprising. Mark's narrative had given no indication that a question had been raised about a woman divorcing her husband. Jesus' addition of a kind of a responsum to a question that had not been asked indicates that the situation of a woman who divorces is similar to that of the husband who divorces. If a man divorces his wife or a woman divorces her husband and remarries, they have committed adultery. What they have done is illegal. They have violated a *mitzvah,* the precept of the Decalogue that prohibited adultery (Exod. 20:14; Deut. 5:18; cf. Lev. 18:20).[8]

That the historical Jesus would have mentioned the situation of a woman divorcing her husband is quite unlikely. Jesus lived and taught in first-century Palestine, where it was all but unthinkable for a woman to divorce her husband. In the social circumstances of the Jewish community of the time, a man married, a woman *was* married. A man could divorce his wife, a woman could *be* divorced. Some decades later rabbis taught that if a husband had deprived his wife of her marital due[9]—"pleasuring her," to use the language of the times—she could petition the council, which would then order the man to give her a certificate of the divorce, the *giṭ.*

Jesus' saying about the woman divorcing her husband is, moreover, not found in the Matthean version of the story (Matt. 19:1–9). Neither is it found in Matthew's other version of Jesus' saying on the subject (Matt. 5:31–32), nor is it in the Lukan parallel (Luke 16:18).[10] Given these facts, it is likely that the historical Jesus spoke only about a man divorcing his wife. The logion about a woman divorcing her husband most likely results from Mark's adaptation of the tradition. His Gospel was written for Gentiles, not Semites or Palestinians. In Mark's Greco-Roman world it was quite possible for a woman to divorce her husband. Mark appended the saying about the woman divorcing her husband so as to make Jesus' exhortation on divorce relevant to those for whom his Gospel was written. If Jesus had exhorted men not to divorce their wives and remarry, why should women not be similarly exhorted?

That Mark would have paralleled a saying about a man divorcing his wife with a saying about a woman divorcing her husband is typical of Mark's style. Duality is one of the characteristic features of Mark's Gospel.[11] In fact, Mark's predilection for duality is to be seen in the way that he has structured his story of Jesus' teaching on divorce. It is

a narrative with two scenes. The first scene is set someplace "beyond
the Jordan," where Jesus is engaged in a controversial dialogue with
some Pharisees (10:2-9). The second scene is set in a house, where the
disciples ask Jesus about the same topic (10:10-12). These two narrative scenes are linked closely together. That Jesus' response to his disciples in 10:11 is a response to the Pharisees' question in 10:2 is one
way that the evangelist links the two scenes together. That he uses a
demonstrative pronominal adjective, "this matter" (*toutou*), in 10:10
is another.

That the evangelist has narrated Jesus' teaching on divorce in the
form of a response to his disciples' question and that he has placed the
scene in the house are other features of Markan style. The response to
a question and the location of significant activity and teaching in the
house are among the noteworthy narrative features of Mark's Gospel.[12]
Thus, it is quite likely that the entire scene has been composed by
Mark. By the time that Mark wrote his Gospel in about 70 C.E., a saying of Jesus on divorce had long been in circulation in the early
church.[13] That saying indicated that a man's divorce of his wife was
tantamount to adultery. In this respect, it was a violation of the Torah.

A question that had been raised in the Gentile Christian communities of the early church concerned the extent to which the precepts of
the Torah were binding on Gentile Christians. The Acts of the Apostles preserves a tradition that indicates that Gentiles were not to be
troubled about the observance of the precepts of the Torah. They had
only to abstain from things polluted by idols, from fornication, from
whatever had been strangled, and from blood (Acts 15:19-20, 28-29).[14]
If Jesus' exhortation to his male Jewish disciples not to divorce their
wives was to have relevance for Gentile Christians of a later generation, it had to be seen as having an authority other than that of the
Torah. Observance of the Torah *per se* was not incumbent upon Gentile Christians. Were they then not bound to avoid divorcing their
wives if the ban on divorce were merely a matter of Torah observance?

To respond to that question Mark composed the narrative found in
10:2-12. Verses 10-12 present the implications of the traditional exhortation for Gentile Christians. Verses 2-9, the first part of the narrative,
use the literary form of the conflict story and a kind of "scriptural
apologetic"[15] to base the authority of Jesus' exhortation not on the
Torah but on the creative will of God.[16]

This part of Mark's narrative features three distinct elements in
Jesus' discourse. The first unit of discourse is the dialogue between

Jesus and the Pharisees over the command of Moses with regard to divorce (vv. 2–4). Jesus answers their question with a question, "What did Moses command you?" The Pharisees quickly respond with a reference to Deut. 24:1, the operative scripture in this regard. The Deuteronomic passage on the certificate of divorce was the basis of rabbinic halakah on divorce. It was the subject of a famous dispute between the school of Hillel and the school of Shammai (see *m. Giṭ.* 9:10). Jesus dismisses the use of this scripture as legitimate grounds for divorce by characterizing it as a provision of the law for those who were hard of heart. In the Jewish understanding of the human person, the heart (*lēb*) was the very core of the human being. The heart was known only to God. In one's heart a human was open to God or closed to God. In effect, Jesus' reply to the Pharisees was that if they were to take advantage of the provision of Deut. 24:1 and divorce their wives, they were no better than Pharaoh of old, who also was hard of heart.

The second part of Jesus' discourse (vv. 5–8) consists of a scriptural reflection on God's creation of the human being. Using a citation from the priestly creation narrative (Gen. 1:27),[17] Jesus reminds the Pharisees that God had created humanity in two genders, male and female. Using a citation from the Yahwist's story (Gen. 2:24), Jesus then draws an inference from God's creation of humanity in two sexes. Because of the sexual difference, the male is to leave the parental home and be joined to his wife. Their sexual union makes them no longer two but one.

In the third part of his discourse (v. 9) Jesus draws a strong inference from his reflection on the divinely intended purpose of human sexuality:[18] "What God has joined together, let no one separate" (Mark 10:9). The Greek word "to separate" (*chōrizō*) was part of the technical divorce language of Mark's day. It was not, however, the word that the Pharisees had used in their question about "divorce" (*apolyō*). Changing the language of the discussion as he did, Jesus chose not to respond directly to the Pharisees' question. Jesus' change of the linguistic register indicated that what was at stake in the discussion was not simply an issue of the law. Something far more important was at stake, namely, the will of God. The language of "separation" produces a direct and vivid contrast to the language of Gen. 2:24, which speaks of "joining" and "becoming one." According to Jesus, a human being must not take it upon him- or herself to divide what God has made one. Any use of the Torah to separate the two-in-oneness created by God comes from the hardness of the human heart.

The second scene in the Markan narrative takes place in the house (10:10–12). There Jesus is engaged in dialogue with his disciples. The disciples pursue the question that the Pharisees had asked. Jesus gives them the answer that he did not give to the Pharisees. His answer is given in the form of a casuistic instruction in which men and women are treated in similar fashion. Jesus speaks about men first of all. "Whoever divorces[19] his wife," he says, "and marries another commits adultery against her" (10:11). With regard to women, Jesus' casuistry affirms that "if she divorces her husband and marries another, she commits adultery" (10:12). The instruction on men divorcing their wives has a relative clause, "whoever divorces his wife and marries another," as its subject. The instruction on women begins with a conditional clause, "if she divorces her husband and marries another." Otherwise the instructions are parallel[20] with the single exception of the phrase "against her" (*ep' autēn*).

The phrase "against her" breaks the structural balance of the two parts of Jesus' instruction to his disciples.[21] The presence of the words "against her" is nevertheless necessary for the semantic balance of the instruction. In the ancient world, adultery was generally considered to be an offense against an aggrieved husband. His wife and her paramour had committed adultery against him. This understanding of adultery was so common that in some societies the aggrieved husband was allowed to determine the punishment for adultery. If he were to do so, he was to treat his adulterous wife and her lover in similar fashion.[22] The man who committed adultery offended not his own marriage but the marriage of his married lover. He committed an offense against the husband of his paramour, but he was not considered to have committed an offense against his own wife. With the addition of "against her," Jesus' instruction states that a man who divorces his wife and marries another woman has committed an offense against his own wife. Conversely, a woman who divorces her husband and marries another man commits an offense against her own husband. Men, like women, offend their own spouses when they are involved in an adulterous tryst. For Jesus to affirm that it is an offense against one's own wife for a man to commit adultery was a new and radical idea.[23] It reflects a situation of parity in marital relationships that had hitherto been unknown in the ancient world.[24]

Jesus' instruction to his disciples moves far beyond the narrow ambit of the Pharisees' question. The Markan Jesus addresses a new situation. The question of the Pharisees made sense in a patriarchal world where only men had the right to divorce their wives. Jesus' words impart some degree of parity to the marriage relationship. In the matter of divorce the situation of a woman is equal to that of a man. If either a man or a woman takes advantage of legal tolerance to divorce his or her spouse and then marry again, the man or woman has committed an adulterous offense against the abandoned spouse, be it wife or husband.

Jesus' instruction of the disciples adds something else to the discussion. In answering the Pharisee's question for the benefit of his disciples, Jesus talks about the man and the woman who divorce and remarry. The offense against the law, that is, adultery, takes place with remarriage. At that point the abandoned spouse is aggrieved and the law is violated. Adultery has been committed. This is the legal response to the Pharisees' question. The larger issue is whether divorce itself should take place. That issue had been aired by Jesus in the public forum in the Pharisees' presence. His response to the question of a married man or woman abandoning his or her spouse is radical: "What God has joined together, let no one separate."

MATTHEW 19:3–12

A decade or so after Mark wrote his story about Jesus, the evangelist Matthew revised the story for the benefit of a Jewish Christian readership that probably lived in Syria. The question about whether or not it was licit for a man to divorce his wife was placed in a different context and rephrased. The new context was the age-long discussion among Jews not about whether or not it was licit for a man to divorce his wife but about the grounds for divorce. Jews knew well that the Mosaic legislation preserved in the book of Deuteronomy legitimated a man's divorcing his wife for cause. The scripture said, "Suppose a man enters into marriage with a woman, but she does not please him because he finds something objectionable about her, and so he writes her a certificate of divorce, puts it in her hands, and sends her out of his house; she then leaves the house and goes off to become another man's wife" (Deut. 24:1–2). What kind of objectionable thing did a man have to find in his wife before it was legitimate for him to dismiss her from his house with a certificate of divorce? That was the question that the Pharisees of Matthew's time were asking.

Around 200 C.E. the Mishnah summarized the discussion. It

invoked the authority of the most important rabbis of Jesus' day, Shammai and Hillel, as well as that of the great rabbi Akiva, a second-century C.E. Jewish martyr and teacher:

> The School of Shammai say: A man may not divorce his wife unless he has found unchastity in her, for it is written, "Because he hath found *indecency* in anything." And the school of Hillel say: (He may divorce her) even if she spoiled a dish for him, for it is written, "Because he hath found in her indecency in *anything*." R. Akiva says: Even if he found another fairer than she, for it is written, "And it shall be if she *find no favor in his eyes*." (*m. Giṭ*. 9:10)

Rabbis of the school of Shammai were rabbis of strict observance. In their interpretation of the Deuteronomic text, the emphasis lay on "objectionable/indecency." Rabbis of the school of Hillel were more tolerant in their interpretation of the demands of the law. They placed the emphasis on "something/anything." Akiva, a disciple of Hillel, continued with the more tolerant interpretation of the law by stressing "does not please/find no favor in his eyes" in the interpretation of Deut. 24:1. Flavius Josephus, the first-century historian of Judaism, refers to a man divorcing his wife "for whatsoever cause" (*Antiquities* 4.8.23 §253).

Within the context of this ongoing halakic debate Matthew rewrote Mark's conflict story about an encounter between Jesus and the Pharisees on the matter of a husband's prerogative to divorce his wife. In Matthew's version of the episode, the Pharisees question was not, "Is it lawful for a man to divorce his wife?" (Mark 10:2). Rather the question was, "Is it lawful for a man to divorce his wife for any cause?" (Matt. 19:3). In the Gospel according to Matthew, it is "the cause" that is the focus of the Pharisees' question. They sought to entrap Jesus by forcing him to opt for one side or the other in the ongoing debate.

In rewriting the story of Jesus' encounter with the Pharisees for his Jewish Christian readership, Matthew placed the emphasis on the interpretation of the law.[25] In his version the scriptural stories of creation serve as an introduction to Jesus' public response to the legal question. This background was not sufficient for the Pharisees, who pressed the legal question saying, "Why then did Moses command us to give a certificate of dismissal and to divorce her?" (19:7).

Jesus' answer is given in the form of a response to each of the Pharisees' questions (vv. 3, 7). To the second question, "Why did Moses command us to give a certificate of dismissal?" Jesus responded, "It was because you were so hard-hearted that Moses allowed you to divorce your wives" (19:8). Jesus' response to the question contains an implicit critique of the Pharisees' attitude. They spoke of a "command" of Moses; Jesus spoke about what Moses "allowed." From Jesus' perspective, Moses merely tolerated a man's divorcing his wife. To make the point even clearer, he added, "but from the beginning it was not so." Jesus relegated the tolerance of divorce to that second tier of *mitzvot* that popular wisdom considered to derive from God's condescension of those who could not fully conform to the rigors of the demands of the law. He reminded the Pharisees that this concession was not in accord with God's creative will. "From the beginning it was not so."

To the Pharisees' initial question, "Is it lawful for a man to divorce his wife for any cause?" Jesus responded, "And I say to you, whoever divorces his wife, except for unchastity, and marries another commits adultery" (19:9). This response is tailored to the Pharisees' question. The Pharisees raised a legal question about a man divorcing his wife. Jesus responds only to this legal question. Unlike the Jesus of Mark's Gospel, the Jesus of Matthew's Gospel does not add a parallel saying about a woman divorcing her husband. Nor does he say anything about divorce and remarriage being an affront to the woman who had been divorced. Matthew's Jesus simply responds to the Pharisees' question. The formal introduction, "And I say to you," identifies Jesus as an authoritative interpreter of the law (cf. Matt. 5:32). What is the legality of a man's divorcing his wife? Jesus' answer is that it is against the law. For a man to divorce his wife and remarry is to commit adultery, a violation of Torah. Jesus responds to the question of law with a legal answer.

The context is one of casuistry. Matthew's Jesus admits one exception to his blanket assertion that a man's divorcing his wife and remarrying is a matter of adultery. The exception is "unchastity" (*porneia*). The Greek word *porneia* is a term that designates sexual misconduct in general or in any of its forms. Throughout the centuries scholars have been debating the meaning of this apparent exception.[26] On balance it would seem that in rewriting Mark's conflict story Matthew has added his own codicil to the legal tradition. He has amended the ruling so that any of his Jewish Christian readers who had availed themselves of a strict interpretation of the law to divorce adulterous wives and remarry should not consider themselves to have committed adultery. At the time that Matthew wrote his Gospel, the law of the land actually required a man to divorce a wife who had committed adultery.[27]

Matthew's revision of the story about Jesus' debate with the Pharisees on the subject of divorce retains the Markan structure of a story with two scenes. In Matthew the second scene, the scene in the house (19:10–12), focuses on the disciples' possibility of living in accordance with the authoritatively explained provisions of the law on divorce. Jesus responds to the disciples' ongoing queries with a seemingly enigmatic saying about eunuchs.[28] His response affirms that God's grace will enable the disciples to fulfill the demands of the law as authoritatively explicated by Jesus. He counters their impetuous outburst that it is better not to marry (19:10) with the offer of God's grace for his disciples as they live their marital lives in fidelity to God's demand. Only a few are impelled by God's rule to live a celibate life.[29] Jesus was one of them. His way of life earned for him the derogatory remark that he was less than a man.[30]

The story about Jesus' conflict with Pharisees on the subject of divorce expands the traditional lore on adultery so that divorce followed by remarriage is considered to be a form of adultery. Both the Markan and the Matthean versions of the conflict reflect the view that human sexuality is an integral element of God's creative plan for humankind. Sexual desire moves a man to leave his parental home and to cling to a woman as his wife. This is the vision of human sexuality on which Jesus' teaching about divorce is based. Mark's version of that teaching goes beyond that of Matthew in that it clearly introduces the notion of parity in sexual relations, an idea that is missing from the Matthean narrative, whose story of the conflict has been revised for the patriarchal society of a Jewish Christian readership.

MATTHEW 5:31–32

Matthew's story of the conflict is not the only place in his Gospel in which he addresses the issue of divorce. Earlier in the Gospel, in the Sermon on the Mount, Jesus explains to his disciples that their righteousness must go beyond that of the scribes and Pharisees. To illustrate, Jesus cites a number of *mitzvot* that he interprets with authority. "But I say to you . . . ." One such *mitzvah* is Deut. 24:1, the regulation concerning the certificate of divorce. Explaining this commandment, Jesus says, "Anyone who divorces his wife, except on the ground of unchastity, causes her to commit adultery; and whoever marries a divorced woman commits adultery" (Matt. 5:32).

The double explanation expands the traditional notion of adultery in two ways.[31] Jesus first states that a husband who divorces his wife is responsible for the guilt of adultery that is incurred in her remarriage. The certificate of divorce was a bill of freedom that allowed a woman to remarry. Both Deut. 24:1–2 and the social circumstances of the time presume that the woman would be remarried. Otherwise she would have been without a significant other in the patriarchal society of the times. According to Matthew's Jesus, this woman's second marriage is adulterous; the husband who divorced her, forcing her into this second union, is the one who is responsible for the adultery. Again, an exception is to be made for the case of "unchastity" (*porneia*). Then Jesus states that a man who marries a divorced woman is guilty of adultery.

The prescriptions on divorce in Matthew are clearly patriarchal; they are written from the perspective of the man. Together with his response to the Pharisees' question in 19:9, Jesus' words identify three circumstances attendant upon a divorce that make a man guilty of adultery: (1) a man divorcing his wife and marrying another; (2) a man virtually forcing his wife into adultery by divorcing her; and (3) a man who marries a divorced woman. According to Matthew, there is an exception to be made in the first two cases. The exception is made when "unchastity" has taken place. This exception is found only in the Gospel according to Matthew.

LUKE 16:18

A tradition of Jesus' logion on divorce is attested also in the Gospel according to Luke. In Luke 16:18 a saying on divorce appears with virtually no narrative context. Almost out of the blue, Jesus says, "Anyone who divorces his wife and marries another commits adultery, and whoever marries a woman divorced from her husband commits adultery."

This version of Jesus' saying on divorce is different from those found in Mark 10:11–12; Matt. 5:32; and Matt. 19:9. Since the logion exists as an isolable saying in Luke's Gospel and has a parallel in Matt. 5:32, scholars generally hold the opinion that Luke 16:18, along with Matt. 5:32, derives from an ancient collection of Jesus' sayings, the Q source.[32] The second part of the saying is substantively the same in Luke 16:18 and Matt. 5:32: any man who marries a divorced woman is guilty of adultery. Luke's version of the first part of the saying on divorce (16:18a) is virtually the same as Mark 10:11 and Matt. 19:9, but it is different from Matt. 5:32.

That the Lukan version of the saying is so different from its parallel in Matt. 5:32 gives rise to scholarly speculation as to the original version of the logion.[33] The pursuit of the original version of Jesus' saying is complex. I would venture that the original version was something like "Anyone who divorces his wife involves her in adultery, and whoever marries a divorced woman commits adultery."[34]

1 CORINTHIANS 7:10–11

A fifth version of Jesus' saying on divorce can be found in Paul's first letter to the Corinthians.[35] Paul's reference to the saying is, in fact, the oldest literary witness to the tradition of Jesus' logion on divorce. Paul's letter was written more than fifteen years before Mark wrote his Gospel story about Jesus. Paul cites the saying because some in the Corinthian community were apparently troubled by a slogan that was circulating within the community: "It is well for a man not to touch a woman" (1 Cor. 7:1). Paul's response to the Corinthians' concern is contained in a long section of his letter, chapters 5–7, in which he deals with a variety of issues related to human sexuality.[36] His response begins with timely advice to those who are married (7:1–7). Then Paul addresses a number of people who are involved in a variety of particular situations, widows and widowers (7:8–9), those who might be contemplating divorce (7:10–11), and those who are involved in a "mixed marriage" (7:12–16). In the last part of the chapter (7:32–40), Paul writes about those who have not yet married (vv. 32–38) and adds a few words on the widow (vv. 39–40).

Paul's words on divorce in 1 Cor. 7:10–11 seem to have been occasioned by a situation that had arisen within the Corinthian community. It concerned a woman who was about to divorce her husband. That Paul's words are case-specific is suggested by the fact that he speaks of a woman separating from her husband before he talks about a man divorcing his wife. Elsewhere in the chapter Paul begins with the man, then addresses the situation of the woman. Writing about divorce in vv. 10–11, however, Paul deals with the situation of the woman before that of the man. Another reason for thinking that Paul was dealing with a real situation of divorce in 7:10–11 is the fact that all the other New Testament passages that offer a version of Jesus' saying on divorce speak to the possibility of a man divorcing his wife. Among the Synoptics Mark alone adds to the traditional saying a complementary saying that makes reference to a woman divorcing her husband (Mark 10:10–12), which follows the saying about a man divorcing his wife.

In this case (7:10–11), Paul strongly urges the wife not to separate from her husband. He does so on the strongest authority, that of the Lord. He contrasts the Lord's authority with his own and reminds the Corinthians that the advice he is offering is not merely apostolic advice; it ultimately comes from the Lord himself. As he makes his plea, Paul appeals not so much to the binding force of a tradition that has been handed down within the community as to the authority of the risen Lord over the community.[37] Paul urges the wife who is contemplating separation from her husband not to do so. If she does separate, says Paul, she must remain unmarried so that she can be reconciled to her husband.[38] Paul's words reflect the traditional sexual taboo, attested in Deut. 24:1–4, according to which a woman who had had sexual intercourse with another man was not allowed to resume a marital sexual relationship with her (former) husband.

Paul's approach to human sexuality holds that there is a parity in the relationship between men and women.[39] In matters of sexuality, the demands of the Lord pertain equally to men and to women. Having exhorted the woman who was contemplating separation from her husband to refrain from doing so, Paul also exhorts husbands not to divorce their wives. The brevity of his exhortation to Christian husbands (7:11b) confirms that the real issue in Corinth is that of a woman divorcing her husband. Because of his conviction that a similar moral responsibility falls on men and on women with regard to the sexual relationship, Paul adds to his exhortation that a woman not divorce her husband the expectation that a man should not divorce his wife (cf. 7:27).

Paul's conviction that spouses should not divorce each other carries over in the exhortation that he addresses to the rest (7:12–16). "The rest" are those men and women who are married to unbelievers. Since Christians are expected to marry "in the Lord" (7:39), it is likely that "the rest" are Christians who had been married before they accepted the Christian faith. Their spouses did not accompany them into the church. Because of the conversion of one of the partners but not of the other, these Christians were involved in an exogamous marriage.

Within all cultures there is a prohibition against someone marrying outside of the normal social group. Sometimes the prohibition is in the form of law; at other times it is in the form of custom or social pressure. Royalty is expected to marry royalty. Jews are expected to marry Jews.[40] Christians are expected to marry Christians. In the Indian caste system, men and women are expected to marry persons belonging to their caste. As far as the law is concerned, one need only remember the laws on miscegenation that were enforced in many southern states until recent decades. Roman Catholic canon law continues to prohibit marriage between Roman Catholics and those who are not Roman Catholic.[41]

In Paul's day marriages between Corinthian Christians and non-Christians were simply anomalous. In the Greco-Roman world a wife was expected to honor her husband's deities. Within Judaism, some rabbis considered that the conversion of a proselyte to Judaism constituted something like a new birth (see *b. Yebam.* 22a). A marriage into which a person had entered prior to conversion to Judaism was nullified by that person's conversion to Judaism. A social concern for endogamy prompted Paul to consider "mixed marriages" as a special case. His view—and he makes it clear that it is his view, not a command of the Lord—is that even in exogamous marriages, marital fidelity is the norm.[42] Christians are not to divorce their non-Christian partners. Since his exhortation in this regard is in fact countercultural, Paul develops a lengthy argument (7:14–16) in which he proposes a series of reasons why Christians should remain wedded to their non-Christian spouses.

Paul's first argument is that the non-Christian is "made holy" because of his or her marriage to the Christian. Because of the marriage, the non-Christian has, as it were, been co-opted into God's plan of salvation. Moreover, children born of such a union are also holy.[43] Another argument advanced by Paul is that Christians have been called to peace. Peace is the sum total of God's gifts to his people. Within Paul's Jewish tradition a happy and fruitful marriage is a blessing from God (see Psalm 128). A good marriage is an important component of the peace that God gives to his people and to which he calls them. Finally, Christians should not divorce their non-Christian spouses because it is possible that their marriage is the means by which God will introduce the nonbeliever to the Christian faith.[44] In sum, Paul not only urges Christians to remain united to their non-Christian spouses; he also explains to them why they should do so.

Where sex and marriage are concerned, Paul is ever the realist.[45] In a brief aside (7:15a), he notes that if the non-Christian refuses to live with the Christian, there is nothing that the Christian can do about it. The Christian must be content to see the non-Christian depart. Paul's realistic attitude toward marriage is such that he realizes that exogamous marriage is countercultural in the world in which he lives, whether that world be the Greco-Roman world in which he preached or the world of the Jewish heritage in which he had his religious roots. In this context Paul could but counsel the Christian who was married to a non-Christian to allow the non-Christian spouse to leave the marital union if he or she chose to do so.

Paul was, however, convinced that the call to peace was such that Christians should remain committed to their spouses in their marriage relationship. He developed a substantial theological argument to convince Christians involved in an exogamous marriage to remain married to their spouses. So convinced was he that marriage was a gift from the Lord (7:7) that carried with it a divinely mandated set of responsibilities that he pleaded with spouses not to abandon their marital partners—whether they were married to non-Christians or in a marriage in the Lord (7:39). If a Christian woman should contemplate divorce it was important that she remain in a state that would allow reconciliation with her husband (7:11b).

In short, Paul has taken from Jesus' traditional logion on divorce a warrant for his own exhortation with regard to divorce. His exhortation is attentive to the various marriage situations in which Christian spouses, men or women, might find themselves. The authority of "the Lord" (7:10) is the perspective from which he develops his argument. Paul invokes the authority of the Lord, but he does not cite the logion of Jesus verbatim.[46] The logion spoke of divorce as a kind of adultery. It places the matter of divorce within the context of the meaning of the Ten Commandments of the law. That is something that Paul, apostle to the Gentiles and writing for a Gentile Christian audience, did not do in his letter to the Corinthians.

Notes

1. See Luise Schottroff, "Sexualität im Johannesevangelium," *EvT* 57 (1997): 437–44 (abstract: "Sexuality in John's Gospel," *TD* 45 [1998]: 103–7).

Noël Lazure's monograph on the moral values of Johannine theology, including the letters, does not pay any particular attention to sexuality. See N. Lazure, *Les Valeurs morales de la théologie johannique (Évangile et Épîtres)*, EBib (Paris: Gabalda, 1965).

2. See Raymond F. Collins, *Divorce in the New Testament*, GNS 38 (Collegeville, Minn.: Liturgical Press, 1992), esp. 65–145, 184–213.

3. Within the New Testament the genre of the conflict story is classic. See Arland J. Hultgren, *Jesus and His Adversaries: The Form and Function of the Conflict Stories in the Synoptic Tradition* (Minneapolis: Augsburg, 1979).

4. The two judicial scenes in John 7:53–8:11 give rise to two such apothegms, John 8:7b, 11b. The punch lines that conclude the story of Jesus' dialogue with the Pharisees about divorce are somewhat different in the Gospels according to Matthew and according to Mark. See Matt. 19:9 and Mark 10:5–9, 11–12.

5. Mark 10:5; cf. v. 3. In the rabbinic tradition of the 613 commandments of the law, Deut. 24:1 was the 222nd among the 247 mandatory commandments.

6. The universal negative imperative, *anthrōpos mē chōrizetō*, is hortatory, not legislative.

7. Note the use of the same verb, *eperōtaō*, "to ask," in vv. 2 and 10.

8. With a reference to Lev. 18:20, the rabbinic tradition of the 613 commandments in the law identified the prohibition of adultery as the 347th prohibition.

9. Exod. 21:10 identifies three rights of a wife: her right to food, to clothing, and to sex (*'ōnah*). There is some dispute as to the exact meaning of *'ōnah*, translated in the NRSV as "marital rights," but rabbinic tradition generally interprets the expression as referring to a woman's sexual rights.

10. See, however, 1 Cor. 7:10–11.

11. Cf. Frans Neirynck, *Duality in Mark: Contributions to the Study of the Markan Redaction*, BETL 31 (rev. ed.; Louvain: University Press/Peeters, 1988), 26, 29.

12. Cf. Mark 4:10–12; see R. F. Collins, "The Transformation of a Motif: 'They Entered the House of Simon and Andrew' (Mark 1,29)," SNTSU 18 (1993) 5–40, 11–13, 17–18; idem, *Divorce*, 70–93.

13. See 1 Cor. 7:10–11. This letter would have been written in about 53 C.E. The saying on divorce in Matt. 5:32 and Luke 16:18 comes from Q, a hypothetical documentary source of Jesus' sayings that may have been compiled in about 50 C.E. (see below, n. 32).

14. See below, pp. 169–70.

15. The terminology comes from Barnabas Lindars. In its widest form it connotes the use of the Jewish scriptures to reflect on the life, ministry, and teaching of Jesus as well as on the experience of the early church itself.

16. The very fact that a rationale is appended to parenesis is a telling indication of the secondary use of parenesis. Normally parenetic exhortations are uttered on the basis of their inherent authority.

17. The priestly narrative of creation is the first story in Genesis, 1:1–2:4a.

18. Note the inferential *oun*, "therefore."

19. The Greek verb "divorces"—the subjunctive *apolysē* in v. 11, the aorist

participle *apolysasa* in v. 12—harks back to the Pharisees' question in v. 2, "Is it lawful for a man to divorce his wife?" which uses the same verb in the aorist infinitive form (*apolysai*).

20. Both Jesus' traditional saying on divorce, in all its New Testament forms, and Mark's additional statement about women divorcing their husbands suppose a situation in which the new "spouse" is a person who was previously married.

21. It is likely that this explanatory phrase does not go back to the historical Jesus. It is not found in the other New Testament passages that speak of a man divorcing his wife (Matt. 5:32; 19:9; Luke 16:18; 1 Cor. 7:11). The phrase was most likely added by the evangelist, who, in composing his story, adapted the traditional saying of Jesus on divorce to the new situation of a Christian community in the Hellenistic world.

22. See above, pp. 2–4.

23. In his study of rabbinic rhetoric on sexuality, Michael Satlow has likewise observed that Jesus' idea that a man can commit adultery against his own wife "differs fundamentally" from rabbinic rhetoric. See Satlow, *Tasting the Dish: Rabbinic Rhetorics of Sexuality*, Brown Judaic Studies 303 (Atlanta: Scholars Press, 1995), 120 n. 6.

24. The parity of relationships within marriage is reflected also in 1 Cor. 7:1–7, 12–14, 16, where a series of six parallel statements indicates that the situations of husbands and wives with regard to their spouses are quite equal. See below, pp. 34–35.

25. On Matthew's revision of Mark, see Collins, *Divorce*, 104–45, 279–97.

26. See the summary of the various interpretations in Collins, *Divorce*, 199–205.

27. That is Roman law, under the provisions of the *Lex Iulia de adulteriis coercendis*. See Corrado Marucci, *Parole di Gesù sul divorzio: Ricerche scritturistiche previa ad un ripensamento teologico, canonistico e pastorale della dottrina cattolica dell'indissolubilità del matrimonio*, Aloisiana 16 (Naples: Morcelliana, 1982), 383–95; Collins, *Divorce*, 212, 229–31.

28. See Collins, *Divorce*, 118–32, 285–91.

29. Francis J. Moloney has observed that it was a "very *precise* [his emphasis] situation in the Matthean Church" that led to the insertion of the eunuch saying in the Matthean narrative. He opines that the situation most likely had to do with the marital situation of recent Gentile converts. See F. J. Moloney, "Matthew 19,3–12: A Redactional and Form Critical Study," *JSNT* 2 (1979): 42–60, 48.

30. See John P. Meier, *A Marginal Jew: Rethinking the Historical Jesus*, vol. 1, ABRL (Garden City, N.Y.: Doubleday, 1991), 343–45; Collins, *Divorce*, 130–32.

31. Following a Jewish catechetical practice, the preceding pericope, Matt. 5:27–30, had expanded the notion of adultery by presenting lust and masturbation as forms of adultery. See below, pp. 45–46.

32. Q is the first letter of the German word *Quelle*, which means "source." In biblical scholarship it is the commonly accepted siglum used to designate a hypothetical collection of sayings of Jesus that may have arisen around 50 C.E. The existence of such a collection is accepted by the vast majority of biblical

scholars. It is a "hypothetical" document insofar as there is no extant manuscript of the document as a discrete text. The 245 verses of discourse material that scholars assign to Q are collated into the hypothetical document on the basis of their presence, in very similar form, in both Matthew and Luke.

33. See Collins, *Divorce*, 146–83.

34. Ibid., 183.

35. Ibid., 9–39, 233–60.

36. On this passage, see chap. 7 below.

37. It is to be noted that Paul but rarely appeals to the tradition of the sayings of Jesus. The memory of the words of Jesus on the night before he died in 1 Cor. 11:23–26 is a notable exception. The only other passages in which a claim can legitimately be made for Paul's appealing to the tradition of the words of the historical Jesus are 1 Thess. 4:15–17; 1 Cor. 9:14; and 1 Cor. 7:10–11. For a discussion, see Frans Neirynck, "Paul and the Sayings of Jesus," in *Evangelica II: Collected Essays by Frans Neirynck*, ed. Frans van Segbroeck, BETL 99 (Louvain: University Press/Peeters, 1991), 511–68; and F. Neirynck, "The Sayings of Jesus in 1 Corinthians," in *The Corinthian Correspondence*, ed. Reimund Bieringer, BETL 125 (Louvain: University Press/Peeters, 1996), 141–76.

38. The aside of v. 11a, "but if she does separate, let her remain unmarried or else be reconciled to her husband," should not be construed as offering a choice to the woman who has separated from her husband, as if she might choose to remain unmarried or choose to be reconciled to her husband. The aside is a single statement that implies that a woman who has separated from her husband should remain unmarried so that she can be reconciled to her husband. A traditional sexual taboo prohibited a woman who had been divorced and remarried from returning to her first husband (Deut. 24:1–4). See further the discussion in Helmut Merklein, "'Es ist gut für den Menschen, eine Frau nicht anzufassen': Paulus und die Sexualität nach 1 Kor 7," in Josef Blank et al., *Die Frau im Urchristentum*, QD 95 (Freiburg/Basel/Vienna: Herder, 1983), 225–53, 236; and Collins, *Divorce*, 36–37, 245–46.

39. It is to be noted that the passages that speak of the subordination of wives to their husbands, Eph. 5:22 and Col. 3:18, are found in the Pauline pseudepigrapha, not in the letters that the apostle himself wrote.

40. This expectation, continued to this day, has its roots in a biblical injunction. See Deut. 7:3–4; cf. 11QTemple 57:15–19, which prohibits a king from marrying a Gentile. By extension this injunction bans the members of the community for whom the text was written from marrying Gentile women.

41. See canons 1086 and 1124 of the 1983 Code of Canon Law: "Marriage between two persons, one of whom is baptized in the Catholic Church or has been received into it and has not left it by means of a formal act, and the other of whom is non-baptized, is invalid" (1086, 1). "Without the express permission of the competent authority, marriage is forbidden between two baptized persons, one of whom was baptized in the Catholic Church or received into it after baptism and has not left it by a formal act, and the other of whom is a member of a church or ecclesial community which is not in full communion with the Catholic Church" (1124).

42. See Collins, *Divorce*, 40–64, 246–59.

43. This element of Pauline teaching was somewhat countercultural. Within the Greco-Roman world, children of Greek and Roman citizens were considered citizens only if both parents were citizens. Among Jews, a child borne by a Jewish woman of a Gentile father—even of a proselyte who had converted to Judaism and had been circumcised, but was not yet immersed—was considered to be a *mamzer/et*. This Hebrew term is usually translated as "bastard." Cf. *b. Yebam.* 46a; par. *b. ʿAbod. Zar.* 59a.

44. See Collins, *Divorce,* 60–62.

45. See chap. 7 below, especially on 1 Cor. 7:1–9, pp. 119–22.

46. The form of Jesus' logion on divorce that might have been known to Paul is another question, one that it may not be possible to resolve.

3

"You Shall Not Commit Adultery"

W HEN HE URGED THE CHRISTIANS of Corinth to avoid divorce, Paul did not cite the authority of the law. It was, however, the authority of the law with regard to divorce that had prompted some Pharisees to ask Jesus about the legitimacy of a man divorcing his wife (Mark 10:2). For his Gentile Christian audience, Mark moved the discussion of divorce away from a discussion on the relevance of the commandments of Torah to the significance of God's creation of man and woman. Back in the house, Jesus had taught his disciples that, notwithstanding this broad theological perspective, divorce was a violation of the law. Rewriting the story for a Jewish Christian audience, Matthew underscored the idea that divorce was to be considered a violation of Torah (Matt. 19:9). In the Sermon on the Mount (Matt. 5:31–32) he would make it clearer still that divorce was a violation of the seventh commandment,[1] "You shall not commit adultery.

THE SERMON ON THE MOUNT

Matthew was heir to a Jewish catechetical tradition in which various ethical demands could be collated under the rubric of the Ten Com- mandments.[2] This is clearly evident in his portrayal of Jesus as the teacher par excellence in the Sermon on the Mount (Matt. 5:1–8:1). The evangelist's narrative setting of the Sermon solemnly and for- mally presents Jesus speaking to and teaching his disciples (5:1–2).

Assuming the posture of the seated rabbi, Jesus offers his disciples a series of catechetical lessons. The disciples of Jesus are presented as his pupils. The master–disciple relationship is such that the disciples must learn from the master teacher so that they in turn can transmit his teaching to their disciples (28:20). Thus there was formed within Matthew's Jewish Christian community a "school of Jesus." Simon, called Peter, was the chief rabbi after Jesus.[3] This school considered itself to be the authentic interpreter of the Jewish tradition in contrast to the schools of Shammai and Hillel, which were vying for leadership among the Pharisees in the generation after the destruction of Jerusalem.[4]

As he sits on the mountain in the presence of the crowds, Jesus gathers his disciples around him (5:1). The crowds, whom Jesus can see, are able to observe the young school at work. Jesus offers a series of catechetical instructions to his students. The first lesson is a series of instructions on happiness. These are the beatitudes of Matt. 5:1–12.[5] The second major catechetical unit has the form of a series of antitheses. The essential outline for the catechetical lesson is provided by the Ten Commandments, to which is appended the commandment of the love of neighbor (Matt. 5:21–48; cf. 22:37–40). The third major unit of Jesus' catechesis is a lesson on the pious works of almsgiving, prayer, and fasting (Matt. 6:1–18).

The second lesson in this long "classroom" session is presented from the perspective of the fulfillment of the law and the prophets.[6] With this perspective the master teacher does not allow his disciples to teach that it is permissible to violate even one of the lesser commandments of the Torah. They must be all that they can be, just as their heavenly Father is all that he can be (5:48). The disciples of the teacher are to be fully responsive to their call to righteousness. This is the demand that they be in right relationship with their God and their neighbor. Their righteousness must exceed that of the scribes and Pharisees, Hillelites and Shammaites alike.

To illustrate his point, Jesus begins with an instruction on the Ten Commandments—not all of them, to be sure, but enough of them for his disciples to grasp the gist of his challenge. From the lectern that Matthew has strategically placed on the mountaintop, Jesus explains the sixth, seventh, and ninth commandments, "You shall not murder," "You shall not commit adultery," and "You shall not swear falsely."[7] Following traditional pedagogical practice, the teacher first presents the commandment as it had been handed down within Jewish tradition and taught in the schools. Then, using an authoritative *egō* that sets his teaching over and against the teaching of other inter- preters, Jesus offers an instruction as to how his disciples are to under- stand the various precepts.

In keeping with the Jewish catechetical tradition that considered "Honor your father and mother" to be the transition between the first series of commandments and the second, Jesus begins his exposition on the commandments with the first commandment of the second group, "You shall not murder" (5:21). The exposition expands the demand of the commandment so that it prohibits various forms of conduct that are destructive of the dignity of the human person. Jesus follows a similar pedagogy in his explanation of "you shall not commit adultery" (5:27).

In his catechetical treatment of this commandment, Philo, Jesus' contemporary, had said that adultery was the greatest of crimes. He noted that adultery arises from fondness for pleasure (*philēdonia*) and passionate frenzy (*oistros*). If that were not enough to characterize adultery as "an abominable and God-detested sin" (*stygēton kai theomisēton pragma*) (*Decalogue* 131), Philo notes that adultery wreaks havoc on the cuckolded husband, "who suffers from the breach of faith, stripped of the promise of his marriage vows and his hopes of legitimate offspring." Adultery harms the adulterer and the adulteress as well. The injury is potentially very serious, for "if their connections include a large number of persons through intermarriages and wide- spread associations, the wrong will travel all round and affect the whole State" (*Decalogue* 127). To these considerations Philo adds another, namely, the fate of the children who might result from an adulterous liaison (*Decalogue* 128–30). If the adultery remains unde- tected, bastard children will usurp the position of legitimate children and the heritage of their putative father. If the adultery is detected, the poor children, who have done no wrong, will be most unfortunate. Children born of an adulterous liaison belong to neither family.

Jesus' catechesis on adultery, as found in Matthew, differs from that of Philo. The philosopher attributes the evil of adultery to its cause, passion, and to the social consequences that result. Matthew's cate- chesis does not explain why adultery is wrong. It does not offer a philo- sophical rationale for the evil of the offense. What it does is to treat the commandment parenetically. It proclaims the demand of the com- mandment on the basis of the authority of the tradition, going back to

Sinai, reinforced by the authority of Jesus, teacher of the circle of his disciples.

Unlike Philo, Matthew does not consider adultery to be the greatest of sins and therefore the first of the "You shall nots." Rather, Matthew follows the Hebrew tradition, in which "You shall not commit adultery" comes after "You shall not murder." The evangelist's treatment of the two commandments is similar. Neither adultery nor murder is said to be a more egregious offense than the other. Both are treated alike. Both are cited and "explained" by the addition of apposite material.

A first addition to the prohibition of adultery, formally promulgated under the rubric of "But I say to you," is that "everyone who looks at a woman with lust has already committed adultery with her in his heart" (5:28). As he does elsewhere in the Gospel, Matthew's Jesus uses hyperbole to drive home the seriousness of his teaching, "If your right eye causes you to sin, tear it out and throw it away; it is better for you to lose one of your members than for your whole body to be thrown into hell" (5:29). The right eye is presumed to be more important than the left eye, as the right hand is presumed to be more useful than the left hand (5:30).[8] The graphic language sharpens the demand of God's command. God's requirements are unconditional, "or else" (cf. Matt. 18:7–9; Mark 9:43–48).

Although this first part of Jesus' exposition on "you shall not commit adultery" is found only in Matthew's Gospel, the sayings probably go back to Jesus himself.[9] The woman (*gynē*) of whom the instruction speaks is a married woman.[10] The language speaks of a deliberate intention, if not an actual result. Jesus teaches his disciples that it really is a case of adultery, within the very depths of one's person, the "heart,"[11] when a man looks at a married woman with the thought of violating her marriage and thus committing an offense against her husband (cf. Deut. 5:21; Exod. 20:17).

Jesus' teaching in this regard is consistent with other Jewish interpretations of the seventh commandment.[12] The ethical exhortation of the *Testaments of the Twelve Patriarchs* is remarkably similar to the teaching of Jesus in the Gospels. Comparable to 5:28 are words attributed to Benjamin, Jacob's youngest son: "For the person with a mind that is pure with love does not look on a woman for the purpose of having sexual relations." By way of explanation, the patriarch comments, "He has no pollution in his heart, because upon him is resting the spirit of God" (*T. Benj.* 8:2–3). A homily contained in *Leviticus Rabbah,* one of the oldest extant Midrashim, proclaims, "Even the one who commits adultery with his eyes is called an adulterer" (*Lev. Rab.* 23). Similarly, the Talmud teaches that "whoever looks at a woman with (lustful) intention is counted as one who sleeps with her" (Tr. Kallah 1; cf. *y. Ḥal.* 2:1).

Were it not for the fact that Matthew is such a careful editor and that so much of his parenetic material reflects similar material in the rabbinic tradition, it would be easy to dismiss Matt. 5:30, "And if your right hand causes you to sin, cut it off and throw it away; it is better for you to lose one of your members than for your whole body to go into hell," as a simple reinforcement of the hyperbole of v. 29.[13] But this is not to be.

The rabbinic tradition spoke of the offense of masturbation as "adultery with the hand" and "masturbation by contact with the limbs" (*b. Nid.* 13b).[14] Tarfon, a rabbinic scholar more or less contemporary with the evangelist, speaks of the hand being cut off, while placed on the offender's stomach, as a punishment for the sin of masturbation. In response to a query from one of his disciples about the severity of the punishment, Tarfon is reported to have said, "It is better that his belly be split but that he did not go down into the pit of destruction" (*b. Nid.* 13b). The parallelism between what Tarfon is reputed to have said and what Matthew reports Jesus to have said is remarkable.

Philo, the Hellenistic Jew who lived earlier in the first century C.E., reflects a similarly harsh response to sexual sins committed with the hand. Commenting on a woman's grabbing one of her husband's opponents by the genitals, Philo writes "while all else might be tolerable, it is a shocking thing, if a woman is so lost to a sense of modesty, as to catch hold of the genital parts of her opponent. . . . And the penalty shall be this—that the hand shall be cut off which has touched what decency forbids it to touch" (*Special Laws* 3.175). As the evangelist does in 5:28–30, Philo juxtaposes a sin of touch with a sin of sight. He continued his exposition with a ban on women attending gymnastic events, in which the male competitors are naked, and concludes: "if it is reprehensible for them to use their sight, their hands are far more guilty" (*Special Laws* 3.177).

Having added lust and masturbation to the offenses that are banned by the seventh commandment, Matthew comes to yet a third kind of conduct that Jesus considered to have been a sin of adultery. This was divorce. Unlike the catechetical tradition that viewed lust and mas-turbation as offenses against the intensified ban against adultery, the idea that divorce was also a form of adultery was something of a nov-elty within Matthew's catechetical tradition (cf. Matt. 19:1–12).

Matthew took the ban on divorce (5:31–32) from a collection of Jesus' sayings known to scholars as the "Q" source (cf. Luke 16:18). The words about divorce being a form of adultery go back to Jesus. Matthew has incorporated them into the framework of the Sermon on the Mount.[15] The shortened form of the introduction, "it was also said,"[16] suggests that the saying on divorce was inserted into a tradi-tional catechetical discussion on the precepts of the Decalogue. The saying on divorce in 5:32 contains language that allows it to be readily linked to the traditional intensification of the prohibition on adultery found in 5:28–30. "Wife" (*gynē*) and "commit adultery" (*moicheuō*) are the catchwords that link 5:32 to 5:28 and allow Jesus' words about adultery to be incorporated into the catechetical exposition on the sev-enth commandment.

Matthew took a traditional Jewish approach to the interpretation of the seventh commandment when he wrote about adultery with the eye and with the hand. He continues to do so as he speaks about a man divorcing his wife and about a man who marries a divorcée. The evan-gelist's perspective is that of the man who is called to be a *bar mitz-vah*, a "son of the commandment," who has taken upon himself the yoke of the law.

The instruction on divorce lacks, nonetheless, the hyperbole that gives rhetorical force to the earlier and later sayings in Matthew's cat-echetical exposition (5:21–30, 33–42). The saying is simply a bit of Jesuanic halakah that Matthew has incorporated into the Sermon because of its traditional importance in the Matthean community's understanding of the ban on adultery. For this community divorce was a form of adultery. Christian Jewish casuistry may have admitted a possible exception,[17] but there was to be no mistaking the thrust of Jesus' logion. Divorce was adultery. Matthew's incorporation of the logion makes this point even more clearly than does the story of Jesus' discussion with the scribes and Pharisees on divorce (19:1–12; cf. Mark 10:2–12) or the isolated saying preserved in Luke 16:18.

The Jesus of the Sermon on the Mount has clearly expanded the meaning of the seventh commandment. According to his interpreta-tion of the law, the seventh commandment prohibits not only adultery in the strict sense of the term—a man having sexual intercourse with another man's wife—but also lust, masturbation, and divorce. This catechesis has been incorporated within a series of antitheses (5:21–48) whose context cannot be overlooked if the import of the teaching is to be fully grasped. Three aspects of the context bear highlighting. First of all, the catechesis is promulgated for the members of a Christian Jewish community called to a form of righteousness, a way of right living, that is different from other Jewish communities. Second, the authority for the promulgation of the teaching is none other than Jesus himself, the venerable teacher par excellence for the community. Third, the epilogue to the series of six antitheses (5:43–48) effectively states that the love command provides the interpretive key for the entire series of antitheses, including the two units that speak about the meaning of the seventh commandment (5:27–30, 31–32; cf. 22:40).

KEEPING THE COMMANDMENTS

As he continues to tell his readers about the meaning of the commandments, Matthew narrates the story of a young man who came to Jesus asking what it was that he had to do in order to gain eternal life (19:16–22; cf. Mark 10:17–22; Luke 18:18–23).[18] The story of this "rich young man"[19] belongs to a group of New Testament stories that speak of the demands of discipleship.[20] The story says something about God and his goodness.[21] Its Christology highlights Jesus as a teacher[22] and contrasts the human Jesus with God, who alone is good. Ultimately, however, it is a story about discipleship.[23]

The story is about a man who had kept all the commandments, including the seventh commandment, but who lacked the one thing that was necessary for discipleship. He was unable to abandon all that he had in order to be a disciple of Jesus. His possessions were the obstacle that prevented him from attaining to the kind of radical commitment that discipleship entails. The story contrasts a self-serving search for eternal life with the demands of discipleship, which brings with it its own heavenly reward. The story speaks of the disciple's concern for the poor and contrasts a would-be disciple with one who is called to discipleship.

In Mark's and Luke's versions of the tale, the man responds to Jesus' presentation of the Ten Commandments with a quick retort, "Teacher, I have kept all these since my youth." The language suggests that the man is relatively mature; otherwise there would have been nothing exceptional about his having kept the commandments. Matthew, however, presents the man as a relatively young *bar mitzvah*. This is possibly due to Matthew's desire to show that the young man was impeccable with regard to his conduct under the law (cf. Phil. 3:6)—something that from a human standpoint would be well nigh impossible for someone of a mature age—but that nonetheless he was lacking in that completeness, that "perfection" (Matt. 19:21), that is normative for the disciples of Jesus (Matt. 5:48). Mark and Luke evidence no scruple in presenting the man as someone who had kept the commandments from his youth. This may be because they were writing for Hellenistic Christian audiences, among whom the commandments were understood in a narrow, literal sense.[24]

In Mark's version of the story a man meets Jesus as he was traveling through Galilee. The man pays homage to Jesus in unusual fashion. Not only does he kneel down in Jesus' presence, but he also calls Jesus "good." These narrative traits enhance the Markan picture of Jesus the teacher. The man's question about an inheritance would have struck a responsive chord in all the bystanders. The idea of a promised inheritance was well known to the Jews. It evoked the memory of that unique relationship between Israel and God which gave them, as it were, the right to an inheritance.[25] Most Jews thought of the land of Israel as the promised inheritance (see Matt. 5:5), but the New Testament authors typically present the kingdom of God or eternal life as the hoped-for inheritance.[26]

Responding to the interlocutor's self-interested question, Jesus underscores the goodness of God. Jesus then cites "the commandments," that is, commandments that have come from God[27] who alone can offer eternal life as an inheritance. Six commandments are mentioned: "You shall not murder; You shall not commit adultery; You shall not steal; You shall not bear false witness; You shall not defraud; Honor your father and mother" (Mark 10:19). Today's reader recognizes the six commandments as precepts of the Decalogue (Exod. 20:2–17; Deut. 5:6–21). In this context, "you shall not defraud" is an unusual formulation.[28] It was surely intended to be a summary of the prohibition of coveting, put into the crisp style that is otherwise characteristic of the precepts of the decalogue.[29] Summarized in this fashion, the tenth commandment does not specifically mention coveting a neighbor's wife in the fashion to which Deut. 5:21 draws attention.[30]

The Ten Commandments were widely used in the Jewish liturgical and catechetical traditions.[31] The Nash papyrus, a second-century

B.C.E. papyrus,[32] and some tefillin found in the excavations at Qumran confirm the liturgical importance of the Ten Commandments. The combination of the Ten Commandments with the Shema in the Nash papyrus suggests that the combined text was read during the daily morning Jewish worship service at the time of the Second Temple.[33] "The officer," says the Mishnah, "said to them, 'Recite a Benediction!' They recited a Benediction, and recited the Ten Commandments, the Shema, and the 'And it shall come to pass if you will only heed,' and the 'The Lord said to Moses'" (*m. Tamid* 5:1; cf. *y. Ber.* 1:5).[34] Some commentators, however, hold that the public reading of the Ten Commandments took place in a synagogal service during the Feast of Weeks.[35]

Rabbinic literature placed the Ten Commandments, along with the affirmation that there is but one God, at the heart of Judaism.[36] The Jewish catechetical tradition considered the Decalogue to be an epitome of the law, a kind of résumé of the chief precepts of the Torah.[37] This tradition typically arranged the Ten Commandments in two groups of five, the second of which is a group of five negative precepts. The last of the positive precepts, "Honor your father and mother" (Exod. 20:12; Deut. 5:16), was considered to be a bridge between the two groups.[38]

Philo observes that, "with these wise words on honoring parents He closes the one set of five which is more concerned with the divine." Philo then goes on to speak of "the second set which contains the actions prohibited by our duty to humans" (*Decalogue* 121). In the Middle Ages Maimonides explained the position of the covenantal stipulation that parents be honored by making reference to their cooperation with God in creating offspring. That tradition is a time-honored one. "The rabbis taught," says the Talmud, that "there are three partners (in the creation) of a man—the lord, his father, and his mother" (*b. Qidd.* 30b; cf. *b. Nid.* 31a).

The order of the six commandments cited by Jesus in Mark 10:19 is a by-product of the Jewish catechetical tradition[39] on the uniqueness of "Honor your father and mother." Mark does not comment on the relative importance of any of the commandments. The one commandment on whose significance Mark writes elsewhere in his Gospel (7:1–13; cf. Matt. 15:1–9) is the commandment on parental honor, identified as "the commandment of God" and "the word of God" (Mark 7:9–13). No special attention is, however, given to the fifth commandment, nor is any particular attention paid to the seventh commandment in the evangelist's account of the dialogue between Jesus and his interlocutor in 10:17–22. What the interlocutor affirms is that he had kept all six of the commandments from his youth. In response to the interlocutor's protestation of innocence, Jesus, who loved him, presents a call to discipleship, with its radical demands. The man was shocked and went away grieving (Mark 10:22).

The interlocutor's response concerning his observance of the traditional commandments is similar to the negative protestations found on the lips of a deceased person in various Egyptian mortuary texts. Concerned with securing eternal beatitude for the dead, these ancient Egyptian texts frequently presented a deceased person protesting innocence before the divine tribunal.[40]

LUKE AND MATTHEW

Luke's version of the story of the man who came to meet with Jesus (Luke 18:18–23) follows the Markan version very closely. A notable difference is that Luke places "You shall not commit adultery" at the head of the list of Ten Commandments. He does so without making any comment. That the prohibition of adultery appears before the other five commandments should not be construed to mean that Luke intended to emphasize the prohibition of adultery any more than did Paul in Rom. 13:9. The Greek Bible also listed "You shall not commit adultery" before the other negative commandments. In the book of Deuteronomy the Septuagint has "You shall not commit adultery" before "You shall not murder" (Deut. 5:17–18 LXX). In the Greek version of Exodus, "You shall not commit adultery" comes at the head of the list of the second set of commandments and "You shall not murder" comes after "You shall not steal" (Exod. 20:13–15 LXX). This kind of variation in the sequence of the Ten Commandments reflects their preservation in the oral tradition[41] and their wide use in various liturgical and catechetical settings.

The sequence of the Ten Commandments in Philo's work on the Decalogue follows that of the Greek Bible. Apropos of the placement of the prohibition of adultery, Philo states that "He begins with adultery, holding this to be the greatest of crimes" (*Decalogue* 121). He goes on to explain why this is so. "In the first place it [adultery] has its source in the love of pleasure which enervates the bodies of those who entertain it, relaxes the sinews of the soul and wastes away the means of subsistence, consuming like an unquenchable fire all that it touches and leaving nothing wholesome in human life" (*Decalogue* 122). Luke makes no such observation with regard to the fact that the ban on adultery comes before the other negative commandments. Luke, in fact, seems to have no particular interest in the commandments as such.

Luke's seeming disinterest in the Ten Commandments is not paralleled in Matthew, who has a consistent notion of the commandments.[42] Matthew presents the story of the man's quest for eternal life in the form of a kind of rabbinic dialogue that features three exchanges between the teacher and a young man.[43] In the Gospel according to Matthew, the commandments about which Jesus speaks are the commandments of the Torah, among which the precepts of the Decalogue are exemplary. All the commandments, including the Ten Commandments, can be summed up in the twofold love commandment. Matthew hints at this summative function of the commandment by adding "You shall love your neighbor as yourself" (Lev. 19:18) to the precepts of the Decalogue cited by Jesus in his dialogue with the young man (Matt. 19:18–19).[44]

Matthew does not emphasize "You shall not commit adultery" any more than do Mark and Luke. He does, however, relativize the seventh commandment and the four other commandments cited in 19:18–19 by adding the love commandment (Lev. 19:18). Placed in the final, emphatic position in the list of commandments, the love commandment is the hermeneutical key that not only summarizes but also interprets all the precepts of the Decalogue—including "You shall not commit adultery." This, Matthew suggests, is the teaching of Jesus. Among the Synoptists Matthew alone places the Ten Commandments on the lips of Jesus. It is Jesus the teacher who explains which commandments must be observed if one is to obtain eternal life. For Matthew, it is Jesus the teacher who explains that "You shall not commit adultery" and all the other precepts of the Law depend on the love commandment (Matt. 22:40).

PAUL'S LETTER TO THE ROMANS

A somewhat similar point of view is found in Paul's letter to the Romans, the longest and most systematic piece of the extant correspondence. The letter treats of what J. Christiaan Beker has appropriately called "the Jewish question."[45] Its formal parenetic section (Romans 12–15) includes a passage on love as the fulfillment of the law (13:8–10). The unit is bracketed within a framework that speaks first of a person who loves as fulfilling the law (v. 8) and then of personified love as fulfilling the law (v. 10).

Between these two variants on a single motif, Paul writes about the Ten Commandments. He quotes four of the commandments, including "You shall not commit adultery." The commandments that Paul cites to illustrate the requirements of the law are the negative commandments of the Decalogue. Paul lists these prohibitions according to the order in the Greek Bible (Deut. 5:17–21 LXX), but he mentions neither the prohibition against coveting nor the prohibition against false witness.[46] The apostle does not, moreover, attempt any individual interpretation of these commandments. He merely cites them as illustrative of the demands of the law.

Paul adds to his short list of commandments an et cetera clause, "and any other commandment," so that his audience will understand that all of the *mitzvot* of the Torah[47] are summed up in the single command "Love your neighbor as yourself" (13:8; cf. Lev. 19:18). Paul's "et cetera" prevents the modern reader of the Letter to the Romans from thinking that the four commandments that he quoted verbatim were somehow more important than other commandments of the law. This is not so. The negative precepts of the Decalogue were important within the Jewish catechetical tradition. Writing on a variety of topics that pertain to the Jewish question, Paul indicates that these important commandments and every other commandment of the Torah are summed up in the single command to love one's neighbor. Calling the love command a "word" (*en tǭ logǭ toutǭ*), as he does, Paul reminds his audience that this word was spoken by God. The saying that summarizes all the commandments is God's own spoken word.

Elsewhere Paul affirms that faith, expressing itself, works itself out in love (Gal. 5:6). In describing the commandments as being summed up in the love command (Rom. 13:8–10), Paul does not mean that it is somehow logically possible to deduce all the commandments from the single command to love one's neighbor;[48] rather he is affirming that those who live by the Christian demand of love fulfill what is required by each of the commandments of the law. A life of love is never harmful to one's neighbor. Those who commit adultery, those who murder, those who steal, those who contrive to spirit away another's possessions harm their neighbor. One who truly loves the neighbor does not commit adultery, nor does he—or she—violate any other precept of the law, for all these precepts are summed up in the single love command.

THE EPISTLE OF JAMES

The Epistle of James has its place in the great current of ancient hortatory literature. Its various exhortations parallel similar appeals in the writings of the Hellenistic moralists and Jewish literature including the Bible, the letters of Paul, and the Sermon on the Mount. Given the general character of its parenesis and its relative lack of a specifically Christian perspective,[49] the epistle is difficult to date. Some authors consider it to be a pseudonymous text, having James the brother of the Lord as its patronym, that was composed toward the end of the first century C.E.[50] Other commentators hold that it was written toward the beginning of the second half of that first century,[51] a period that would allow for the epistle to have been written by James the brother of the Lord or by one of his contemporaries.

One of the principal themes of this hortatory collection of some 108 verses is "the law" (*ho nomos*). This is the theme of the reflective exhortation contained in 2:8–13. The author's initial exhortation is "You do well if you really fulfill the royal law according to the scripture, 'You shall love your neighbor as yourself'" (2:8; cf. Lev. 19:18). The final exhortation is "So speak and so act as those who are to be judged by the law of liberty" (2:12). To this last injunction is appended an explanatory comment on the relationship between judgment and mercy, the topic of v. 13.

"James" writes about the royal law. From his Jewish perspective the royal law is the law of the kingdom (*nomon basilikon*), the law to be fulfilled by those who are called to the kingdom of God (cf. 2:5). Promulgated for Israel at the time of the exodus, the law is a perfect law, a law of liberty (*nomou eleutherias;* cf. 1:25). The law that frees was given at the time that Israel was freed from its bondage so that it could live in freedom as God's children. Writing about the law of freedom as he does, the author of the epistle reflects Jewish tradition.[52] "The tablets were the work of God, and the writing was the writing of God, engraved upon the tablets," says the Mishnah. In its commentary, the Mishnah appropriates a remark attributed to R. Joshua ben Levi, who was reputed to have taught "Read not 'engraved' (*haruth*) but 'freedom' (*heruth*), for thou findest no freeman excepting him that occupies himself in the study of the Law" (*m. ʾAbot* 6:2). Philo, moreover, affirmed that the friends of God are free and that they are bound to have absolute felicity (see *Every Good Man Is Free* 41, 44). What is the role of law in all of this? Philo says that people are like cities: "Those which have laws to care for and protect them are free" (ibid., 45).

Freedom, as a quality of the law, was in the air at the time that the author of James compiled his anthology of exhortative dicta.[53] In the Hellenistic world freedom was particularly associated with royal figures. Kings are those for whom "all things are lawful," said Dio Chrysostom (*Discourse* 3.10).[54] "The familiars of kings," remarks Philo, "enjoy not only freedom but authority, because they take part in their management and administration as leaders" (*Every Good Man Is Free* 42).

The author's exhortation to really (*mentoi*, 2:8) fulfill the royal law is one that urges constancy in the fulfillment of the law that liberates. One who practices favoritism,[55] judging people by their outward appearances, violates the law. One who does not observe the law in its entirety violates the law. To illustrate this point, the author cites two of the Ten Commandments, identifying them as logia, words that have been uttered. The seventh commandment, "You shall not commit adultery," and the sixth commandment, "You shall not murder," are the two commandments that he cites. He cites them in the order in which they appear in the Greek Bible.[56] His point is not to imply that they are more important than any of the others nor that one is more important than the other. It is likely that he has simply chosen the first two "you shall nots" in the catechetical tradition's series of five negative commandments.

Unlike Matthew, the author of the Epistle of James does not identify these two as "commandments" (*entolai*), a term that he resolutely avoids. James has a holistic view of the law that does not atomize its individual precepts. James affirms that one cannot pick and choose among the demands of the law. If one commits adultery, one violates the law. If one commits murder, one violates the law. The law is an entire package that must be "really" fulfilled if it is to be the law of liberty.[57] It is the entire law that he considers to be the royal and freeing law. The royal law, whose fulfillment imparts freedom, can be summed up in the love command.[58] Like Matthew's Jesus, Paul (cf. Rom. 13:8–10), and the great rabbi Hillel,[59] the author of the epistle suggests that the love command sums up the entire law. This is a point of view not far removed from what is suggested by Matt. 5:48; 19:19; 22:40.[60]

The epistle echoes the theme of the unity of the law when, in the middle of a topos on envy, he addresses those who sin as "adulterers" (*moichalides,* in the feminine).[61] This unexpected form of address harks back to biblical imagery in which the covenant relationship between God and the people is likened to a marital relationship.[62] Within the metaphor the people's infidelity to God is frequently described as adultery or whoredom. Hosea's relationship with an adulterous wife was a living parable of Israel's infidelity to God. In James it is not Israelites who are derisively addressed as adulteresses. Envious Christians are called by this name. In one sense what they are called makes little difference; one who violates any of the demands of the law has become a transgressor of the law. Envious Christians violate the law. So do murderers and adulterers.

NOTES

1. On the enumeration of the Ten Commandments, see n. 7 below.

2. See R. F. Collins, "Jesus Within the Jewish Catechetical Tradition: Matthew's Portrayal of a Teacher at Work," in *The Echo Within: Emerging Issues in Religious Education,* ed. Catherine Dooley and Mary Collins (Allen, Tex.: Thomas More, 1997), 89–102.

3. See R. F. Collins, "The Transformation of a Motif: 'They Entered the House of Simon and Andrew' (Mark 1,29)," SNTSU 18 (1993) 5–40, 36–48.

4. See J. Andrew Overman, *Matthew's Gospel and Formative Judaism: The Social World of the Matthean Community* (Minneapolis: Fortress, 1990).

5. In English translation Matthew's sixth beatitude, "Blessed are the pure in heart, for they will see God" (Matt. 5:8), contains language that may appear to connote sexual purity. In the Synoptic tradition "pure" (*katharos*) is cultic language. It describes persons and things that are ritually pure (cf. Matt. 23:26; 27:59). In the New Testament the expression "pure in heart" is found only in Matthew. The phrase connotes a single-mindedness in one's devotion to the Lord in contrast to a merely superficial cultic devotion to the Lord (cf. Matt. 23:25–29; etc.). See Jacques Dupont, *Les Béatitudes,* 3, *Les Évangélistes,* EBib (rev. ed.: Paris, Gabalda, 1973), 567–90; Donald A. Hagner, *Matthew 1–13,* WBC 33A (Dallas: Word, 1993), 94; Ulrich Luz, *Matthew 1–7: A Commentary* (Minneapolis: Augsburg, 1989), 238–41.

6. Christoph Burchard rightly suggests that 5:17–20 must be read as a preamble to the antitheses, not to the body of the Sermon as a whole ("The Theme of the Sermon on the Mount," in Luise Schottroff et al., *Essays on the Love Commandment* [Philadelphia; Fortress, 1978], 57–91, esp. 68; similarly,

John P. Meier, *The Vision of Matthew: Christ, Church and Morality in the First Gospel*, Theological Inquiries [New York: Paulist, 1979], 222–23).

7. Given Matthew's familiarity with the Jewish catechetical tradition and the fact that that tradition divides the commandments into two groups of five, it seems preferable in this discussion of a Matthean text to speak of the sixth, seventh, and ninth commandments, even though my own Roman Catholic and other Christian traditions would refer to them as the fifth, sixth, and eighth commandments. The language of Matt. 5:33 is closer to that of Lev. 19:12 than it is to that of Exod. 20:16 and Deut. 5:20. Lev. 19:11–13 is a short pericope that deals with stealing and bearing false witness. It echoes the concerns of the seventh and eighth commandments.

8. See Daniel J. Harrington, who notes that, "The right side was considered the more respectable in antiquity" (*The Gospel of Matthew*, SacPag 1 [Collegeville, Minn.: Liturgical Press, 1991], 87).

9. See the discussion in Luz, *Matthew 1–7*, 292. See also Hagner (*Matthew 1–13*, 119–20), who, however, sees no reference to a sexual sin in the hyperbolic challenge of 5:29.

10. That "a woman" is a married woman is suggested both by the traditional sphere of the commandment's application and the expression "has committed adultery" (*emoicheusen*).

11. The Greek *kardia* reflects the Hebrew *lēb*. The idea that sin lies within the heart is found in rabbinic literature: see, e.g., the extracanonical tractate Kallah 1, cited on p. 46, and *b. Yoma* 29a. See also Matt. 15:19; Mark 7:21.

12. See Str-B 1:298–301.

13. See Hagner, *Matthew 1–13*, 120–21.

14. For the text, see below, pp. 65–66. Robert H. Smith, however, suggests that adultery by the hand is a matter of seizing another man's wife (*Matthew*, ACNT [Minneapolis: Augsburg, 1989], 99).

15. The parallel saying to Matt. 5:32, Luke 16:18, exists as an isolated saying in the Lukan text. On the saying in Matthew, see Raymond F. Collins, *Divorce in the New Testament*, GNS 38 (Collegeville, Minn.: Liturgical Press, 1992), 160–69, 182–83, 302–5, 309.

16. Instead of "you have heard that it was said" (Matt. 5:27, 38, 43) or the fuller form, "you have heard that it was said to those of ancient times" (Matt. 5:21, 33). The fact that Matt. 5:31 has a shortened introduction and the fact that Matt. 5:33, with its longer form, represents a kind of getting back to the principal task at hand, indicate that the divorce intensification represents a later addition to the catechetical tradition represented by Matthew.

17. See the discussion in Collins, *Divorce*, 184–213, 309–23.

18. See R. F. Collins, "The Ten Commandments and the Christian Response," in *Christian Morality: Biblical Foundations* (Notre Dame, Ind.: University of Notre Dame Press, 1986), 64–81; idem, "Matthew's *Entolai*: Towards an Understanding of the Commandments in the First Gospel," in *Four Gospels 1992: Festschrift Frans Neirynck*, ed. Frans van Segbroeck et al., 3 vols., BETL 100 A, B, C (Louvain: University Press, 1992), 2:1325–48, esp. 1326–31.

19. The familiar title, the story of the "rich young man" is the result of a

conflated reading of the three Gospels. From Mark one learns that Jesus' interlocutor was a male (Mark 10:17). From Matthew one learns that he was young (Matt. 19:20). From Luke one learns that he was very rich (Luke 18:23; and a few Greek manuscripts of Mark 10:17) and a "ruler" (18:18). Luke does not indicate what he means by "a certain ruler" (*tis archōn*). The way that this evangelist uses the term elsewhere—apart from 11:15, where it is used of Beelzebul, the ruler of the demons—suggests that Luke was thinking of a leader among the Pharisees. See 8:41; 12:58; 14:1; 23:13, 35; 24:20. By stating that the man was "very rich" the evangelist has made explicit what is implicit in the parallel stories that speak of the man's possessions.

20. See Matt. 8:19–22; 10:34–39; 16:24–27; Mark 8:34–38; Luke 9:23–25, 57–62; 14:25–33.

21. See R. F. Collins, "Good," *ABD* 2:1074.

22. The man addresses Jesus as "Teacher" (Matt 19:16). This form of address harks back to the portrayal of Jesus as the teacher par excellence in the Sermon on the Mount.

23. See "come, follow me" in Matt. 19:21; Mark 10:21; Luke 18:22. Cf. Matt. 4:20, 22; 8:22; 9:9; Mark 1:18; [1:20]; 2:14; Luke 5:11, 27–28.

24. Cf. Matt. 5:21–48, above, pp. 43–48. See also the formulation of Matt. 22:40, in comparison with Mark 12:31, apropos of which see Collins, "Matthew's *Entolai*," 1342–43.

25. In the New Testament, the idea of the inheritance evokes the idea of Jesus as the Son and Christians as co-heirs. See, e.g., Rom. 8:17.

26. The notion of the inheritance is one that appears throughout the New Testament, with the exception of the Johannine corpus, where it appears but once (Rev. 21:7). As a word group, "inherit" and its cognates appear almost fifty times in the New Testament writings.

27. The Jewish tradition was strong in affirming that God had spoken the Ten Commandments (see *b. Ber.* 12a). Exod. 34:28 and Deut. 4:13; 10:4 refer to the Ten Commandments as the "ten words" of Yahweh. See Moshe Greenberg, "Decalogue (The Ten Commandments)," *EncJud* 5:1435–46.

28. The Greek *mē aposterēsēs* uses a verb that is not otherwise used in the four Gospels (cf. 1 Cor. 6:7, 8; 7:5, 1 Tim. 6:5). Since the wording is not found in Exod. 20:17 and Deut. 5:21 (cf. Deut. 24:14; Sir. 4:1), it may have seemed inappropriate in a listing of some of the Ten Commandments. Thus, it does not appear in Matthew or Luke. Some scribes have also omitted it from their manuscripts of Mark (thus, B, K, W, Δ, Ψ, and the minuscules of the Lake and Farrar families). For modern readers of the text, the summary formulation obviates the discussion as to whether the prohibition of coveting is one or two commandments.

29. Josephus summarizes the prohibition of coveting with "to covet nothing that belongs to another" (*Antiquities* 3.5.5 §92). He also notes that it was not permissible for Jews to state the precepts of the Decalogue "explicitly and to the letter" (*Antiquities* 3.5.4 §90).

30. Deut. 5:21 is a revision of Exod. 20:17. By taking the "wife" out of the list of possessions and making the coveting of the wife the object of a specific prohibition, the Deuteronomist has created, as it were, an eleventh commandment. His revision of Exod. 20:17 has led to different enumerations of the

Ten Commandments among the churches. The revision does, however, point to a development in the understanding of the relationship between a man and his wife.

31. See R. F. Collins, "Ten Commandments," *ABD* 6:383–87.

32. See Moshe Greenberg, "Nash Papyrus," *EncJud* 12:833. The papyrus is possibly of Egyptian origin.

33. Alfred Rubens, however, contends that the Ten Commandments were originally intended to be included in the daily temple service, but that outside the temple it was forbidden to include the Ten Commandments in a daily service lest the contention of the *minim,* heretical groups, that only the Ten Commandments had been given by God be enhanced ("Decalogue [The Ten Commandments]," *EncJud* 5:1446–47).

34. The three Torah texts to be recited after the Ten Commandments were Deut. 6:4–9; Deut. 11:13–21; and Num. 15:37–41. Rabbinic tradition considered Deut. 11:13–21 and Num. 15:37–41 to be part of the Shema along with Deut. 6:4–9, from which the confession derives its name.

35. Cf. Exod. 34:22; Deut. 16:10. The Feast of Weeks, considered in Jewish tradition to be the anniversary of Moses' encounter with Yahweh on Mount Sinai (see *b. Meg.* 31a; *t. Meg.* 4:5), when the Ten Commandments were given to Moses, was the Jewish celebration of Pentecost (see Lev. 23:16). In the early twentieth century Sigmund Mowinckel suggested that there had existed in ancient Israel a covenant renewal festival during which the Ten Commandments were recited (see Deut. 31:11). In any case it is likely that the recitation of the Ten Commandments would have been an addition to any celebration of a liturgical feast. The addition would have been facilitated by the preservation of the stone tablets in the ark of the covenant in the tabernacle at Shiloh, later in the temple of Jerusalem (see Exod. 25:16, 21; 40:20; Deut. 10:2–5; 1 Kgs. 8:9).

36. See Roger Brooks, *The Spirit of the Ten Commandments: Shattering the Myth of Rabbinic Legalism* (San Francisco: Harper & Row, 1990), 34.

37. See Moshe Greenberg, David Kadosh, and Alfred Rubens, "Decalogue [The Ten Commandments]," *EncJud* 5:1435–49, passim. The observation is first found in Hellenistic Jewish writings. The "Instructions" (*Azharot*), hymns for the Feast of Weeks, distributed the 613 commandments of the Torah under the rubric of the Ten Commandments. See I. Davidson et al., *Siddur R. Saʿadyah Gaʾon* (Jerusalem: Mekize Nirdamim, 1941), 191–216. This method of classifying the 613 commandments is mentioned several times in the midrashim (*Num. Rab.* 13:15–16, etc.) and in the works of several important medieval scholars, including Saadiah Gaon (882–942), the leader of Babylonian Jewry. Maimonides' collation of the 613 commandments associates with the commandment "You shall not commit adultery" thirteen other commandments, including those prohibiting bestiality (Lev. 18:23); homosexuality (Lev. 18:7, 14, 22; and prostitution (Deut. 23:18). See Abraham H. Rabinowitz, "Commandments, The 613," *EncJud* 5:760–83.

38. Apropos of this commandment, see Gerald Blidstein, *Honor Thy Father and Mother: Filial Responsibility in Jewish Law and Ethics,* Library of Jewish Law and Ethics (New York: KTAV, 1975).

39. See *The Sentences of Pseudo-Phocylides* 8.

40. Often the dead person's protestation of innocence included an affirma-

tion that he had not been guilty of sexual transgression. For example, "I have not had sexual relations with the wife of [another] male; . . . I have not defiled myself; . . . I have not had sexual relationship with a boy" (see *ANET,* 34–35).

41. Josephus reflects that it was not lawful to set down directly the words that Moses wrote on the two tablets, shortly thereafter observing that the writing was by the hand of God. What Jews were expected to do was to declare their import (Josephus, *Antiquities* 3.5.4, 8 §§90, 101). On other "adaptations" of the text for public use, see Greenberg, "Decalogue," 5:1442.

42. See Collins, "Matthew's *Entolai.*"

43. Ibid., 1326–31.

44. In Matt. 22:34–40, where a question is also addressed to Jesus as "Teacher," Jesus responds that all the law and the prophets hang on two commandments, love of God (Deut. 6:4) and love of neighbor (Lev. 19:18). In Matt. 19:19, only Lev. 19:18 is cited. This is most likely because the Markan text that Matthew was editing had a list that consisted only of one's obligations to one's neighbor.

45. See J. C. Beker, *Paul the Apostle; The Triumph of God in Life and Thought* (Philadelphia: Fortress, 1980), 77–78.

46. Scribes frequently accommodate the texts that they are transcribing to other well-known texts. A number of New Testament manuscripts show that the phenomenon was operative in the transcription of Rom. 13:9. Various manuscripts have "you shall not bear false witness" (*ou pseudomartyrēseis*) after Paul's "you shall not steal" (see ℵ, P, 048, various minuscules, along with ancient Latin, Coptic, Armenian, and Ethiopian versions).

47. Joseph A. Fitzmyer notes that the immediate referent of this phrase is the other precepts of the Decalogue and adds, "but Paul's typically rhetorical generalization has a more remote sense, which extends what he says about love to any legal system" (*Romans,* AB 33 [New York: Doubleday, 1993], 679).

48. Pace Helmut Merklein, who writes, "they are brought together in the single major and fundamental statement from which they can be deduced or to which they can be reduced" (*"anakephalaioō," EDNT* 1:82–83, esp. 82). "Sum up" (*anakephalaioō*) is a word that is used only twice in the New Testament (Rom. 13:9; Eph. 1:10). Here it reflects the rabbinic notion of the summation of the law. See Str-B 1:357, 907–8.

49. Jesus Christ is mentioned only in 1:1 and 2:1.

50. See Bo Reicke, *The Epistles of James, Peter, and Jude,* AB 37 (Garden City, N.Y.: Doubleday, 1964), 6.

51. See Luke Timothy Johnson, *The Letter of James,* AB 37A (New York: Doubleday, 1995), 118–22.

52. Cf. Psalm 119, the great hymn of praise of the law.

53. For the Hellenistic moralists, freedom was a quality of the truly wise person (see Philo, *Every Good Man Is Free* 40). Stoics associated this freedom with freedom from passion (*pathos, epithymia*). Cf. 4 Macc. 5:22–25.

54. Cf. Dio Chrysostom, *Discourses* 62.2.4; Seneca, *Mercy* 1.8.5; 4 Macc. 14:2.

55. The verb "to show partiality" (*prosōpolēmpteō*) appears in Greek literature for the first time in Jas. 2:9. Thereafter it appears in a limited number of Christian writings, apparently in dependence on James.

56. See above, p. 51.

57. Cf. 4 Macc. 5:20–21: "to transgress the law in matters either small or great is of equal seriousness, for in either case the law is equally despised."

58. See Martin Dibelius, *A Commentary on the Epistle of James,* rev. ed. by Heinrich Greeven, Hermeneia (Philadelphia: Fortress, 1976), 144–48.

59. The menorah in the Knesset bears an image of Hillel teaching the Torah to a heathen standing on his right foot, while holding up the left foot with his hand. Jewish tradition has it that Hillel was once approached by a Gentile who was willing to become a Jewish proselyte on the condition that Hillel teach the Torah while standing on one foot. Hillel is said to have replied, "What is hateful to you, do not unto your neighbor; this is the entire Torah, all the rest is commentary."

60. See Collins, "Matthew's *Entolai,*" 1342–43.

61. The word *moichalides,* the NRSV's "adulterers," is a substantivized noun in the feminine. Its literal meaning is "you adulteresses."

62. See Dibelius, *James,* 220; Johnson, *James,* 278.

4

Teaching the Disciples

I N THEIR RESPECTIVE VERSIONS of the story of the dialogue between the "rich young man" and Jesus, each of the Synoptic evangelists presents the episode as one in which a man comes to Jesus and calls him "Teacher." As teacher, Jesus reminded the rich young man of the importance of the commandments of the law. As teacher, Jesus taught his disciples about the meaning of some of the commandments of the Decalogue, especially the seventh commandment, "you shall not commit adultery."

In the Synoptics "teacher" is a familiar form of address for Jesus: Matthew, six times; Mark, ten times; and Luke, twelve times. Each of the evangelists has a different way of fleshing out the picture of Jesus the teacher. Matthew does so in the Sermon on the Mount; Mark in his description of Jesus' conversations with his disciples back in the house; and Luke when he presents Jesus as a guest who has been invited to dinner, thereafter engaging his host in constructive dialogue.

One of the longest household conversations that Mark narrates in his Gospel story about Jesus is in Mark 9:33–50. The scene is set in Capernaum (9:33) after the journey through Galilee which culminates in the third prediction of the passion (9:31). Mark presents the prediction itself as something that Jesus "taught." In the house (9:33) John, one of the disciples, addresses Jesus as teacher before asking him about the exorcist who has been casting out demons in the name of Jesus but does not belong to the tightly knit circle of Jesus' disciples (9:38–41). John's intervention comes after Jesus teasingly inquires about the subject of the argument that engaged the disciples as they traveled with

Jesus through Galilee. They are embarrassed to tell Jesus the answer and fall strangely silent (9:34). They had, in fact, been arguing among themselves as to who was the greatest among them. Assuming the seated posture of a teacher, Jesus gathers the Twelve around him and teaches them that if they are to lead, they must become as servants.

As Mark continues to describe this teaching moment in the life of Jesus, he includes in Jesus' discourse a number of sayings that appear to have circulated among the early disciples of Jesus apart from their present narrative context in the Gospel of Mark (9:42–50). The reader of his Gospel has the impression that the evangelist intended to collate a number of sayings that stem from Jesus' Galilean ministry before he describes his hero moving into Judea, where he will soon be put to death. Placing them on the lips of Jesus while he was in a house in Capernaum is a convenient way of preserving these sayings for posterity.

Matthew and Luke treat these sayings as somewhat isolable, as once they were. Matthew has taken over virtually the entire series of sayings, modifying them in the manner of his own style and placing them at convenient places in his story about Jesus. The first four sayings in the Markan collection (9:42–48) deal with cases of "stumbling." The first talks of someone who causes "one of these little ones" to stumble. The other three present the offense as stumbling because of one's hand, one's foot, or one's eye. Matthew has compressed the sayings about the hand and the foot (Mark 9:43–45)[1] into a single logion (Matt. 18:8) and has included the entire group in the discourse on church leadership (Matthew 18; see 18:6–9). Matthew modified the sayings on salt (Mark 9:49–50) even more radically and located them within the Sermon on the Mount (Matt. 5:13).

The sayings of Mark 9:42–50 were also incorporated into the Gospel according to Luke. Like Matthew, Luke divided them into two groups, the "stumble" group and the "salt" group. As did Matthew, Luke also placed the modified salt sayings at an earlier point in his narrative than the salt sayings. In Luke these sayings are found in 14:34–35, immediately after a series of sayings on discipleship (14:25–34). The sayings about stumbling have been reduced into one general statement about temptation, which Luke uses as part of the conversation (17:1–2) between Jesus and his disciples as they are on the way to Jerusalem, toward which Jesus has turned his face. In the Lukan narrative this part of the conversation takes place just after the parable of Lazarus and the rich man (16:19–31).

STUMBLING

The sayings about stumbling in Mark 9:42–48 are roughly parallel in form with one another, but the last three (9:43–48) are more closely parallel with one another than they are with the first saying (v. 42). The three use a conditional clause to present the case, while the first uses a relative clause for the same purpose. The final three sayings describe an eternal punishment; the first suggests a form of temporal punishment, even one as severe as death.

It is all but certain that the first saying on stumbling circulated in the early Christian community independently from the last three sayings. Matthew's addition of a double "woe" to the first saying and the fact that Luke has made use of the first saying, but not of the last three, suggest that Matthew and Luke, respectively, were aware of the relative independence of the first statement from the latter three. It may well be that Matthew and Luke found the first saying about stumbling not only in Mark but also in another source that they used, the Q source.[2]

The Markan sayings on stumbling are characterized by oriental hyperbole. The first logion suggests that it is better (*kalon estin*) for someone to be drowned in the sea, a weighty millstone around his neck, than to cause "one of the little ones" to stumble. The second, third, and fourth state that it is better to go though life maimed than to have an integral body and ultimately be cast into hell. The millstone was the *mylos onikos*,[3] literally, "the donkey-driven millstone." This kind of millstone, much heavier than the smaller hand-held grinding stones, was generally worked by a mule. "Hell" is Gehenna, the Greek transliteration of the Hebrew, *gê-hinnōm*. This is the Valley of Hinnom, located to the south of Jerusalem, near the Dung Gate. It was the municipal dump, whose fires provided the imagery for eternal hell fires. Mark's Greek also serves to locate the original *Sitz im Leben* of these sayings in the ancient Orient. The syntax of the second, third, and fourth sayings is that of "translation Greek." This suggests that the original language of the logia was Hebrew or Aramaic.[4]

"Stumbling" (*skandalisē, skandalizē*) is obviously a metaphor. Jesus was not talking about someone tripping over their own feet. Nor was he talking about someone putting an obstacle in front of a young child so that it would trip and fall. To stumble is to commit an offense.

In theological terms, it is to sin. Elsewhere in Mark's Gospel, stumbling is used as a metaphor for apostasy (4:17; 14:27, 29) and disbelief (6:3). What sort of sin is evoked by the imagery of Mark 9:42–48?

ENLIGHTENING PARALLELS

A striking parallel to the Markan sayings is found in the Babylonian Talmud, a commentary on the Mishnah completed in the fifth and sixth centuries C.E. In comparison with the New Testament, the Talmud is a relatively recent document. It is, however, deeply rooted in Jewish tradition and is the beneficiary of traditions that were faithfully passed on from generation to generation. The authorities it cites in a passage parallel to Mark lived in late New Testament times. This parallel suggests that the sayings in Mark 9:42–48 related to various kinds of sexual sins.[5] The Mishnaic tractate *Niddah* ("The Menstruous Woman") states: "The hand that oftentimes makes examination is, among women, praiseworthy; but among men—let it be cut off" (*m. Nid.* 2:1).

The passage then goes on to give various instructions as to how a woman should attend to her hygiene during her menstrual period. It was necessary for a woman to examine herself with some frequency lest she defile herself and her partner by having sexual intercourse during the menstrual period (*m. Nid.* 2:2–3). With men, things are different. If a man touches his penis, his hand is to be cut off. "But among men—let it be cut off," says the Mishnah. The Talmud has a long commentary on this Mishnaic injunction. A major portion of the commentary deals with masturbation (*b. Nid.* 13a–b).[6] The Talmud says:

> The question was raised: "Have we learned this teaching of the Mishnah as a law to be carried out, or have we learned it as a mere curse?"
>
> Have we learned the Mishnah's law as a law to be carried out, in the case in which R. Huna had a hand cut off, or is it a mere curse?
>
> Come and take note of that which we have learned on Tannaite authority. R. Tarfon says, "It should be cut off while lying on his belly button." They said to him, "Lo, his belly will be split open." He said to them, "Indeed, I intended exactly that." It is better that his belly be split but that he did not go down into the pit of destruction" (cf. *t. Nid.* 2:8b–d).
>
> . . . This is the sense of the statement of R. Tarfon: "Whoever puts his hand below his belly button—his hand should be cut off" (*b. Nid.* 13b).

This passage shares with the saying in Mark 9:43 a reference to a sin of the hand, mutilation as a punishment, and the avoidance of hell as a result. The similarities are striking. They are all the more striking in the light of what immediately precedes this talmudic passage:

> And said R. Eleazar, "What is the meaning of the verse of Scripture, 'Your hands are full of blood' (Isa. 1:15)? This refers to those who commit adultery with their hand."
>
> A Tannaite authority of the household of R. Ishmael [said], "You will not commit adultery" (Exod. 20:14)—you will not be subject to adultery, whether by hand or by foot."
>
> Our rabbis have taught on Tannaite authority: Proselytes and those who "play" with children postpone the coming of the Messiah.[7]
>
> Now the statement with respect to proselytes poses no problems, since it is in accord with what R. Helbo said. For said R. Helbo, "Proselytes are as hard for Israel as a scab." But what is the point of the reference to those who "play" with children?
>
> If I should say that what is at stake is pederasty, such men are subject to the death penalty by stoning. If it is those who masturbate by contact with the limbs, they are deserving of destruction by flood! Rather, the statement refers to those who marry young girls who are not yet ready to bear children. . . . (b. Nid. 13b)

If "one of these little ones" (Mark 9:42; par. Matt. 18:6; Luke 17:2) originally meant a child, as it probably did,[8] the talmudic text appears to address three of the offenses to which Mark's collection of sayings makes reference in 9:42–46, causing a little one to stumble, stumbling because of one's hand, and stumbling because of one's foot.

To cause one of the little ones to stumble is to commit a sexual offense against a child. The rabbis called the offense "playing with children." Today the same offense would be labeled "child molestation." For a grown man to have sex with a young boy was abhorrent to many living in the ancient Near East.[9] Praising the ethos of Jews, the *Sibylline Oracles* say that "they do not engage in impious intercourse with male children, as do Phoenicians, Egyptians, and Romans, spacious Greece, and many nations of others, Persians and Galatians and all Asia, transgressing the holy law of immortal God, which they transgressed" (*Sib. Or.* 3:595–600; cf. 3:185–87; 5:166, 387).

The Slavonic *Apocalypse of Enoch*, of unknown date but likely to have been composed toward the end of the first century C.E., contains the story of the visionary Enoch seeing a cruel place of detention, with merciless angels carrying instruments of torture. "This place," it is said, "has been prepared for those who do not glorify God, who practice on the earth the sin which is against nature, which is child corruption in the anus in the manner of Sodom" (*2 Enoch* 10:4, MS P). The saying of Mark 9:42, "If any of you put a stumbling block before one of these little ones who believe in me, it would be better for you if a great millstone were hung around your neck and you were thrown into the sea," reflects the ancient Near East's abhorrence of pederasty.

HAND AND FOOT

The second saying of Jesus in Mark's household collection of sayings about stumbling refers to an offense committed with the hand: "If your hand causes you to stumble, cut it off; it is better for you to enter life maimed than to have two hands and to go to hell, to the unquenchable fire" (9:43). In the talmudic passage cited above, Rabbi Eleazar and rabbis who had studied in the school of Ishmael talked about adultery with the hand. This was the sin of masturbation, punishment for which was severe.[10] Rabbi Tarfon stipulated that the one who masturbates should have his hand cut off. But even this was not enough. The offending hand was to be placed upon the man's stomach as it was being cut off, for "it is better[11] that his belly be split but that he did not go down into the pit of destruction."

Any scholar who studies an ancient text, be it the Bible, a work of history, or the Talmud, must approach the text with a certain amount of methodological skepticism. The texts are not always to be taken "literally." What is recounted does not always correspond to historical reality. It is, however, noteworthy that the three scholars mentioned in the talmudic passage on the tractate *Niddah*, which speaks about masturbation as "adultery by the hand," were among the foremost Jewish scholars of the tannaitic era (early second century C.E.). Eleazar was one of the great sages of Yavneh and may have succeeded Gamaliel II in the leadership of the school. Ishmael was a priest and martyr of the same era. Tarfon, "the teacher of all Israel," was one of the leading scholars in the second generation of Tannaim. The witness of these early rabbinic scholars, combined with the protestation "I have not defiled myself"[12] in the Egyptian *Book of the Dead* is of some importance for the interpretation of Matt. 9:43. These texts suggest that the logion was originally a very strong and hyperbolic saying on the evil of masturbation.

The third saying (9:45) in Mark's household collection is relatively easy to interpret. The rabbis talked about committing adultery with the hand and with the foot. The Markan sayings about the hand and the foot (9:43, 45) follow the same sequence. In the Hebrew Bible the "foot" is a well-attested euphemism for the male sex organ (see Exod. 4:25; Isa. 6:2; Ruth 3:4, 7, 8, 14). When rabbis of the school of Ishmael spoke about committing adultery with the foot, they were talking about a man having sexual intercourse with a married woman who was not his wife.

In Matthew's parallel to 9:43–45, the sayings about the hand[13] and the foot have been combined into a single logion. In the tradition that the Talmud attributes to the school of Ishmael there is likewise one saying on both the hand and the foot.

THE EYE THAT CAUSES ONE TO STUMBLE

The aforementioned talmudic passage (*b. Nid.* 13b) does not offer a parallel to Mark's fourth stumbling saying, "And if your eye causes you to stumble, tear it out; it is better for you to enter the kingdom of God with one eye than to have two eyes and to be thrown into hell" (Mark 9:47).

This saying about the eye that causes one to stumble is the final logion in the triad of closing parallel sayings in 9:43–47. Appended to it is a graphic description of hell (*tēn geennan*, 9:43, 45, 47). The imagery comes from the city dump, "where their worm never dies, and the fire is never quenched" (9:48).[14] This graphic conclusion is not found in Matthew's rendition of the four stumbling sayings. The graphic finale has a fitting place in Mark, where the sayings on stumbling are manifestly hortatory. In Matthew the sayings appear in a didactic collection, an address to church leaders (Matthew 18). The different literary genre of the collection in which Matthew has placed the stumbling sayings may have precluded the evangelist's taking over the imagery of garbage in the city dump. Such graphic imagery might well seem to be a bit out of place in a didactic piece. Matthew has dropped Mark's hortatory finale, but he has taken over the saying on the eye that causes one to stumble. Matt. 18:9, "If your eye causes you to stumble, tear it out and throw it away,"[15] is a very close parallel to Mark 9:47.

Earlier in his Gospel than the address to church leaders in chapter

18, Matthew records a logion that sheds considerable light on the saying about the eye that causes one to stumble. Interpreting the seventh commandment, "You shall not commit adultery," for the benefit of his disciples and students, Jesus says, "But I say to you that everyone who looks at a woman with lust has already committed adultery with her in his heart. If your right eye causes you to sin, tear it out and throw it away; it is better for you to lose one of your members than for your whole body to be thrown into hell" (5:28–29). With the exception of the detail that it is the right eye that causes the problem,[16] 5:29 is textually the same as 18:9.

In the Sermon on the Mount the traditional saying about the eye that causes one to stumble is appended to a statement about lust, "adultery in the heart." The rabbis also spoke about adultery with the eye and in the heart.[17] The offense that is implied in the intriguing metaphor of the eye that causes one to stumble is none other than the sin of lust, a man's leering at a woman, reducing her to the level of a desirable possession that he would like to have for his very own. In reality, if not in imagery, the saying about the eye that causes one to stumble evokes an old biblical tradition, "neither shall you covet your neighbor's wife" (Deut. 5:21a).

SEXUAL OFFENSES

Each of the sayings in Mark 9:42–48 was originally a very powerful statement about sexual offenses. Reflecting the moral standards of the Jewish people, Jesus urged his listeners in very strong terms to avoid child abuse, masturbation, adultery, and lustful glances. From the perspective of that tradition, it was better to be mutilated or killed than to commit one of these sins. Jesus' language is hyperbolic. It is not to be taken literally, but it does underscore the abhorrence with which he and the Jewish people of his time viewed these kinds of sexual offense. In their original setting, the four sayings were prophetic and eschatological denunciations of conduct held in abhorrence by the people. In his preaching Jesus urged his listeners to turn from various kinds of egregious conduct. Child abuse, masturbation, adultery, and making a woman an object of one's lust were among such sins.

The double woe[18] that Matthew has added to the saying on child abuse (18:6–7) speaks of the inevitability of sin, even the horrible sin of child abuse, in the evil generation that precedes the coming of the End. Despite the inevitability of even this kind of sin, its perpetrators, Matthew reminds his readers, are liable to very severe judgment.

By the time that the Gospel story was written and rewritten in the last few decades of the first century, some forty and fifty years after Jesus' death, the eschatological urgency of the message had been lost. Even though Jerusalem had been destroyed, the parousia had not come. The fervor of apocalyptic expectation that had taken hold of Jesus' disciples receded as his apocalyptic movement gave way to the church that settled into the world. The Hellenistic Gentiles for whom Mark's story was written were people whose standards of sexual conduct were different from those of the Jewish people.

Separated from their Palestinian context and having lost their eschatological urgency, Jesus' stumbling sayings became general sayings on discipleship.[19] They were used to urge "the little ones," the disciples of Jesus, to avoid temptation no matter its source. Their hyperbole imparted rhetorical force to Jesus' exhortation to avoid temptation. In their naiveté Mark's Gentile audience were most likely unaware that various forms of sexual misconduct lay at the origin of the traditional sayings.[20]

NOTES

1. The words of Mark 9:44 and 9:46, "where the worm never dies, and the fire is never quenched," are found in some of the ancient New Testament manuscripts, including some majuscules (A, D, Θ), the minuscules of the Farrar family, the majority of the medieval manuscripts, and some of the Old Latin translations. They were taken over into Jerome's Vulgate edition [= Mark 9:43, 45] and are to be found in the Revised Version and in the New King James Version. Since they are absent from a wide range of ancient manuscripts and do not appear in Matthew, textual critics generally agree that the words are a scribal addition to the text, appended in 9:44 and 9:46 under the influence of 9:48. They are not found in most of the modern translations of the text.

2. See above, chapter 2 n. 32.

3. The expression is found in the New Testament only in Matt. 19:6 and Mark 9:42. Luke 17:2 has the more elegant *lithos mylikos*, a stone for a mill.

4. See Klaus Beyer, *Semitische Syntax im Neuen Testament*, 1/1, SUNT (Göttingen: Vandenhoeck & Ruprecht, 1962), 78–81.

5. See Will Deming, "Mark 9.42–10.12, Matthew 5.27–32, and *B. NID.* 13b: A First Century Discussion of Male Sexuality," *NTS* 36 (1990): 130–41; Robert H. Gundry, *Mark: A Commentary on His Apology for the Cross* (Grand Rapids: Eerdmans, 1993), 524–25. In an unlikely reading of the text, Ched Meyers sug-

gests that the set of sayings addresses the problem of apostasy within the community (*Binding the Strong Man: A Political Reading of Mark's Story of Jesus* [Maryknoll, N.Y.: Orbis, 1988], 263). A fair number of modern commentators avoid the issue of the interpretation of the metaphors, preferring to limit their remarks to considerations of the tradition history of the sayings.

6. See Jacob Neusner, *The Talmud of Babylonia: An American Translation*, 36A, *Tractate Niddah Chapters 1-3*, Brown Judaic Studies 221 (Atlanta: Scholars Press, 1990), 65–69. Among other things, the talmudic passage attributes to R. Yohannan the judgment that "whoever emits semen purposelessly is liable to the death penalty, as it is said, 'And the thing that he did was evil in the sight of the Lord, and he slew them also' [Gen 38:9]." The Talmud attributes to Rab the statement, "He who deliberately makes himself hard should be excommunicated."

7. The rabbis taught that the faithful observance of the law on the part of God's people would lead to an earlier coming of the Messiah. Conversely, failure to observe the law meant that the coming of the Messiah would be delayed.

8. On the basis of the rabbinic parallel and the absence of the qualifying "who believe in me" from Luke 17:2, Deming argues that "one of these little ones" originally meant a young boy (see Deming, "Mark 9.42–20.12," 132; and Vincent Taylor, *The Gospel According to St. Mark* [London: Macmillan, 1952], 411). "Who believe in me" would have been added when the saying, removed from its original Palestinian context in the oral tradition, was used as a general instruction for disciples. Bruce Malina and Richard Rohrbaugh state that "these little ones" are "lowborn persons committed to following Jesus" (*Social-Science Commentary on the Synoptic Gospels* [Minneapolis: Augsburg, 1992], 239). It may have been the phrase "one of these little ones" that led the evangelist to incorporate the stumbling sayings into the short discourse in the house in Capernaum. The discourse begins with Jesus talking about a child (9:35–36).

9. A collection of sayings in the Egyptian *Book of the Dead*'s "Protestation of Guiltlessness" includes the declaration, "I have not had sexual relations with a boy" (Saying A20; *ANET*, 34). A similar assertion, in somewhat different form is found in another collection of Egyptian sayings, "O His-Face-Behind-Him, who comes forth from *Tep-het-djat*, I have not been perverted; I have not had sexual relations with a boy" (Saying B27; *ANET*, 35).

10. Some authorities in rabbinic Judaism considered masturbation to be the most severe of all the sins recorded in scripture. R. Johanan, for example, says that one who practices self-abuse "is guilty of a capital crime" (*b. Nid.* 13a). See Louis M. Epstein, *Sex Laws and Customs in Judaism* (New York: KTAV, 1967), 146–47.

11. Compare Mark's "it is better" (*kalon estin*, literally, "it is good").

12. Saying A21; cf. B21: "O *Maa-Intef*, who comes from the Temple of Min, I have not defiled myself" (*ANET*, 34–35, following protestations of innocence with regard to pederasty and adultery).

13. J. Duncan M. Derrett has argued that the right hand was not used for sexual contact in the East and that "the right hand" must therefore refer to property transactions. In his analysis, stumbling with the hand is a matter of

theft, fraud, or forgery; stumbling with the foot refers to a case of robbery, theft, or perhaps that of a runaway slave. The amputation of hand and foot was the typical penalty for these crimes in the ancient East. See Derrett, "Law in the New Testament: *Si scandalizaverit te manus tua abscinde illam* (Mk. IX.42) and Comparative Legal History," in *Studies in the New Testament*, vol. 1, *Glimpses of the Legal and Social Presuppositions of the Authors* (Leiden: Brill, 1977), 4–31. Derrett uses the Matthean text to interpret Mark 9:42. In weighing the validity of Derrett's observations for the interpretation of the text, one must note that the "right" hand is a Matthean addition to the tradition and that Matthew has incorporated the saying into a catechetical pericope that deals with sexual sin.

14. The saying provides an emphatic conclusion to the entire series. In some manuscripts, it was reproduced at 9:44 and 9:46. See above, n. 1.

15. Matthew the evangelist is a careful editor. He has replaced Mark's simple "tear it out" (*ekbale auton,* Mark 9:47) with "tear it out and throw it away" (*exele auton kai bale apo sou,* Matt. 18:9). He has also changed the mood of the verb "stumble" from Mark's subjunctive to an indicative. In this way he has made the saying in 18:9 conform to that of 5:29. Matthew preserves the saying in two places in his Gospel, as he often does when he finds material in two of his principal sources, Mark and Q. On the presence of the saying in Q, see Frans Neirynck, *Q-Synopsis: The Double Tradition Passages in Greek*, Studiorum Novi Testamenti Auxilia 13 (Leuven: University Press/Peeters, 1988), 56–57.

16. The detail of the "right" eye has probably been introduced into the saying because of the parallelism between 5:29 and 5:30. It would have been natural to speak of the right hand in a society in which the right hand was considered to be the more active hand.

17. See, e.g., the *Mekilta of R. Simeon,* "he is not to commit adultery . . . either by the eye or by the heart" (111). Cf. *Pesiq. R.* 4:2; *T. Iss.* 4:4; 7:2; *T. Benj.* 8:2; *Jub.* 20:4; *Pss. Sol.* 4:4–6.

18. See Ronald E. Clements and R. F. Collins, "Woe," *ABD* 6:945–47.

19. See Urban C. von Wahlde, "Mark 9.33–50: Discipleship: The Authority that Serves," *BZ* 29 (1985): 49–67. A similar fate attended other sayings of Jesus. For example, the first beatitude, "Blessed are you who are poor," a radical prophetic and eschatological statement that is essentially reproduced in Luke 6:20 (cf. Luke 6:24), became a catechetical item in Matt. 5:3, "Blessed are the poor in spirit.

20. In a somewhat similar vein, Gundry has written, "He [Mark] is interested in the explosive force of Jesus' teaching, not in its ethical content" (*Mark*, 525).

5

Conduct to Be Avoided

ARK'S GOSPEL STORY ABOUT JESUS was written for a Gentile Christian audience at about the time that the temple in Jerusalem was destroyed. It includes an episode in which provocative Pharisees and scribes come from Jerusalem and ask Jesus why it was that his disciples had broken the tradition of the elders by eating with defiled hands (Mark 7:1–15).[1]

In response to the provocation, Jesus contrasts the concern of the Pharisees and scribes for the tradition of the elders with their lack of concern for the commandments of God. The commandment of God that Jesus cites as an illustration of how his opponents really transgress God's demands even as they are apparently concerned with the tradition of the elders is the fifth commandment, "Honor your father and your mother" (Exod. 20:12; Deut. 5:16), the *mitzvah* that was considered to be the link between the righteous Israelite's obligations toward God and the obligations toward one's neighbors. Jesus shows how the law was used as a means to violate the commandments of God. Instead of honoring their parents by taking care of them in their old age, some people offered their goods to God. Goods that could have been used to provide care for elderly parents were offered instead to God as corban. This, said Jesus, was honoring God with the lips rather than honoring God from the depths of one's being, one's very heart.

Having confronted the Pharisees and their scribes, Jesus calls the crowds to himself to explain what it is that really defiles a person. "Listen to me," he says, "there is nothing outside a person that by going in can defile, but the things that come out are what defile (7:15). Back in the house, Jesus' disciples asked him what all this really meant (7:17). Jesus chided them because they were dense. Then he explained what he meant. "It is what comes out of a person that defiles. For it is from within, from the human heart (*ek tēs kardias tōn anthrōpōn*), that evil intentions come: fornication, theft, murder, adultery, avarice, wickedness, deceit, licentiousness, envy, slander, pride, folly. All these things come from within, and they defile a person" (7:20–23).

What defiles a person are the evil actions and the vices that rise from deep within. Mark's list is hardly exhaustive, but it does include a variety of things that defile the person. The first seven items are plural in Greek; they evoke activities that consist of evil scheming,[2] fornication, theft, murder, adultery, avarice, and wickedness. The last six items on Mark's list are singular—deceit, licentiousness,[3] envy, slander, pride, and folly. The reader should think of these as vices, rather than as evil acts *per se*.[4]

Mark's list of thirteen vices is similar to a number of such lists that appear in the writings of Greco-Roman authors more or less contemporary with the evangelist himself. Lists of vices are found, for example, in the writings of Cicero (*Tusculan Disputations* 4.11–27), Epictetus (*Discourses* 3.20.5–6), and Dio Chrysostom (*Discourses* 69.9). They are not often found in the Hebrew Bible, but they are common in Hellenistic Judaism.[5]

In the Pseudepigrapha, lists appear in a wide variety of writings. Typical of the list of vices is *3 Apoc. Bar.* 8:5: "The sun sees all the lawlessness in the world; he does not countenance lewdness, adultery, jealousy, rivalry, theft, murder, all of which are not acceptable to God." See also *3 Apoc. Bar.* 4:17; 13:4; *1 Enoch* 10:20; 91:6–7; *2 Enoch* 10:4–6; 34:1–2; *Apoc. Abr.* 24.6–9; *Jub.* 21:21; 23:14; *4 Macc.* 1:3–4, 26–27; 2:15; *Sib. Or.* 1:175–79; 2:255–66; 3:220–29, 377–80; 8:182–89; *T. Abr.* 10:5; *T. Mos.* 7:3–4; *T. Reub.* 3:2–8; *T. Sim.* 4:7–9; *T. Levi* 17:11; *T. Jud.* 13:2; 16:1; 16:3; 18:2–6; 23:1; *T. Iss.* 4:2; 6:1–3; 7:2–4;[6] *T. Dan* 5:1–6; 6:8; *T. Gad* 3:3; 5:1; *T. Benj.* 6:4–5; 1QS 4:9–11.

Such lists seem to have made their way into Hellenistic Judaism under the influence of the Stoics. From there they made their way into the writings of the early Christians, particularly those that were intended for Gentile Christian readers. Within the New Testament lists of vices are found in Rom. 1:29–31; 13:13; 1 Cor. 5:10–11; 6:9–10; 2 Cor. 12:20–21; Gal. 5:19–21; Eph. 4:31; 5:3–5; Col. 3:5–8; 1 Tim. 1:9–10; 6:4–5; 2 Tim. 3:2–5; Titus 1:7; 3:3; 1 Pet. 2:1; 4:3, 15; Rev. 9:21; 21:8; 22:15; and Matt. 15:19, which is dependent on Mark 7:21–22.[7]

In rewriting Mark's instruction about what it is that really defiles a person, Matthew reduces Mark's list of thirteen vices to seven. "Out of the heart," Matthew writes, "come evil intentions, murder, adultery, fornication, theft, false witness, slander" (15:19). The reader of this Jewish Christian Gospel quickly recognizes that the things that defile a person are violations of one or another of the Ten Commandments. Matthew has arranged the seven vices on his short list so that they follow the catechetical sequence of the Ten Commandments. The list of things that defile—murder, adultery (+ fornication), theft, and false witness (+ slander)—is parallel to the order of activities prohibited by the Decalogue's set of negative commandments.

That Matthew has reordered the vices according to the order of the Decalogue is clear when the reader considers that Matthew has not only shortened the list but also placed murder and adultery before fornication and theft. Matthew has placed false witness,[8] an activity that does not appear on Mark's list but is the activity prohibited by the ninth commandment, before slander.[9] He has omitted the short list of seven vices that appear in Mark, namely, avarice, wickedness, deceit, licentiousness, envy, pride, and folly. The seven nouns on Matthew's short list are plural, indicating acts of murder, acts of adultery, acts of fornication, and so forth.

In his list of vices, Matthew has expanded the content of the seventh commandment so that it includes fornication (*porneiai*) as well as adultery. The purview of the ninth commandment is similarly extended so that it includes slander (*blasphēmiai*) as well as false witness. That Matthew has added fornication to adultery and slander to false witness suggests that he has a view of the ancient commandments that goes beyond the letter of the law (cf. 5:27–32).[10] Not only adultery but also fornication, not only false witness but also slander come from the heart and defile a person.

Since Matthew's presentation of the vices is so clearly dependent on the Ten Commandments, it is likely that what Matthew intended by "evil intentions" is not simply a general introduction to the whole list of offensive activities.[11] The first item on Matthew's list, "evil intentions" (*dialogismoi ponēroi*), designates activities that violate the fifth commandment, the kind of thing that the evangelist has just described in his version of the story of the confrontation between Jesus and the Pharisees on the tradition of the elders (15:3–11). "Intentions" (*dialogismoi*) suggests scheming calculations. In the immediately preceding dispute with the Pharisees and their scribes, Jesus had shown how these Pharisees schemed so as to avoid taking care of their elderly parents as the fifth commandment of God required them to do. "Evil intentions" are acts that do not honor one's father and mother (15:4).

VICE LISTS

Mark's list of thirteen vices is one of the longest in the New Testament, where only four lists contain more than thirteen vices. Of these, Rom. 1:29–31 is the longest, with twenty-one vices. 2 Tim. 3:2–5 lists eighteen vices. There are fifteen vices in Gal. 5:19–21 and fourteen in 1 Tim. 1:9–10. The shortest catalogues of vices in the New Testament are those found in 1 Pet. 4:15 and Rev. 9:21. These two lists contain only four vices. Titus 1:7 and 1 Pet. 2:1 contain five vices. The other lists have six (Rom. 13:13; Eph. 4:31; 1 Pet. 4:3), seven (Rev. 22:15), eight (Titus 3:3;[12] Rev. 21:8), nine (1 Tim. 6:4–5), ten (1 Cor. 5:10–11; 6:9–10; Eph. 5:3–5[13]), and eleven (2 Cor. 12:20–21 [= 8 + 3]; Col. 3:5–8). In comparison, the typical vice list in Iranian literature, among the earliest literature to make use of such lists, contains five items.

Two of the longer lists of vices in the New Testament, Gal. 5:19–21 and 1 Tim. 1:9–10, have an et cetera clause at the end of the list. This finale indicates that neither Paul nor the author of 1 Timothy intended to include all the vices known to them. In fact, the vices listed in Rom. 1:29–31 are only twenty-one of the 110 vices cited in the New Testament's various lists of vices.[14] Were all of these vices to be compiled into a single list it would still not be an exhaustive list of the vices known in the Hellenistic world. Philo has 146 vices on a single list.

Mark cites three sexual vices among the thirteen vices on the list that he gives in 7:21, fornication (*porneiai*), adultery (*moicheiai*), and licentiousness (*aselgeia*). These three vices are named in several different New Testament lists. Vices of a sexual nature are, in fact, a stock item on the classic lists of vices. All but five of the New Testament's twenty-two catalogues of vices list one or another sexual vice. One of these five is Rom. 1:29–31, where a long list of vices has been appended to a discussion on homoerotic activity.[15]

Several words that appear on the New Testament vice lists are not used by their respective authors in any context other than a vice list.[16] This makes it difficult to determine what precisely an author had in mind when he cited one or another vice. The context simply lets the reader know that the author was writing about "a vice." Sometimes an interpreter is hard pressed to say anything more than that. That the New Testament vice lists contain words that appear only in the lists confirms that this material is "borrowed." The proper literary context of some of the vocabulary is simply the vice list itself.[17]

The vice lists found in the writings of Jewish authors, including the New Testament's Jewish Christian authors, typically include idolatry, the root of all evil. The book of Wisdom has a list of twenty vices (Wis. 14:23–26).[18] The list says that those who err about the knowledge of God no longer keep their marriages pure. They grieve one another by adultery. There is sexual perversion, disorder in marriages, adultery, and debauchery. Explaining the origin of these vices, the wise man said that "the worship of idols not to be named is the beginning and cause and end of every evil" (Wis. 14:27).[19] According to the sage, the worship of idols is the source of sexual perversion, marital disorder, adultery, and debauchery. The author notes that just penalties will overtake these evil persons for two reasons. The first is that "they thought wrongly about God in devoting themselves to idols" (Wis. 14:30). The second is that with contempt they swore unrighteously.

LISTS OF VIRTUES

In form and function the New Testament's twenty-two lists of vices are comparable to its lists of virtues. Altogether there are nineteen catalogues of virtues: 2 Cor. 6:6–7a; Gal. 5:22–23; Eph. 4:2–3; 4:32; 5:9; Phil. 4:8; Col. 3:12; 1 Tim. 3:2–4; 3:8–10; 3:11–12; 4:12; 6:11; 6:18; 2 Tim. 2:22–25; 3:10; Titus 1:8; Heb. 7:26; 1 Pet. 3:8; and 2 Pet. 1:5–7. As is the case with the catalogues of vices, the distinctive vocabulary of the virtue lists sometimes consists of abstract nouns, sometimes of descriptions of activities, and sometimes of epithets for those involved in the activity. Some of the words on these lists are not otherwise used by the author who cites them in a list and some of them appear in the New Testament only on the lists. The words themselves, of course, suggest just the opposite of the words that appear on the vice lists.

The array of literature in which lists of virtues and vices appear attests to a practice that was widespread in the ancient Mediterranean world.[20] In the Hellenistic world such lists are found in both literary and nonliterary sources. These lists were used for a wide variety of purposes, most commonly to praise the good person, to set forth the ideal of the moral life, or to castigate evil persons as thoroughly reprobate.

In diatribe and satire, lists of vices were used to characterize evil persons or to describe the masses, the *hoi polloi*, as irrational and impious. On the other hand, lists of virtues were used in exhortation and instruction to portray the ideal of a good or wise person. As funereal epitaphs, such lists served as a permanent testimony to the deceased's good life.

Lists of virtues and vices are found in Iranian cosmological traditions, in Mesopotamia, in Egypt,[21] in the Greco-Roman world, in Hellenistic Judaism, and in the New Testament. In the Greek-speaking world their use goes back to Plato. This academic philosopher divided virtue into the four cardinal virtues of prudence, temperance, justice, and fortitude. Philosophic moralists of Stoic persuasion subdivided Plato's four virtues into various subcategories. In their exhortations that good be pursued and evil avoided, they often made use of lists of virtues and lists of vices.

Illustrative of Hellenistic Judaism's use of lists of virtues is a commentary on Plato's list of cardinal virtues in 4 Maccabees. The author writes that "the forms of wisdom consist of prudence, justice, courage, and temperance. Of all these, prudence is the most authoritative, for it is through it that reason controls the passions" (4 Macc. 1:18–19).[22] Other lists of virtues appear in *2 Enoch* 9:1; 66:6; and *Jub.* 7:20–21.

Philo contrasts the virtues of the proselytes with the vices of rebels from the holy laws (*Virtues* 182). In the *Sacrifices of Abel and Cain*, this Jewish philosopher describes a pleasure-lover as one who will be "all these things." He brings his description to a close by describing the pleasure-lover as "a mass of misery and misfortune without relief." The list in this description of the pleasure-lover contains 146 vices (§32).

In a fashion reminiscent of the way that Philo contrasted the virtues of proselytes with the vices of rebels, the apostle Paul sets out in contrast a list of virtues, the "fruits of the Spirit" (Gal. 5:22–23) and a list of vices, "the works of the flesh" (Gal. 5:19–21). Paul's antithetical use of the two lists was imitated by his disciples who wrote the New Testament's Deutero-Pauline epistles. Following the example of their mentor, these authors listed the vices before the virtues so as to underscore the idea that the Christian life is to be found in the avoidance of vice and the pursuit of virtue. These epistles contain perhaps five examples of contrasting lists of vices and virtues: Eph. 4:31; 4:32; Col. 3:5–8; 3:12; 1 Tim. 6:4–5; 6:11; [2 Tim. 3:2–4; 3:10]; and Titus 1:7; 1:8.

In Hellenistic Judaism and in the New Testament, catalogues of vices were often used to portray, almost as a caricature, the moral turpitude of Gentiles or of those who refused to follow the law of God. A characteristic feature of this caricature was the association between a run-on series of vices and the accusation of idolatry. A model of the use of the genre in this fashion is the apostle Paul (cf. Col. 3:5–8; 1 Pet. 4:3; Rev. 21:8; 22:15). In his letter to the Romans he writes about those who do not acknowledge God. Because of this, says Paul, God gave the idolaters up not only to degrading passions but to a whole host of immoral activity. He describes that activity by means of his longest list of vices, the twenty-one vices cited in Rom. 1:29–31.

A General List or a Specific Description?

Any one of the classic catalogues of vices contains but a selection from among the many known vices of antiquity. Some selections are longer, some are shorter, but all are only a selection. A question that is often asked in the interpretation of the ancient texts concerns the degree to which a given list of vices represents a self-conscious choice on the part of the author. Is a given list merely a literary convention, or is it "tailor-made" for the circumstances? Should the modern reader assume, for example, that vices mentioned on any particular list point to specific problems within the community for which the text was intended? Or is the vice list simply a standard literary form whose individual components need not reflect such circumstances? Many New Testament scholars, inspired by the classic work of Martin Dibelius and Hans Conzelmann on the "bourgeois ethic" of the Pastoral Epistles, express the view that vice lists are indiscriminate in their selection.

The fact of the matter is that the editorial hand of an author is at work in any literary presentation of a list of vices. Yet this does not mean that the community for which the author was writing was beset by all the evils that are cited on the list of vices in that particular text. A mixture of cultural commonality and compositional specificity characterizes the literary use of the vice list. The comparison of Matt. 15:19–20 with Mark 7:21–22, for example, shows not only that Matthew has chosen from the Markan list those vices that serve his purpose, but that he has also added to the list a vice whose mention serves his redactional interest. He has, moreover, arranged the whole group in such a way that it will make a strong impact upon his Jewish readers. Matthew, like Mark before him, used the whole list for his own rhetorical purpose.

Similar remarks are to be made apropos of the other vice lists in the New Testament. A comparison of Col. 3:5–8[23] with Eph. 4:31–5:5 proves the point.[24] The Epistle to the Ephesians is dependent on Colossians; it is, in fact, almost a new revised edition of the earlier epistle. Col. 3:5 reads "Put to death, therefore, whatever in you is earthly: fornication, impurity, passion, evil desire, and greed (which is idolatry)." In Eph. 5:3, 5 the text has been revised to read: "But fornication and impurity of any kind, or greed, must not even be mentioned among you. . . . Be sure of this, that no fornicator or impure person, or one who is greedy (that is, an idolater). . . ."[25] Both texts mention fornication, impurity, greed, and idolatry, but the author of the Epistle to the Ephesians has omitted "passion" (*pathos*) and "evil desire" (*epithymian kakēn*) from the new list. On the other hand, this churchman[26] has underscored fornication, impurity, and greed by repeating these three vices.

Eph. 4:31, "Put away from you all bitterness and wrath and anger and wrangling and slander, together with all malice" is an editorial rendition of Col. 3:8, "but now you must get rid of all such things— anger, wrath, malice, slander, and abusive language."[27] The author of Ephesians has dropped "abusive language" from the earlier list and has added "bitterness" (*pikra*) and "wrangling" (*kraugma*). He has emphasized that all forms of the vices that he lists are to be avoided by the Christian. He begins and ends his list with the word, "all" (*pasa, pasę̄*).[28] The author of the Epistle to the Colossians had used a list of virtues (Col. 3:12) to contrast the kind of life that is appropriate to Christians with one that is not. The reviser also employed such a contrast (4:31, 32; 5:3–4).

"SEXUAL IMMORALITY"

Among the many vices to be avoided, none is more frequently mentioned than "fornication" (*porneia*). Among the 110 vices in the New Testament catalogues, "fornication" is the only vice that appears in the majority of texts. "Fornication" is cited in twelve of the twenty-two lists: Matt. 15:19; Mark 7:21; 1 Cor. 5:10, 11; 6:9; 2 Cor 12:21; Gal. 5:19; Eph. 5:3, 5; Col. 3:5; 1 Tim. 1:10; Rev. 9:21; 21:8; 22:15. It appears twice in 1 Cor. 5:10–11 and Eph. 5:3–5. It is the first named on the lists in 1 Cor. 5:10, 11; 6:9; Gal. 5:19; Eph. 5:3, 5; Col. 3:5.[29] Fornication is first among the "works of the flesh" (Gal. 5:19). Paul repeatedly told the Corinthians to have nothing to do with those who are "sexually immoral," be they pagan or Christian (1 Cor. 5:9–11).[30] Those who are sexually immoral[31] will not inherit the kingdom of God, Paul says in 1 Cor. 6:9. The presence of those who are sexually immoral is a source of grief for the apostle (2 Cor. 12:21; cf. 1 Cor. 5:1–8). This evidence indicates that fornication is a vice that the Apostle Paul especially urged his neophyte Christians, born as Gentiles, to avoid.

Paul's strong statements about sexual immorality made an impact on his disciples. The author of the Epistle to the Colossians exhorted those to whom he was writing to put sexual immorality to death; those who do not are subject to the wrath of God (Col. 3:5). Echoing a thought that the apostle himself had expressed in his letter to the Corinthians, the author of Ephesians told them that sexually immoral persons would not inherit the kingdom of God (Eph. 5:5). The abhorrence with which the community should view sexual immorality is such that they shouldn't even talk about it (Eph. 5:3). The pastor who wrote the first letter to Timothy[32] set down a rule of life for the community in which he reminded them that sexual immorality is contrary to the sound teaching that is in conformity with the glorious gospel of God that had been entrusted to the apostle (1 Tim. 1:8–11). According to the pastor, the law was given because of those who were sexually immoral.

Paul urged Christians in Thessalonica and Corinth to shun sexual immorality (1 Thess. 4:3; 1 Cor. 6:18). Luke tells us that when the apostles and elders of the early church gathered in Jerusalem they decided under the inspiration of the Holy Spirit to tell Gentile Christians to avoid sexual immorality. They did this by means of a circular letter that was sent to Gentile Christians in Antioch, Syria, and Cilicia, Paul's home region (Acts 15:20, 29).

The way that Luke writes about sexual immorality in Acts 15 suggests that Jewish Christians almost took it for granted that Gentiles would be involved in sexual immorality much as they ate food that was not kosher and participated in idolatrous worship. If Gentile Christians were to associate with Jewish Christians, they, as the resident aliens in Israel of old, had to abstain from eating three kinds of food: food that had been defiled as a result of being offered to idols, meat that had not been properly or ritually slaughtered, and food that contained or was made from blood—and they had to abstain from sexual immorality![33]

The book of Revelation links sexual immorality to the worship of idols (cf. *Sib. Or.* 3:34–45; *T. Naph.* 3:3–4). Those who have not abandoned idolatry are caught up in sexual immorality (Rev. 9:21). They are doomed to the "second death," a place of sulphurous fire (Rev. 21:8). They will be banned from the holy city forever (Rev. 22:15). In comparison with these strong images, what Jesus had to say about sexual immorality, as reported by Mark and Matthew, is relatively mild. The two evangelists tell us that sexual immorality comes from the human heart and that it defiles the whole person (Mark 7:21; Matt. 15:19).

What did Matthew, Mark, Luke, Paul and his disciples, and the pseudonymous author of the book of Revelation mean when they wrote about "sexual immorality," *porneia?* The meaning of the term is somewhat ambiguous.[34] Like many modern translations of the Bible, the New Revised Standard Version translates *porneia,* as well as the related personal nouns *pornos* (a sexually immoral person) and *pornē* (a prostitute) and the related verb *porneuō* (to indulge in sexual immorality), in various ways. Etymologically the term *porneia* meant fornication or prostitution, but the word was often used in a broader sense. In its wider sense *porneia,* from whose root we have the English word pornography ("writing about *porneia*"), connoted any and all forms of sexual misconduct. The ambiguity of the terms *porneia* and *pornos* can be seen in the NRSV's translation of the various lists of vices. These words are translated as "sexual immorality" and "sexually immoral" in 1 Cor. 5:9, 10, 11 and 2 Cor. 12:21. They are translated as "fornication" and "fornicator" in Matt. 15:19; Mark 7:21; 1 Cor 6:9; Gal. 5:19; Col. 3:5; Eph. 5:3, 5; 1 Tim. 1:10; Rev. 9:21; 21:8; and 22:15.

Some translations of the New Testament's catalogues of vices must necessarily give a translation of *porneia* that has a more specific connotation than "sexual immorality." This is because, in addition to *porneia,* other forms of sexual immorality are cited on these lists. For example, in Mark 7:21–22 "adultery" (*moicheia*) appears as well as *porneia.* In Matthew's revision of the list (Matt. 15:19) *porneia* is cited as a catechetical expansion of the seventh commandment's prohibition of adultery. In 1 Cor. 6:9 "adulterers" (*moichoi*) appears along with *pornoi.* Apart from the catalogues in Matthew, Mark, and 1 Corinthians, "adultery" does not appear in the New Testament's lists of vices. It is, nonetheless, the subject of much New Testament discourse.[35]

In sum, within the New Testament *porneia* generally means sexual immorality in a general sense; in a particular context the Greek term may denote one or another particular form of sexual misconduct. In any case, whether the term *porneia* is to be understood generally or specifically, New Testament authors urged Christians to avoid *porneia* altogether.

OTHER SEXUAL VICES

Paul the apostle shared with many Jewish writers of his time the conviction that with regard to sex the mores of Gentiles were reprehensible (cf. Rom. 1:21–32; 1 Thess. 4:5).[36] This prejudice may lie behind what Paul wrote to the Corinthians when he said to them, "I fear that when I come again, my God may humble me before you, and that I may have to mourn over many who previously sinned and have not repented of the impurity, sexual immorality, and licentiousness that they have practiced" (2 Cor. 12:21).

The same triad of sexual vices, impurity (*akatharsia*), sexual immorality (*porneia*), and licentiousness (*aselgeia*) occurs at the beginning of the list of the works of the flesh in Gal. 5:19.[37] In Galatians the order is, first, sexual immorality [= "fornication," NRSV], then impurity and licentiousness. "Impurity" and "licentiousness" are terms that generally characterize immoral sexual behavior. Each of the two vices appears in three additional catalogues, "impurity" in Eph. 5:3, 5 and Col. 3:5; "licentiousness" in Mark 7:22; Rom. 13:13; and 1 Pet. 4:3.

"Impurity" essentially evokes the idea of some reality—persons, places, things, or behavior—that is under the influence of evil and demonic powers rather than under the influence of God. It is a cultic term, from which an ethical meaning has been derived. Philo, for example, interprets ritual impurity, which prevents a person from participating in the Passover ritual during the first month (Num. 9:6–14), as moral impurity (see *Allegorical Interpretation* 3.94). Something similar is seen in Mark 7:1–23, where a discussion of ritual impurity (7:1–13) gives way to the two-part instruction on morality in 7:14–23.

In the New Testament, the word "impurity" (*akatharsia*) evokes moral deficiency in a serious and general way. The juxtaposition of the word with "sexual immorality" (*porneia*) in the catalogues of vices suggests, however, that its primary allusion in these lists is to sexual immorality.[38] As is the case with *porneia*, it is only from the context that one can determine the specific meaning of *akatharsia*. That context is lacking when the word appears in a catalogue of vices.

Long before the term "licentiousness" (*aselgeia*) was used by Paul, it had been used by classical authors such as Plato and Demosthenes. In two of Paul's triads of sexual vices (2 Cor. 12:21; Gal. 5:19) "licentiousness" appears as the third item in the group. Etymologically the term suggests wanton, outrageous, or brutal behavior. In the New Testament, and especially in its catalogues of vices, the word means debauchery, voluptuousness, or sexual excess.[39] This sense is retained in the *Shepherd of Hermas*'s list of vices. The glorious man who was lord[40] is reported to have said to the shepherd:

> Hear the names of the women who wear the black garments. Of these . . . four are more powerful than the rest; the first is Unbelief; the second, Intemperance; the third, Disobedience; the fourth, Deceit; and their followers are called, Sadness, Wickedness, Wantonness (*aselgeia*), Irascibility, Falsehood, Folly, Slander, Hatred. (*Herm. Sim.* 9.15)

The classic terms of "sexual immorality," "impurity," and "licentiousness," along with "adultery," were not the only words used in the Greco-Roman world to denote sexual immorality. Stoics held that there were four principal passions or emotions (*pathoi*) that destroyed a human being. These were grief (*lypē*), fear (*phobos*), desire (*epithymia*), and pleasure (*hēdonē*). In the Hellenistic world "desire" and "pleasure" were sometimes used specifically of sexual desire (see 1 Thess. 4:5; cf. Rom. 13:14; Gal. 5:16) and lust.[41] The two terms occur together in the list of eight vices in Titus 3:3. The epistle uses a list of vices in order to describe a Christian's former way of life. Christians, the author notes, were once "slaves to various passions and pleasures (*epithymiais kai hēdonais poikiliais*)" before their acceptance of the faith. Passion (*epithymia*) appears on the list of vices in Col. 3:5, where it is associated with fornication and impurity,[42] and in 1 Pet. 4:3, where it is associated with licentiousness.

In sum, the New Testament's vice lists include a number of terms that describe sexual deviation in a general manner. Some of these terms identify kinds of behavior, such as sexual immorality, impurity, and licentiousness. Others get to the heart of the matter by pointing to illicit desire and sexual lust. The various lists in which these terms are found are generally used in a summary exhortation. They describe the manner of life that Christians are to have left behind as they have embraced the faith.[43] That behavior is radically different from life in the Spirit (Gal. 5:16, 18, 22; Eph. 4:30; cf. Titus 1:8) and is incompatible with the acceptance of the gospel of Jesus Christ (1 Tim. 1:10–11; 6:3). To urge them to stand fast in their determination to turn from that form of deviant behavior, the New Testament authors often state that those who practice those forms of misconduct cannot enter the kingdom of God.[44]

The Christian use of the catalogues of vices derives from Hellenistic Judaism. The matrix is clearly reflected in the New Testament's lists, where vices are often associated with idolatry (Eph. 5:5; Col. 3:5; 1 Pet. 4:3; Rev. 21:8; 22:15) and are sometimes offered as a "profile" of the pagan life (Rom. 1:29–31; 13:13; 1 Cor. 5:10–11; 2 Tim. 3:2–4; 1 Pet. 4:3; cf. 1 Thess. 4:5). Among the various terms used to describe sexual deviance, one term definitely describes a very specific type of conduct. That term is "adultery" (*moicheia*), the sexual misdeed cited in Matt. 15:19; Mark 7:22; and 1 Cor. 6:9. There are, however, additional terms in the New Testament vice lists that seem to designate specific forms of deviant sexual behavior. These terms are "debauchery" (*koitai,* Rom. 13:13; cf. Luke 11:7; Rom. 9:10; Heb. 13:4), "male prostitutes" (*malakoi,* 1 Cor. 6:9; cf. Matt. 11:8; Luke 7:25), and "sodomites" (*arsenokoitai,* 1 Cor. 6:9; 1 Tim. 1:10). What kind of conduct is identified with this nomenclature?

DEBAUCHERY

"Debauchery" appears in the list of vices in Rom. 13:13. The Greek term translated as "debauchery" in the NRSV is *koitai,* the plural form of the Greek word *koitē.* The word *koitē,* in the singular, denotes the marriage bed. The word was used with this meaning by such classical authors as Herodotus, Sophocles, and Euripides. The term continued to have this meaning during the Hellenistic era and is used to denote the marriage bed in the New Testament (Luke 11:7; Heb. 13:4). A related idiomatic expression was for a woman to have a marriage bed from someone. The saying meant that she had become pregnant by that man. Paul uses the expression in Rom. 9:10 to describe Rebecca's pregnancy and motherhood.

When the apostle uses the same term in the plural and incorporates it into a list of vices as he does in Rom. 13:13, the term is used in a metaphorical sense to connote some sort of violation or defilement of the marriage bed. A widely used lexicon translates the Greek term by "lasciviousness."[45] "Lasciviousness" is, however, not much more useful than "debauchery" to help the modern reader who wants to understand what particular kind of sexual misdeeds Paul had in mind when he included *koitai* in a catalogue of vices.

Although the Epistle to the Hebrews was written years after Paul's death, Heb. 13:4 might provide some clue to what the apostle meant when he included *koitai*, debauchery, among the vices to be avoided by the Christian. Toward the end of his exhortation, the author of the epistle wrote, "Let marriage be held in honor by all, and let the marriage bed (*koitē*) be kept undefiled; for God will judge fornicators (*pornous*) and adulterers (*moichous*)" (13:4).[46] "Fornicators," an ambiguous term whose precise meaning can be inferred only from the context in which it is used, seems to describe people who have engaged in acts of sexual immorality, other than adultery, that defile the marriage bed. If this is the case,[47] one might argue that the vice of "debauchery" (Rom. 13:13) consists of adultery and other forms of sexually immoral conduct that are harmful to a marriage relationship.

"MALE PROSTITUTION"

Since most of Paul's letters were written to Gentile Christian communities, the apostle mentions but rarely the powerful biblical symbol of the kingdom of God (Rom. 14:17; 1 Cor. 4:20; 6:9, 10; 15:24, 50; Gal. 5:21; 1 Thess. 2:12). One of the few times that he does so is in 1 Corinthians (6:9, 10). He uses the metaphor to frame a short plea that includes a rhetorical question, an exhortation, and an explanation:

> Do you not know that wrongdoers will not inherit the kingdom of God? Do not be deceived! Fornicators, idolaters, adulterers, male prostitutes, sodomites, thieves, the greedy, drunkards, revilers, robbers—none of these will inherit the kingdom of God. And this is what some of you used to be. (1 Cor. 6:9–11a)

Paul employs a list of vices to explain what he means by "wrongdoers" (*adikoi*). The apostle frequently adopts this literary genre in his moral exhortation.[48] The list that appears in 1 Cor. 6:9–10 contains nine vices, covering a wide range of immoral behavior,[49] that are associated with idolatry. Paul firmly states that those who are engaged in those forms of behavior will be excluded from the kingdom of God. The motif of the kingdom is reinforced by being repeated. It serves as the literary "bookends" for the entire passage.[50]

The list of vices in 6:9–11 is atypical in its concentration on sexual vices, both in the number of such vices and in the placement of these vices at the head of the list.[51] The sequence "fornicators, idolaters, adulterers, male prostitutes, sodomites" could be read as if Paul were saying that sexual immorality results from idolatry and that the forms of sexual immorality that result from idolatry are adultery, male prostitution, and sodomy. This reading of the text is not simply to be rejected. In his letter to the Romans Paul clearly affirms his conviction that sexual immorality, especially homoerotic activity, is the result of idolatry.[52]

One feature of the list of vices in 1 Cor. 6:9–10 has captured a great deal of attention in recent years. This is the appearance on Paul's list of "male prostitutes" (*malakoi*) and "sodomites" (*arsenokoitai*). Paul does not use these terms in any other place of the extant correspondence. This lack of usage makes it difficult for the modern reader to understand what Paul meant when he used the terms *malakoi* and *arsenokoitai*. The NRSV translates the terms respectively as "male prostitutes" and "sodomites," but these translations are only the editors' attempt to understand what Paul meant. It is usage that allows one to understand the meaning of a word. When a term is not used very much, it is very difficult, and sometimes impossible, to know what an author or a speaker intended to say by using that particular word.

As the modern reader engages in the effort to understand what Paul meant by *malakoi* and *arsenokoitai*, he or she must hold fast to two principles. One is hermeneutical; the other is ethical. The hermeneutical principle is that any translation is an interpretation.[53] The ethical principle is that the vices of "male prostitution" and "sodomy" are only two of the 110 vices identified in the New Testament as forms of conduct to be avoided by the committed Christian.

Trying to understand what Paul meant by *malakoi* and *arsenokoitai*, the reader should bear in mind that the word *malakoi* is an adjective that Paul uses as a noun.[54] Elsewhere in the New Testament the adjective appears only in Matt. 11:8 and Luke 7:25, where it refers to fancy clothing. The word *arsenokoitai* appears elsewhere in the New Testament only in 1 Tim. 1:10—that is, in a vice list cited in a text that is dependent on Paul's writings.

The difficulties in understanding what Paul meant by *malakoi* and *arsenokoitai* are apparent when a reader looks at the various ways that these Greek terms have been translated in widely used versions of the New Testament.[55] The Revised Standard Version and the Revised English Bible lump the two terms together in an inclusive "sexual perverts."[56] The revised edition of the New American Bible reads "boy prostitutes" and "practicing homosexuals," but has changed the translation of *arsenokoitai* to "sodomites" in the most recent printings.[57] The New International Version gives "male prostitutes" and "homosexual offenders." The Contemporary English Version writes about one who "is a pervert or behaves like a homosexual." The King James Version has "effeminate" and "abusers of themselves with mankind," while the New King James Bible has "homosexuals" and "sodomites."

These different translations point to some of the difficulties that modern readers have when they try to understand precisely what it was that Paul was talking about in 1 Cor. 6:9. What did he mean by *malakoi* and *arsenokoitai?* He was undoubtedly thinking about activity, not about a condition or an orientation. The ancients were unable to distinguish homosexuals from heterosexuals.[58] Their typology was different from ours. When the ancients wrote about sexuality, it was sexual activity, not sexual orientation, that occupied their attention. Undoubtedly, too, Paul had in mind some form of sexual perversion.[59] The cluster of five vices in 1 Cor. 6:9 is embedded in a long section of the letter that deals almost exclusively with human sexuality (1 Corinthians 5–7). The cluster includes four kinds of sexual misbehavior and idolatry. In his letter essay, the letter to the Romans, Paul links idolatry to sexual misconduct, specifically lesbian and homoerotic activity.[60]

In 1 Cor. 6:9, Paul states that, in addition to those people who engage in "fornication" and "adultery," those who are so involved in sexual misconduct that he can label them as *malakoi* and *arsenokoitai* are excluded from the kingdom of God.[61] The word *malakos* is an adjective that means "soft," as its use in the New Testament to describe "fancy" clothes indicates.[62] In Greek the adjective was used of a soft cushion or a freshly plowed field. Used of persons, the expression had a pejorative meaning. Found in the writings of Thucydides, Xenophon, and others, the term evoked a person who was soft, yielding, or remiss; alternatively, someone who was fainthearted, effeminate, or cowardly, a "softy."[63] Plutarch associated "softness" with greed (*pleonexia*). Writing of the downfall of Sparta, he said that "when once the love of silver and gold had crept into the city, closely followed by greed and parsimony in the acquisition of wealth and by luxury, effeminacy (*malakia*), and extravagance in the use and enjoyment of it, Sparta fell away from most of her noble traits."[64] Had *malakoi* followed *pleonektai* on Paul's list of vices in 1 Cor. 6:9, one might argue that what Paul had in mind was the kind of soft living that comes from too much money.[65]

Sandwiched between "adulterers" and "sodomites," however, the word *malakoi* seemingly refers to persons who have been engaged in some form of sexual misbehavior other than that indicated by "fornicators," "adulterers," and "sodomites." The *Exegetical Dictionary of the New Testament* describes the *malakoi* as "reprehensible examples of passive homosexuality."[66] Dale Martin takes issue with this understanding of *malakoi*. He writes:

> There is no historical reason to take *malakos* as a specific reference to the penetrated man in homosexual intercourse. It is even less defensible to narrow that reference down further to mean "male prostitute." The meaning of the word is clear, even if too broad to be taken to refer to a single act or role. *Malakos* means "effeminate."[67]

Martin argues that the term referred to a rather broad social category of people in a world that devalued the feminine. More often than not, it referred to men who prettied themselves up in order to further their heterosexual exploits.[68]

Philo of Alexandria, the Hellenistic Jewish writer contemporary with Paul, clearly distinguishes, however, the active from the passive partner in male homosexual activity.[69] He claims that both are rightly judged worthy of death (see *Special Laws* 3.38–39). In writing about homosexual activity between males, Philo uses language that is similar to Paul's *malakoi*. He speaks of men who emasculate the bodies of their passive partners by "luxury (*malakotēti*) and voluptuousness" (*Abraham* 136). He speaks of "unmanliness and effeminacy" (*anandrias kai malakias*) and prizes for "licentiousness and effeminacy" (*akrasias kai malakias*) (*Special Laws* 3.39, 40). Passages such as these seem to suggest that the word group associated with the Greek root *malak-* was used to describe the passive partner in homosexual activity among males.

If the connotation of *malakoi* is difficult to identify, the meaning of *arsenokoitai* is even less clear. Etymologically the term means "bedding down with a man."[70] Paul may have coined the word, since 1 Cor. 6:9 is the oldest literary indication of its use.[71] The neologism may have been Paul's way of referring to the prohibitions cited in Lev. 18:22 and 20:13.

The rare uses of *arsenokoitai* in ancient Greek literature are principally confined to catalogues of vices. In two second-century catalogues, in the *Acts of John* and Theophilus of Antioch, respectively, *arsenokoitēs* (the singular of *arsenokoitai*) appears on a list with others beholden to economic vice. In an exhortation in the *Acts of John* the *arsenokoitēs* is sandwiched between the robber and swindler, on the one hand, and the thief and all of this band, on the other:

> So also the poisoner, sorcerer, robber, swindler, and sodomite (*arseno-koitēs*), the thief and all of this band, guided by your deeds you shall come to unquenchable fire and utter darkness and the pit of torments and eternal doom. So, men of Ephesus, change your ways. (*Acts of John* 36).[72]

Theophilus of Antioch cites the thief, plunderer, and robber before the *arsenokoitēs*.[73] Then he moves on to savagery and abusive behavior.

"Do not practice homosexuality" (*mē arsenokoitein*) is an exhortation contained within a long exhortation on justice in the second book of *Sibylline Oracles* (see 2.56–77, esp. 73).[74] This evidence, slight as it may be, seems to suggest that a century or so after Paul first used the word it had the connotation of paying a man for sex. In the light of this, it may well be that *malakoi* and *arsenokoitai* denote the passive and the active partners in sex for a price among males. Nonetheless, "sodomites" seems well on its way to becoming the commonly accepted translation of *arsenokoitai* in the New Testament's catalogues of vices (1 Cor. 6:9; 1 Tim. 1:10).[75]

HOMOEROTIC ACTIVITY

Homosexual activity was a subject of discussion among the ancients. Not everyone agreed that it was morally wrong. Some three or four centuries before Paul, the great historian Xenophon had written about different cultures' tolerance of pederasty in this way:

> I think I ought to say something also about intimacy with boys, since this matter also has a bearing on education. In other Greek states, for instance among the Boeotians, man and boy live together, like married people; elsewhere, among the Eleians, for example, consent is won by means of favors. Some, on the other hand, entirely forbid suitors to talk with boys.
>
> The customs instituted by Lycurgus were opposed to all of these. If someone, being himself an honest man, admired a boy's soul and tried to make of him an ideal friend without reproach and to associate with him, he approved, and believed in the excellence of this kind of training. But if it was clear that the attraction lay in the boy's outward beauty, he

banned the connection as an abomination; and thus he purged the relationship of all impurity, so that in Lacedaemon it resembled parental and brotherly love.

I am not surprised, however, that people refuse to believe this. For in many states the laws are not opposed to the indulgence of these appetites. (*Lacedaemonians* 2.12–14)

A century and a half after Paul died, Sextus Empiricus wrote of various societies' tolerance of homoerotic activity. He even drew attention to the fact that some of the classic philosophic moralists held that homoerotic activity was morally indifferent:

And perhaps it may not be amiss . . . to dwell more in detail, though briefly, on the notions concerning things shameful and not shameful . . . for thus we shall discover a great variety of belief concerning what ought or ought not to be done.

For example, amongst us sodomy is regarded as shameful or rather illegal, but not by the Germani,[76] they say, it is not looked on as shameful but as a customary thing. It is said, too, that in Thebes long ago this practice was not held to be shameful, and they say that Meriones the Cretan was so called by way of indicating the Cretans' custom, and some refer to this the burning love of Achilles for Patroclus. And what wonder, when both the adherents of the Cynic philosophy and followers of Zeno of Citium, Cleanthes and Chrysippus, declare that this practice is indifferent? (*Outlines of Pyrrhonism* 3.198–200)

In contrast with other societies' tolerance of homoerotic activity, Jews did not abide either pederasty or homosexual activity. They prided themselves on being different from Gentiles in this respect. Praising Jews, the *Letter of Aristeas*[77] says that righteousness, as the aim of conduct, "explains why we are distinct from all other men. The majority of other men defile themselves in their relationships, thereby committing a serious offense, and lands and whole cities take pride in it: they not only procure the males, they also defile mothers and daughters" (*Ep. Arist.* 151–52).[78]

Another Jewish work of Egyptian origin, the third book of *Sibylline Oracles*, tells about Romans who come from the western sea. "Male," it says, "will have intercourse with male and they will set up boys in houses of ill-fame and in those days there will be a great affliction among men and it will throw everything into confusion" (*Sib. Or.* 3.185–87). The *Sibylline Oracles* praise Jews in these terms:

Greatly surpassing all men, they are mindful of holy wedlock, and they do not engage in impious intercourse with male children, as do Phoenicians, Egyptians, and Romans, spacious Greece, and many nations of others, Persians and Galatians and all Asia, transgressing the holy law of immortal God, which they transgressed. (*Sib. Or.* 3.594–600)

In the light of these Jewish parallels and with what Paul himself has to say about the relationship between idolatry and homosexuality in Rom. 1:18–28, it may well be that pederasty and sodomy[79]—perhaps not so much sodomy in general as sex that has been paid for—are the vices to which Paul refers in his use of *malakoi* and *arsenokoitai* in 1 Cor. 6:9. That these two vices occur so rarely in the New Testament's lists of vices should serve as a word of caution to those who would draw from their appearance in 1 Cor. 6:9 the conclusion that these are among the most egregious of human vices. In 1 Cor. 6:9–10, "male prostitutes" and "sodomites" are listed alongside thieves, the greedy, drunkards, revilers, and robbers, as well as fornicators, idolaters, and adulterers. The appearance of "male prostitutes" and "sodomites" on a list of ten vices puts them on a par with the other eight vices. On the basis of their appearance in the catalogue of 1 Cor. 6:9–10, "male prostitution" and "sodomy" are no more egregious than fornication, adultery, greed, and drunkenness.

THE CALL TO HOLINESS

To understand Paul's use of the vice list in 1 Cor. 6:9–10, the reader must consider the context within which it is found. The context is not only Paul's worldview, in which he shares a vision of the "Jewish difference." It is also the context of the perspective from which the apostle has written his first letter to the Corinthians. Paul's emphasis on sexual vices and their implicit connection with idolatry is part of a broad argument in which Paul appeals to the Corinthian assembly as the church of God, a people called holy (1 Cor. 1:2). The image of the church of God evokes the memory of Israel at the time of the exodus when it was designated as the assembly of Yahweh, the church of God. As Israel was called to live out its holiness, so too the church of God at Corinth has been called to live as God's holy people.

1 Corinthians 8–10 deal with one of the issues facing the Corinthians, that of food offered to idols. Were Corinthian Christians to eat food offered to idols, they might give the impression of participating in idol worship. Paul treats the matter at some length and even mentions some of the specific circumstances in which the problem might arise

(1 Cor. 10:25–29). His bottom-line exhortation is "flee from the worship of idols" (1 Cor. 10:14).

Immediately before chapters 8–10, there is an equally long section of the letter in which Paul deals with a variety of issues pertaining to human sexuality (chapters 5–7). He begins with a case of incest, of a kind that is not even tolerated among Gentiles (1 Cor. 5:1). The case was that of a man having an affair with his father's wife, his own stepmother. If such a thing is not tolerated even among pagans, says Paul, why should it be tolerated among Christians? He takes the community to task for not dealing with the issue (1 Cor. 5:2–13) and strongly encourages them to shun people who live immorally (1 Cor. 5:13). Immorality is to be expected among pagans; it is not to be tolerated among Christians.

Then, after a brief interlude—in which he again takes the Corinthians to task, this time for appealing to secular courts when they should have addressed the issues among themselves (1 Cor. 6:1–8)—Paul returns to the topic that he introduced in 5:1, sexual immorality (*porneia*). His treatment begins in a rather classical manner, with a catalogue of vices in which sexual offenses are highlighted. The list is exploited within a framework that uses the Jewish-Christian notion of the kingdom of God (6:9–11).

Paul then takes up a classic topos, fornication and sex with prostitutes (6:12–13). Only then does he treat the issue of sexuality about which some Corinthians had written to him, the idea that it was good for a man not to touch a woman (7:1). He had learned about the case of the incestuous man from an oral report (5:1). His letter dealt with two specific problems of sexual ethics about which Paul had been informed.[80] These problems were incest and undue sexual abstinence.

Between his pastoral responses to the two problematic issues, Paul offered some rather classic advice on sexual activity. He uses the literary form of a catalogue of vices to tell the Christians of Corinth that they were to avoid fornication, adultery, male prostitution, and sodomy, for these were associated with idolatry (1 Cor. 6:9–10). He made use of the example of prostitution, the topos of the philosophic moralists, to get into a heady discussion on human sexuality. Paul brought a Jewish-Christian perspective to bear on the classic topoi that he used. He placed the catalogue of vices within the framework of the kingdom of God and wrote about sexual union with a prostitute from the perspective of the Christian's union with Christ.

Paul was the first author to produce a written witness to the Chris-

tian message. His letters indicate that a Christian lifestyle was to follow upon the acceptance of the Christian gospel. In writing to the
churches, the apostle reiterated his message that there was a way of
acting that was appropriate for anyone whose being was Christian. His
use of catalogues of vices and his long discourse on human sexuality in
1 Corinthians bear witness to his conviction that proper sexual conduct is an important component of being a Christian in the real world
of human beings.

NOTES

1. So that his Gentile readers might understand the episode, the evangelist
wrote a note that interpreted the phrase "defiled hands" (7:3–4).

2. The Greek form of Mark's "evil intentions" (*dialogismoi kakoi*) is somewhat different from Matthew's "evil intentions" (*dialogismoi ponēroi*). Work-
ing with Mark's list of thirteen vices, Matthew has employed the language of
the seventh vice (*ponēriai*) to characterize intentions as "evil." Unlike the
RSV and many other modern translations, including the NIV, the NRSV has a
colon after "evil intentions" in Mark 7:21. On this reading, "evil intentions"
would be the designation of a general category that includes twelve specific
items. On my reading of the text, "evil intentions" (see further the comment
above, p. 75, on Matt. 15:19) is the first of thirteen forms of evil identified as
coming from the human heart.

3. The English word "licentiousness" connotes a lack of legal or moral
restraint, particularly with respect to sex. The Greek term that Mark uses is
aselgeia, a term that is absent from the parallel Matthean text. The term
appears ten times in the New Testament, often in lists of vices (e.g., Mark 7:22;
Rom. 13:13; 2 Cor. 12:21; Gal. 5:19; 1 Pet. 4:3).

4. Mark uses the gender-inclusive *anthrōpos,* "person," three times in his
introduction to the list of vices (Mark 7:20–21). Matthew uses the term only
once (Matt. 15:18). Neither of them uses the gender-exclusive *anēr,* "man."

5. See also the contrast between the spirit of those whom God loves in 1QS
4:3–8 and the ways of the spirit of deceit in 1QS 4:9–14.

6. This is a confession somewhat similar to those found in the Egyptian
Book of the Dead.

7. See G. Mussies, *Dio Chrysostom and the New Testament,* SCHNT 2
(Leiden: Brill, 1972), 172. To Mussies's list it is possible to add Jude 16.

8. Among New Testament authors only Matthew uses the noun "false witness" (*pseudomartyria,* 15:19; 26:59). The related noun, *pseudomartys,* a person who is a false witness, appears only in Matt. 26:60 and 1 Cor. 15:15. In
26:60, Matthew presents Jesus as someone against whom false witness is
borne. In 5:11 he describes Jesus' disciples as those against whom people will
speak falsely (*pseudomenoi*).

9. In place of Mark's singular *blasphēmia,* Matthew has the plural, *blasphēmiai,* that is, "acts of slander" rather than the vice itself.

10. See above, pp. 45–48.

11. Almost as if there were a "that is" after "evil intentions"—thus "evil intentions, that is, murder, adultery, fornication, theft, false witness, slander."

12. The word "despicable" (*stygētoi*) is a *hapax legomenon* in the New Testament. Because of its passive connotation I have not counted it among the vices of Titus 3:3 although it might be possible to do so.

13. In 1 Cor. 5:10, the first four vices are repeated; thus, the list of ten vices contains but six distinct vices. With its repetition of three vices, Eph. 5:3 contains but seven distinct vices.

14. The list of 110 would include "the dogs" (*kynas*) of Rev. 22:15. In the Bible "dogs" generally has a negative connotation. In Rev. 22:15 it is most likely a derogatory metaphor used of heretics (cf. Phil. 3:2; 2 Pet. 2:22). See Sigfred Pedersen, "*kyōn*," *EDNT* 2:332.

15. See chap. 8 below, esp. p. 131.

16. Some of the words on the New Testament vice lists are quite rare. One of the rarest is the *bdelyssomai*, found in the New Testament only in Rom. 2:22 and in the vice list of Rev. 21:8. It is translated as "polluted" by the NRSV. *EDNT* 1:20 comments: "alongside *deiloi, apistoi,* etc., apparently of those who are stained with (Gentile) abominations and are thus *polluted*." The difficulty of understanding the word is reflected in the manuscript tradition, particularly in that of the medieval Byzantine texts. A large number of manuscripts, together with the commentary by Andreas of Caesarea, have "sinners" (*kai hamartōlois*). Most of the manuscripts omit "polluted."

17. In all cultures there is some vocabulary that is characteristic of a given literary or oral form, whether that be "ETA" as characteristic of a schedule in an airport or train station, or "Pat and Mike" as characteristic of an ethnic joke.

18. A short list of virtues is found in Wis. 8:7.

19. Paul takes a similar tack in Rom. 1:18–32. See below, pp. 140–41.

20. See Anton Vögtle, *Die Tugend- und Lasterkataloge im Neuen Testament* (Münster: Aschendorffschen Buchdruckerei, 1936); Erhard Kamlah, *Die Form der katalogischen Paränese im Neuen Testament* (Tübingen: Mohr, 1964).

21. On the Egyptian *Book of the Dead*, see above, pp. 51, 67.

22. In 4 Macc. 5:22–24 piety replaces prudence as one of the cardinal virtues. Piety is cited, "so that we most highly reverence the only living God."

23. On Col. 3:5–8, see below pp. 147–49.

24. This is the only other case in the New Testament where we have an instance of an author's use of a vice list in dependence on the vice list in another extant document. On the dependence of Ephesians on Colossians, see R. F. Collins, *Letters That Paul Did Not Write: The Epistle to the Hebrews and the Pauline Pseudepigrapha,* GNS 28 (Wilmington, Del.: Glazier, 1988), 132–36, 143–44; Raymond E. Brown, *An Introduction to the New Testament,* ABRL (New York: Doubleday, 1997), 627–29.

25. A comparison of these two lists from the redactional point of view is interesting in other respects as well. Ephesians has a syndetic construction with a repeated "and" (*kai*) and "or" (*ē*) in vv. 3 and 5, respectively. Colossians has an asyndetic construction with no connectives. The catalogue in Eph. 5:3

uses abstract nouns, as does the list in Col. 3:8. The catalogue of Eph. 5:5 uses personal nouns. These various stylistic forms are to be found also in other New Testament and extrabiblical lists of vices in the Hellenistic world.

26. The church is the principal theme of the Epistle to the Ephesians. On the pseudonymity of Ephesians and Colossians, see Collins, *Letters*, 133–50, 171–88.

Despite the idea that is sometimes floated as a trial balloon that Mary Magdalene was the author of the Fourth Gospel, my conviction is that the New Testament texts were written by male authors. To leave open the question of the gender of their author, I will try to use "author" rather than a personal pronoun to refer to the "writer" of the text. "He" or "his" is often less cumbersome than "author" or "author's." As a result I shall occasionally use the personal pronoun to refer to a New Testament author.

27. Once again the construction in Ephesians is syndetic, that of Colossians asyndetic.

28. The word "all" appears also in the vice lists of Eph. 5:3 and 5:5. In the first list the adjective qualifies "impurity"; in the second list it qualifies "fornicator" (but is not translated in the NRSV). The mobility of the adjective is a sign of the all-encompassing character of the vice lists in the Hellenistic world.

29. See also Mark 7:21, where "evil intentions" is sometimes taken to be a general term illustrated by a list of twelve vices. See n. 2 above.

30. The list of vices in 1 Cor. 5:9–10 enhances the rhetorical argument of 1 Cor. 5:1–8. Paul had become aware of at least one case of sexual immorality in the community, that of a man having a sexual relationship with his father's wife (1 Cor. 5:1). He chides the community for tolerating this case of incest by failing to deal with the man who was guilty of sexual immorality. Thereupon he tells the community to have nothing to do with sexually immoral persons (5:9). The fact that these sexually immoral persons are Christian should not deter the community from shunning them. Paul underscores this point in vv. 9–10 by giving a double list of vices, each of which begins with "sexual immorality" (*porneia*).

31. The NRSV translates *pornoi* in 1 Cor. 6:9 as "fornicators," rather than as "sexually immoral," the translation of the same Greek word in 1 Cor. 5:9, 10, 11.

32. See Collins, *Letters*, 88–111.

33. The four things are found mainly in Leviticus 17–18. See the discussion in Joseph A. Fitzmyer, *The Acts of the Apostles*, AB 31 (New York: Doubleday, 1998), 556–57.

34. Terms of the classic discussion between Bruce Malina and Joseph Jensen on this subject are outlined in Malina, "Does Porneia mean Fornication?," *NovT* 14 (1972): 10–17; and Jensen, "Does *porneia* mean Fornication? A Critique of B. Malina," *NovT* 20 (1978): 161–84.

35. See above, pp. 1–10 and esp. chap. 3. What the ancients understood by adultery was a married woman's sexual intercourse with a man other than her husband.

36. See *T. Reub.* 4:6; *T. Dan* 5:5; *T. Naph.* 4:1; *Sipra Lev.* 9:8 (85c–d); 13:8, 10 (85a); *Ep. Arist.* 152; *Jub.* 16:7–9; *Sib. Or.* 7:40–45; Philo, *Special Laws* 3.12–23; Josephus, *Antiquities* 20.7.3 §145 (comp. Juvenal 6.156–60). The

Sipra takes Lev. 18:3 to mean that Egyptians and Canaanites, and by extension all Gentiles, commit the sexual misdeeds described in Leviticus 18.

37. It may be that the three terms were commonly used together to describe sexual debauchery, *porneia* pointing to its specifically sexual character, *akatharsia* pointing to its incompatibility with religious commitment and social behavior, and *aselgeia* to its out-of-order and excessive character.

38. See Frederick Hauck, "*katharos, ktl.,*" *TDNT* 3:413–31, esp. 429; Hartwig Thyen, "*katharotēs,*" *EDNT* 2:218–20.

39. See 2 Pet. 2:2, 7 (with its reference to Sodom and Gomorrah), 18; Jude 4, and Eph. 4:19, where "licentiousness" is associated with "impurity" (*akatharsia*) and greed (*pleonexia*). See Otto Bauernfeind, "*aselgeia,*" *TDNT* 1:490; Horst Goldstein, "*aselgeia,*" *EDNT* 1:169–70.

40. The identification of the speaker is given in *Herm. Sim.* 9.7.

41. Cf. 2 Tim. 3:4, which speaks of those who are "lovers of pleasure (*philēdonoi*) rather than lovers of God (*philotheoi*)." "Lovers of pleasure" is a *hapax legomenon* in the New Testament.

42. The NRSV translation of Col. 3:5 is "Put to death, therefore, whatever in you is earthly: fornication, impurity, passion, evil desire, and greed (which is idolatry)." On this list "passion" renders the Greek *pathos*. The word *epithymia*, which appears elsewhere in the NRSV as "passions," is here translated "evil desire." The ambiguity of the terms used in the New Testament and in the Hellenistic world at large to describe sexual immorality is reflected in these various attempts at translation.

43. See 1 Cor. 6:9–10; Col. 3:5–8; Titus 3:3; 1 Pet. 4:3; Rev. 9:21. Cf. 1 Cor. 5:10–11, where Christians are urged not to fall back to an earlier way of life.

44. See 1 Cor. 6:9, 10; Gal. 5:21; Eph. 5:5; Rev. 21:8; and Rev. 22:15, where those who do such things are characterized as "outsiders." Another metaphor is used by the author of Colossians, who speaks of the malefactors as being subject to the wrath of God (3:6).

45. Henry George Liddell and Robert Scott, *A Greek-English Lexicon,* 9th ed., revised and augmented by Henry Stuart Jones (Oxford: Clarendon, 1968).

46. See below, pp. 167–68.

47. In the list of vices, the cumulative effect of the entire list is more significant than the identification of any particular vice. The readers would not have needed to distinguish one vice from another. In Heb. 13:4, it may well be that the author's use of "fornicators" and "adulterers" is simply a matter of *repetitio,* that is, repetition for rhetorical effect—in which case the two vices would be essentially synonymous rather than distinguishable.

48. See above, p. 74.

49. The ten vices are linked by a syndetic construction. The first seven are joined by the compound negative, *oute,* "and not." The last three are linked by a simple negative, *ou,* "not."

50. This is the literary device of *inclusio.*

51. See Col. 3:5, the only other New Testament catalogue of vices that seems to include four sexual vices.

52. See chap. 8 below.

53. A translation is an attempt to make the meaning of a word, with all of its cultural conditioning understandable for people of another culture. The dif-

ficulties are apparent when one attempts to translate a text from one modern
language into another modern language. How, for example, does one translate
"it's raining cats and dogs" into French or German, Chinese or Russian? What
kind of centigrade temperature is evoked when a young person says, "That's
cool!"? The difficulty is compounded when the two cultures involved in a
work of translation are not contemporary but are separated by two thousand
years, as is the case with modern English translations of the New Testament.

54. In the technical jargon of the exegete, *malakoi* is a substantivized
adjective.

55. That is, other than the NRSV, whose translations are used throughout
this book. The Latin Vulgate rendered Paul's words as *"neque molles, neque
masculorum concubitores."*

56. In 1 Tim. 1:10 the RSV translates *arsenokoitai* as "sodomites."

57. A footnote explains. "The Greek word translated as *boy prostitutes*
designated catamites, i.e., boys or young men who were kept for purposes of
prostitution, a practice not uncommon in the Greco-Roman world. In Greek
mythology this was the function of Ganymede, the 'cupbearer of the gods,'
whose Latin name was Catamitus. The term translated *practicing homosexuals* refers to adult males who indulged in homosexual practices with such
boys. See similar condemnations of such practices in Rom 1,26–27; 1 Tm
1,10." In the later printings of this note, "practicing homosexuals" has been
changed to "sodomites."

58. Taking issue with David F. Wright, William L. Petersen has convinc-
ingly argued that *arsenokoitai* cannot be translated as "homosexuals." See
D. F. Wright, "Homosexual or Prostitutes? The Meaning of *arsenokoitai*
(1 Cor. 6:9; 1 Tim. 1:10)," *VC* 38 (1984): 125–53; W. L. Petersen, "Can
arsenokoitai be translated by 'Homosexuals'? (I Cor. 6.9; I Tim. 1.10)," *VC* 40
(1986): 187–91. Wright offered his rebuttal in "Translating *arsenokoitai* (1 Cor.
6:9, 1 Tim. 1:10)," *VC* 41 (1987): 396–98. Similarly, Athalya Brenner has noted
that "'homosexuality', as a category, does not obtain in biblical as well as talmudic culture" (*The Intercourse of Knowledge: On Gendering Desire and
'Sexuality' in the Hebrew Bible,* Biblical Interpretation Series [Leiden: Brill,
1997], 141); cf. Daniel Boyarin, "Are There Any Jews? in 'The History of Sexuality'?" *Journal of the History of Sexuality* 5 (1995): 333–55.

59. In an article entitled "The Condemnation of Homosexuality in
1 Corinthians 6:9" (*BibSac* 150 [1993]: 479–92), David E. Malick has argued
that in 1 Cor. 6:9 Paul condemns all forms of sexual relationships between persons of the same sex, not merely pederasty or sexual abuse.

60. See Rom. 1:18–28 (see below, chap. 8). There is no reason to believe that
either *malakoi* or *arsenokoitai* refers to lesbian activity. The etymology of the
arsenokoitai excludes acts in which females alone participate. *Arsēn,* "male,"
indicates that a man is involved.

61. In 1 Cor. 6:9–10 Paul's mention of the kingdom of God has a hortatory,
not a dogmatic, function.

62. See Matt. 11:8 [twice] and Luke 7:25. Liddell-Scott-Jones's *Greek-
English Lexicon* notes the affinity between *malakos* and the Latin *mollis,*
"soft." The word *malakos* does not rate an entry in the *Theological Dictionary
of the New Testament.* The cognate noun *malakia* (Matt. 4:23; 9:35; 10:1) is

simply identified as a synonym of *nosēma,* sickness or disease. See Albrecht Oepke, *"nosos, ktl.," EDNT* 4:1091–98.

63. Dionysius of Halicarnassus writes that a person is called *"malakos . . .* because, when a boy, he was effeminate and allowed himself to be treated as a woman" (*Roman Antiquities* 7.2.4).

64. Plutarch, "Agis and Cleomenes," 3.1; *Moralia* 796. See also 10:3, *Moralia* 799, where he writes of their "luxury, effeminacy, and greed."

65. The next two vices on the list are "thieves" and "the greedy" (*oute kleptai oute pleonektai,* 6:10). "Greed" (*pleonexia*) is a vice that Plutarch associates with *malachia,* "effeminacy" in "Agis and Cleomenes."

66. *EDNT* 2:381.

67. Dale B. Martin, *"Arsenokoitēs* and *Malakos:* Meanings and Consequences," in *Biblical Ethics & Homosexuality: Listening to Scripture,* ed. Robert L. Brawley (Louisville: Westminster John Knox, 1996), 116–38, esp. 128.

68. Ibid., 125–26.

69. See *Special Laws* 3.37: "now it is a matter of boasting not only to the active but to the passive partners (*ou tois drōsi monon, alla kai tois paschousin*). Similar language is used to describe the active and passive partners in male sexual intercourse in Philo's *Abraham* 135.

70. See Liddell-Scott-Jones, "lying with a man." Paul's neologism seems to be a Greek translation of the Hebrew *miškab zākûr.* This Hebrew terminology is found in rabbinic texts based on Lev. 18:22.

71. See, however, MM 79, citing Th. Nägeli's 1905 work which claimed that Paul's word was first found among poets of the imperial period.

72. See Knut Schäferdiek, "Acts of John," in E. Hennecke, *New Testament Apocrypha,* ed. W. Schneemelcher, vol. 2, *Writings Relating to the Apostles. Apocalypses and Related Subjects* (London: Lutterworth, 1965), 224.

73. *PG* 6:1028.

74. The *Oracles'* exhortation on justice appears to be based on the *Sentences of Pseudo-Phocylides* 9–21. This passage in Pseudo-Phocylides, probably composed in Alexandria between 30 B.C.E. and 40 C.E., does not include the exhortation to avoid homosexual activity. In the immediately preceding summary of the Decalogue, however, to "you shall not commit adultery" is appended "nor rouse homosexual passion" (*Pseudo-Phocylides* 3). Similar prohibitions come together in *Sib. Or.* 3.764, "Avoid adultery and indiscriminate intercourse with males."

75. See the translations of *arsenokoitai* in the NRSV, rev. NAB, and NKJ.

76. The "Germani" were a Persian tribe, not the residents of the territory now known as Germany.

77. The work, which probably came from Alexandria, was written in Greek sometime between 250 B.C.E. and 100 C.E.

78. Cf. Philo, *Special Laws* 2.50; 3.37; Josephus, *Against Apion* 2.38 §275.

79. See Brown, *Introduction* 529–30.

80. See chap. 7 below.

6

Advice for New Christians

AUL'S INCLUSION OF TWO LISTS of vices in the first of his letters to
the church at Corinth was not the first time that he had written
to one of the communities that he had evangelized about sexual
ethics. In the first of his extant letters, the first letter to the Thessalonians,[1] Paul had encouraged the members of that new Christian community to avoid sexual immorality (1 Thess. 4:3–8). What Paul had to
say about sexual immorality in that letter is important not only
because of the specifics of the exhortation but also because his letter
to the Thessalonians is the oldest of our extant Christian texts. The
first letter to the Thessalonians was written in the middle of the first
century C.E., approximately twenty years after Jesus' death and resurrection, some twenty years before Mark wrote the short story that has
come to be known as the Gospel according to Mark.

Paul had evangelized the community at Thessalonica a relatively
short period of time before he wrote his letter to them. The letter shows
the depths of his affection for the neophyte Christians in Thessalonica
(1 Thess. 2:17–20; 3:9–11). Unable to visit them as he had wanted to do,
Paul says that he felt like an orphan deprived of its parents (2:17). His
love for the community prompted him to send Timothy, his trusted
aide, to Thessalonica (3:1–5). Timothy returned with glowing reports of
the faith and love of the community (3:6). The Thessalonians apparently had as much love for Paul as he had for them. They yearned to see
him again, even as he wanted ever so much to see them.

There was only one thing lacking in their faith. Their hope was
insufficient. This was a result of the grief that they had experienced

because some members of the community had died, perhaps as a result of rough treatment that they had received from the people in town who did not believe in Christ (2:14; 4:13–18). Would those who had died be able to share in the joyful parousia of Jesus, when his presence as Lord would be fully experienced? The Thessalonians may even have been worried about themselves. If they, the living, were also to die before the parousia, what would be their fate? It was to answer these questions and to enable the Thessalonians to grow in hope that Paul wrote his letter.[2]

Before explaining to them that the resurrection of the dead is yet to come and that this resurrection will make it possible for all who belong to Christ to participate in the parousia, Paul fondly recalls his visit to the Thessalonians (1:2–2:16) and why it was that he had sent Timothy to them (2:17–3:5). Even after receiving Timothy's glowing report about the mutual affection between Paul and his beloved Thessalonians, Paul still wanted to visit them again—perhaps even more so! In the meantime a letter would have to make do for his presence.

His letter was to be informational and exhortative. Paul lauded the Thessalonians for following his previous instructions as well as they had.[3] They were truly commendable in this regard. Then, before dealing with the issue of the Thessalonians' grief and how they were to live while waiting for the parousia (4:13–5:11), Paul followed up his earlier oral exhortation with a written exhortation on sanctification and sibling love (4:3–12).[4] His advice is in two parts. The first treats of sanctification (4:3–8); the second is devoted to *philadelphia,* sibling love (4:9–12). In some ways this two-part parenetic unit should be seen as an exhortation to the newly converted Thessalonians to live as God's holy people (4:3–8), followed by an exhortation to live as a Christian community among God's people (4:9–12). Thereafter, Paul treats of what it means for them to believe and live in Christ as he deals with the expectation of the parousia (4:13–18) and how the Thessalonians were to live even as they waited (5:1–11).

The exhortation to live as God's holy people has sanctification as its theme (4:3–8). The passage begins and ends with a reference to God, a reference to holiness,[5] and a reference to the Thessalonians (the personal pronoun, "you"). Beginning and ending a passage in the same way was a well-known literary device used by Paul and other ancient authors to frame a passage as a single literary unit.[6] Sanctification or holiness is Paul's agenda for the Thessalonians as he writes to them in 1 Thess. 4:3–8.

They have learned from Paul how they ought to live their lives so as to please God. Paul's intention is to encourage them to continue to do so. His perspective is Jewish. Paul contrasts their behavior with that of the Gentiles, who do not know God (4:5).[7] His opening pastoral remarks (4:1–2) are firmly rooted within his Jewish tradition. Using the technical language of the rabbis, he speaks to them of what they have learned.[8] He speaks to them of how they ought to live, using the verb *peripatein,* which literally means "to walk," echoing the Jewish tradition of walking in the way of the Lord.[9] In his encouragement he reminds the Thessalonians that they have lived so as to please God, a reminder of their single-minded devotion to the God to whom they had turned (1:9). For these neophyte Christians there was to be no separation of the ethical and the cultic, behavior and worship, as there was in the pagan world, in which religious practice did not necessarily require the adoption of a particular moral code.[10] Having turned from idolatry to the one living and true God, the Thessalonian Christians were to serve God by the way that they lived. This is what Paul continues to explain to them in 4:3–8.

"This," he writes to them, "is the will of God: your sanctification." The notion of God's will is one that was common in the Judaism of the time. Paul tells the newly converted Gentile Christians of Thessalonica that God's will for them is that they live as people who belong to the God to whom they have turned. This is their calling; they have been called not to impurity (*akatharsia*) but in holiness (*hagiasmǭ,* 4:7). In responding to this call, Christians have not been left to their own devices. God gives his sanctifying Spirit to them (4:8).[11] This is the God-given power to live in accordance with their calling. That the Thessalonians live as God's holy people is not without sanction. Paul reminds them that the Lord "is an avenger in all these things, just as we have already told you beforehand and solemnly warned you" (4:6). When Paul writes about the "Lord" he is implicitly reminding the Thessalonians of the authority that the Lord has over them.[12]

When Paul writes to the Thessalonians about their call to holiness, he makes it clear that living in holiness is a "contrast experience." They are to live "in holiness and honor, not with lustful passion, like the Gentiles who do not know God" (4:4–5). God did not call them "to impurity but in holiness" (4:7). Whoever among the Thessalonians rejects Paul's exhortation rejects "not human authority, but God, who also gives his Holy Spirit" (4:8). After his opening statement that God's will for the Thessalonians is their holiness, Paul contrasts holiness with the lust of the Gentiles, with impurity, and with a way of life that is normed by mere human authority. The Thessalonians' way of life was to be different from that.

What does it mean for the Thessalonians to live as God's holy people? Paul's opening exhortation is that they "abstain from fornication" (*porneia*). If they are to live as God's holy people, they must avoid sexual misconduct. To explain, Paul writes, "that each one of you know how to control your own body in holiness and honor, not with lustful passion, like the Gentiles who do not know God" (4:4–5). In a footnote the editors of the NRSV explain that the Greek phrase *to heautou skeuos ktasthai* could be rendered "how to take a wife for himself." In this case Paul's explanation would read in translation, "that each one of you know how to take a wife for himself in holiness and honor, not with lustful passion, like the Gentiles who do not know God."

The New King James Version of the Bible, echoing the King James Version,[13] translates the Greek phrase as "possess his own vessel." This very literal translation illustrates the problem of trying to understand what it was that Paul was encouraging the Thessalonians to do in order to avoid sexual misconduct. The word *skeuos* means "vessel"; the verb *ktasthai* means "to acquire"; and the reflexive pronoun *heautou* means "one's own." It is obvious that Paul's language is metaphorical. Buying a plate is hardly a remedy for concupiscence!

In 1 Thess. 4:4 "vessel" is a metaphor. To what does it refer? The RSV, the revised edition of the NAB, and the Contemporary English Version understand the metaphor to be a reference to one's wife. The NRSV, the NIV, and the Revised English Bible take the metaphor to be a reference to one's body. Following a similar line of thought, but with a narrower focus, some interpreters take "vessel" to be a metaphor for the male sexual organ. This interpretation is generally not reflected in the published editions of the Bible. It does, however, appear in the NAB and is accordingly read in Roman Catholic churches on a Friday in late summer[14] when the congregation is exhorted to "abstain from immorality, each of you guarding his member in sanctity and honor."

The problem of understanding Paul's exhortation is further compounded when one pays careful attention to the verb and the reflexive pronoun. The verb *ktasthai* means "to get, acquire, or procure." How does a man acquire his sexual organ or come to possess his own body? The male child, like the female, is born with a body and its sexual organs. Accordingly, those who take "vessel" to be a metaphorical reference for the body or the penis understand the verb to mean "gain control over." This makes sense, but it would be the only instance in extant Greek literature when the verb *ktaomai* would mean "gain control of."

The three different translations found in the modern English-language versions of 1 Thess. 4:4 reflect an ongoing exegetical discussion that cannot easily be resolved.[15] The Jewish context of Paul's exhortation[16] and the fact that rabbinic literature uses the Hebrew term for vessel as a metaphor for a woman in specifically sexual contexts (see *b. B. Mes.* 84b; *b. Meg.* 12b; *b. Sanh.* 22b) suggest that "woman" is the intended referent of Paul's metaphor. Some support for this interpretation might be found in 1 Pet. 3:7, "Husbands, in the same way, show consideration for your wives in your life together, paying honor to the woman as the weaker sex." The first epistle of Peter lies within the broad stream of late-first-century Pauline thought. Writing about marriage in 3:7, its pseudonymous author uses two terms that Paul uses in 1 Thess. 4:4, "vessel" (*skeuos*) and "honor" (*timē*).

Paul exhorts the Thessalonians to keep their passions under control. They are to live as God's holy people. They are not to live as do the Gentiles, "with lustful passion." Rather, to avoid fornication, the men among the Thessalonians are urged to take a wife. James Rhodes has suggested that the ingressive sense of Paul's verb is maintained when one takes Paul's words to mean "consummate a union in holiness and honor."[17] This understanding of Paul's words gets to the heart of his message to the Thessalonians.

Paul writes about the Gentiles, who do not know God[18] as treating their women, including their wives, with "lustful passion" (*en pathei epithymias*). Paul's observation is not based on any sociological analysis of the role of passion in the sexual lives of Gentiles. He uses the common bias of Jewish opinion to set the sexual mores of his Thessalonian community over and against the sexual behavior of Gentiles.[19] His language reflects that of the vice lists, where "lust" (see Titus 3:3; 1 Pet. 4:3; cf. Col. 3:5) and "passion" are part of the stock description of those who do not acknowledge the one true God. According to Paul, if the Thessalonians are to live as God's holy people, they must avoid sexual misconduct. Taking a wife and living with her in a truly conjugal relationship orients one's sexuality in the proper direction.

Paul continues his exhortation on holiness with another instruction, "that no one wrong or exploit a brother or sister in this matter" (4:6). As was the case with 1 Thess. 4:4, a footnote in the NRSV indicates that the translation of Paul's words is not as simple as it might seem to be at first sight. In a formula of direct address, Paul commonly appeals to those to whom he is writing as his "brothers and sisters" (*adelphoi*). It is one thing for Paul to address a group gathered to listen to the reading of one of his letters as my "brothers and sisters." It is another thing for him to use a singular masculine form of the noun *adelphos* as the object of the verbs "to wrong" and "to exploit." In this case should *adelphos* be translated "brother and sister" or simply "brother"?

The paraphrase found in the Contemporary English Version avoids the problem by rendering Paul's words as "you must not cheat any of the Lord's followers in matters of sex." Other translations are not so direct. The King James Version rendered Paul's words as "that no man go beyond and defraud his brother in any matter," while the NIV has "that in this matter no one should wrong his brother or take advantage of him." The Revised English Bible follows along the same lines when it translates Paul's words as, "no one must do his fellow-Christian wrong in this matter, or infringe his rights." "In matters of sex" is a more explicit referential phrase than is "in this matter." Similarly, "cheat" is clearer than "do wrong."

"Infringe his rights" (REB) and "defraud" (KJ) imply that Paul is talking about justice when he writes as he does in 1 Thess. 4:6. Consequently, some exegetes take Paul's words as an exhortation to avoid taking advantage of a fellow Christian by some kind of economic injustice directed against him. The basis for their reasoning is that Jews tended to look upon Gentiles not only as being sexually immoral but also as being greedy and avaricious. That opinion is reflected in the vice lists. In the New Testament "fornication" is the vice most frequently mentioned. Then comes "idolatry." "Greed" (*pleonexia*) is the third of the three vices that appear most often in the New Testament catalogues (Mark 7:22; Rom. 1:29; 1 Cor. 5:10, 11; 6:10; Eph. 5:3, 5; Col. 3:5). The general point of view is summarized in Eph 5:5, "Be sure of this, that no fornicator or impure person, or one who is greedy (that is, an idolater), has any inheritance in the kingdom of Christ and of God."

In determining what exactly Paul had in mind when he wrote the exhortation of 1 Thess. 4:6, the reader must understand what Paul meant by "to wrong" (*hyperbainein*), "to exploit" (*pleonektein*) and "in this matter" (*en tǭ pragmati*). Once again Paul's Greek is not particularly helpful to the modern reader. "To wrong" (*hyperbainein*), a term that appears in the New Testament only in 1 Thess. 4:6, literally means "to step over." Metaphorically, it can mean "to overstep," "to transgress." Among New Testament authors, it is only Paul who uses the verb "to exploit" (*pleonektein*).[20] It means "to claim more than one's due." Used of persons, it means "to take advantage of" (see 2 Cor. 12:17, 18).

"In this matter" (*en tō pragmati*) uses a noun that can mean, when it is used in the plural, "business matters." Paul, however, uses the singular. What is "this matter" to which he refers? The easiest reading of the text is to take "this matter" as a reference to sex or, more specifically, to sexual immorality (*porneia*, 4:3). How does one avoid sexual immorality by not wronging and taking advantage of one's "brother," a man who is a fellow Christian? The answer would seem to be by not committing adultery with his wife. According to the traditional Jewish perspective, adultery was committed when a man had sexual intercourse with the wife of another man.[21] It was an offense against the cuckolded husband.

In sum, Paul's exhortation to the Christians of Thessalonica is that they live as God's holy people. In order to do so, it was imperative for them to avoid sexual immorality. Writing from his Jewish perspective and influenced by the common Jewish understanding of the sexual mores of the Gentiles, Paul gave the Christian men at Thessalonica two practical directives as to how they were to avoid sexual immorality. If they are to be holy, as God has directed them to be, they must marry and consummate their union with their wives (4:4). If they are to respond to the power of God's Holy Spirit in their lives, they must take care to avoid violating the marriage of their fellow Christians (4:6).[22] By living a full marital relationship and not infringing on the marital relationships of other Christians, the men of Thessalonica could avoid sexual immorality and live as members of God's holy people.

NOTES

1. A very small number of scholars hold that 2 Thessalonians was written before 1 Thessalonians. At the present time a clear majority of New Testament scholars hold that 2 Thessalonians was not written by Paul. See R. F. Collins, *Letters That Paul Did Not Write: The Epistle to the Hebrews and the Pauline Pseudepigrapha*, GNS 28 (Wilmington, Del.: Glazier, 1988), 209–41. In the years following my publication of *Letters*, the tide of scholarly opinion turned even more strongly in favor of the pseudepigraphic character of 2 Thessalonians.

2. See R. F. Collins, *The Birth of the New Testament: The Origin and Development of the First Christian Generation* (New York: Crossroad, 1993), esp. 150–53.

3. In recent decades a number of scholars have argued that the canonical first letter to the Thessalonians is a composite document. Jerome Murphy-O'Connor, for example, has argued that 1 Thess. 2:13–4:2, "Letter A," was written from Athens in the spring of 50 C.E. some ten weeks or so after Paul's departure from Thessalonica. "Letter B," 1 Thess. 1:1–2:12; 4:3–5:28, would have been written from Corinth, perhaps in the summer of that same year. See J. Murphy-O'Connor, *Paul: A Critical Life* (Oxford: Clarendon, 1996), 104–14. In this case, the exhortation of 4:1–2 concludes the earlier missive. In various writings I have argued that extant 1 Thessalonians is a single composition. On my reading of the text, 4:1–2 serves as an introduction to the hortatory material in 4:3–12.

4. On the function of the hortatory material in the letter, see R. F. Collins, "The Function of Paraenesis in 1 Thess 4,1–12; 5,12–22," *ETL* 74 (1998): 398–414.

5. Many synonyms in modern English are due to the fact that one word, liberty, for example, comes from a Latin root, and its synonym, freedom, comes from a Germanic root. The phenomenon is experienced in translations of the New Testament, including 1 Thess. 4:3–8, where a variety of words with the Greek root, *hagi-*, are sometimes translated with a Latin root, "sanctification," "sanctify," "saints," and at other times are translated with a Germanic root "holiness," "make holy," "holy ones." On "holiness" in 1 Thessalonians, see T. J. Deidun, *New Covenant Morality in Paul*, Analecta Biblica (Rome: Biblical Institute Press, 1981), 18–28, 86–87.

6. Technically the device is known as *inclusio*, or ring construction. A well-known New Testament example of the use of this device is Matthew's collection of beatitudes. The collection ends as it begins, with the refrain "for theirs is the kingdom of heaven" (Matt. 5:3–10).

7. With regard to the Jewish prejudice about the sexual behavior of Gentiles, see Rom. 1:21–32 and above, p. 83. See also Michael Satlow, *Tasting the Dish: Rabbinic Rhetorics of Sexuality*, Brown Judaic Studies 303 (Atlanta: Scholars Press, 1995), 146–52.

8. The Greek verb that the NRSV translates as "you have learned" is *parelabete*. This verb reflects the Hebrew *qibbēl*. The verbs *māsar* and *qibbēl* were used in Jewish tradition to describe the process in which teaching was passed on by rote from one generation to the next. Teaching received (*māsar*) by the rabbi was delivered (*qibbēl*) to the disciples (cf. 1 Cor. 15:3).

9. Halakah, derived from the Hebrew verb *hālak*, "to walk," is the term used to describe the body of Jewish law supplementing the Torah and instructing the people how they ought to live. The Haggadah was the narrative lore of the Jews, the halakah their code of conduct.

10. One element of the religious genius of Israel was its joining together religious dedication to God and moral obligation, as is seen in the Ten Commandments (Exod. 20:2–17; Deut. 5:6–21) and Jesus' twofold law of love (Matt. 22:37–40; Mark 12:29–31; Luke 10:27–28). This was not the case in the pagan world, where social obligation was dissociated from cultic observance.

11. Note the use of the present participle, "who gives" (*didonta*). The use of the present tense implies that the gift is ongoing. The Spirit continues to be poured out on them.

12. Given the fact that Paul's reference to the vengeance of the Lord echoes Ps. 94:1, but that "Lord" is normally used of the parousiac Lord in Paul's writings, it is difficult to determine whether the referent of "Lord" in 4:6 is God or Jesus. The issue is moot, but on balance I believe that it is preferable to take "Lord" in 4:6 as a reference to Jesus, who is to appear as Lord at the parousia. See Collins, *Birth of the New Testament*, 68, 247 n. 204.

13. The King James Version reads "possess his vessel," a translation that does not capitalize on the reflexive nature of *heautou*, "his own."

14. 1 Thess. 4:1–8 is the first lection in the eucharistic liturgy for Friday of the twenty-first week of the liturgical year.

15. See, for example, my own contributions to the discussion in *Studies on the First Letter to the Thessalonians*, BETL 66 (Louvain: University Press/ Peeters, 1984), 299–335; and O. Larry Yarbrough, *Not Like the Gentiles: Marriage Rules in the Letters of Paul*, SBLDS 80 (Atlanta: Scholars Press, 1985), with critical remarks by Michael McGehee, "A Rejoinder to Two Recent Studies Dealing with 1 Thess 4:4," *CBQ* 51 (1989): 82–89. McGehee argues that "keep your own body in holiness and honor" is the preferred translation.

16. The Jewish background from which Paul is writing to the Thessalonians is clear not only in his introductory remarks (4:1–2) but also in his use of holiness language and the contrast with the Gentiles' way of life, which he establishes in 4:5. The holistic anthropology of Judaism would not abide the notion of one's mind gaining control over one's body as if the body were simply the instrument of the *logos*.

17. See James N. Rhodes, "Translating 1 Thessalonians 4:4: Making Sense of a Euphemism," *BT* 50 (1999): 246–48.

18. Paul's universe consists of Jews and Gentiles, respectively, the chosen people and those who do not know God. In this simple division of the universe ethnic and religious categories overlap. 1 Thessalonians is written to Gentile Christians. They have, however, been co-opted into the chosen people (1:4) and have turned to God (1:9). Although ethnically Gentiles, the Christians of Thessalonica stand over and against those who are (religiously) Gentiles and do not know God.

19. Commenting on the Jewish ethos, in contrast to those who do not honor the law of Moses, Josephus had a variety of things to say about the way that Jews conducted themselves in marriage. Among other things he wrote: "It [the Law] commands us also, when we marry, not to have regard to portion, nor to take a woman by violence, nor to persuade her deceitfully and knavishly" (*Against Apion* 2.25 §220).

20. Apart from 1 Thess. 4:6 Paul uses this verb only in his second letter to the Corinthians (2 Cor. 2:11; 7:2; 12:17, 18). The verb *pleonektein* is related to *pleonexia*, the noun "greed" on the vice lists.

21. See above, pp. 2–4, 28.

22. The parenesis of 1 Thess. 4:1–12 is directed to the Christian community. In telling Christian males at Thessalonica not to violate another Christian's marriage, Paul was not condoning other acts of adultery. His focus was on the community at Thessalonica, a people called to holiness.

7

The Church at Corinth

THE PRAGMATIC AND DOWN-TO-EARTH ATTITUDE toward sex that Paul reflected when he wrote to the Thessalonians about 50 C.E. was again manifest when he wrote his first letter to the Christians of Corinth some three or four years later. This letter, treating a variety of issues and questions confronting the community, is the work of a pragmatic pastor. It was addressed "to those who are sanctified in Christ Jesus, called to be saints" (1 Cor. 1:2). The apostle made it clear that he wanted the Corinthians to be aware of their call to holiness.

Two situations that involve human sexuality had been brought to the apostle's attention. The first was a serious case of incest (5:1). A man was involved in a sexual relationship with his father's wife. Some people from Corinth, most probably Chloe's people (1:11), had told Paul about this situation. The other concern was a slogan that was making its rounds in Corinth. People were saying, "it is well for a man not to touch a woman" (7:1). The matter of sexual abstinence was something about which the Corinthians wrote to Paul. The letter had most likely been brought to Paul by Stephanas and his companions, Fortunatus and Achaicus, the trio commended by Paul in 16:15–18. Responding to both of the issues about which he had been informed, Paul uses an ethos argument, citing himself as an example (6:12; 7:7).

INCEST

Paul had heard that there was an egregious case of sexual immorality in the Corinthian community. So outrageous was it that it would not have been tolerated in a community of Gentile pagans. It was a case of incest. A man was sleeping with his father's wife. This was something that would have been shocking in a pagan community, presumed by Jews and Jewish Christians alike to be characterized by its loose sexual morals (see Rom. 1:24–27; 1 Thess. 4:5). Paul wrote, "It is actually reported (*holōs akouetai*) that there is sexual immorality (*porneia*) among you, and of a kind that is not found even among pagans;[1] for a man is living with his father's wife" (5:1).

Among Jews, incest was something to be abhorred (*niddah*) (see Lev. 20:21). The Jewish historian Flavius Josephus considered incest to be the greatest of evils (*Antiquities* 3.12.1 §274). The *Psalms of Solomon* attributed Pompey's capture and destruction of Jerusalem to the sins of the city, incest being specifically identified as one of them (8:9). The Jewish legal tradition underscored its abhorrence of incest by decreeing various punishments for incest: death (Lev. 20:11, 12; cf. Deut. 27:20; *Jub.* 33:10, 13–14, 17), burning (Lev. 20:14), or alienation (Lev. 18:29; 20:17). Sterility, too, was viewed as God's punishment for incest (Lev. 20:20, 21). To be sure, such punishments were not always meted out in systematic fashion. Later on rabbinic authorities would use the penalties for incest stipulated in the Torah as categories for the discussion of various forms of adultery.

The Mishnah indicates that death by stoning was the punishment to be meted out to both the man and the woman involved in this kind of incestuous liaison.[2] The Mishnah stipulates that this is to be the penalty when a man has intercourse with his mother. It is also the penalty when a man has intercourse with a woman who is his father's wife but not his own mother. In stipulating that the penalty is to be inflicted on a man who has intercourse with his own mother as well as on a man who has intercourse with a wife of his father other than his own mother, the Mishnah follows Leviticus 18, which bans both sexual intercourse with one's own mother (18:7) and sexual intercourse with another wife of one's own father (18:8). If a man has sexual intercourse with his mother, he is guilty of violating two *mitzvot,* that is, both Lev. 18:7 and Lev. 18:8. A man who has sexual intercourse with a woman who is his father's wife but not his own mother also commits a double offense. He violates both Lev. 18:8 and Lev. 18:20, which bans adultery.[3]

For Jews, incest was something that Gentiles did.[4] In its prohibition of incest, Leviticus 18 cites sexual intercourse with one's mother and with one's father's wife as the first two of the sexual offenses to be avoided. Since Gentiles are presumed to have been involved in incestuous relationships (Lev. 18:3), one might infer that Jews considered these two forms of incest to be among the most egregious of the sexual offenses commonly assumed to be rampant among Gentiles. "There is no greater sin," says the book of *Jubilees*, "than the fornication which they commit upon the earth because Israel is a holy nation to the Lord his God, and a nation of inheritance, and a nation of priests, and a royal nation, and a special possession. And there is nothing which appears which is as defiled as this among the holy people" (*Jub.* 33:20). Avoiding incest was one of the distinguishing characteristics of Israel as God's own people. Having asked the rhetorical question, "What form of unholiness could be more impious than this?" Philo developed old folkloric traditions to show that incest had led to civil strife and the destruction of great cities in Greece and Persia (see *Special Laws* 3.14–17). Philo considered that it was the defilement of the father's marriage couch that caused this kind of destruction.

Jewish tradition had a difficult time dealing with Gen. 35:22, "Reuben went and lay with Bilhah his father's concubine; and Israel heard of it." The book of *Jubilees* dramatizes the incident (33:1–17), noting Bilhah's regret and Jacob's anger. Jacob did not have a sexual relationship with Bilhah after that single nocturnal encounter because she had become polluted for him. According to *Jubilees*, despite the evilness of his action, neither Reuben nor Bilhah was put to death, "For the ordinance and judgment and law had not been revealed till then as completed for everyone" (*Jub.* 33:16). In the absence of the law, the gravity of Reuben's offense was somehow mitigated. Another Jewish work, the *Testament of Reuben* is essentially a confession by Reuben, who admits having indulged in the ignorant ways of youth and sexual promiscuity and defiling the marriage bed of his father, Jacob (*T. Reub.* 1:6). Although the *Testament of Reuben* portrays women as weak and scheming to entice men, the book exonerates Bilhah, who had become drunk and had fallen asleep. She was unaware of the act of incest that had taken place (see 3:13–14; 4:1–4). The rabbis had similar difficulties with the biblical story of Reuben's incestuous liaison with his father's concubine. The Babylonian Talmud cites the names of Samuel b. Nahman, Yohanan b. Zakkai, and Simeon b. Eleazar as Palestinian authorities who dismissed the possibility of Reuben's having had sexual intercourse with Bilhah (*b. Shab.* 55b).

From the beginning of his letter to them, Paul reminded the newly converted Corinthian Christians that they were the church of God, sanctified in Christ Jesus, people called saints (1 Cor. 1:2). They were God's holy people. The outrageous kind of incest in which one of their number had become involved was something that should have shocked the community and moved it to tears. They should have expelled the evildoer. They did not do so; instead they boasted. Their own arrogance was at the root of their intolerable acceptance of this evil. Paul reminded the Corinthians that he would be with them in spirit when they extirpated the sinner from their midst so that they could continue to exist as a holy and spiritual community.[5] As a peroration to his passionate exhortation Paul cited the biblical exclusionary formula, "Drive out the wicked person from among you" (1 Cor 5:13; cf. Deut. 17:7).

Underscoring his point, Paul used the classical topos of a catalogue of vices,[6] to say that the community should not allow itself to associate with sexually immoral persons (*pornois*). Paul did not intend that the Corinthians have no dealings whatsoever with the sexually immoral persons of this world—in that case the community would have to leave the world entirely! Rather he was concerned that the Corinthian Christians who strove to follow their calling as God's holy people should avoid those sexually immoral persons who claimed to be Christian.

Reference to those who are sexually immoral occurs three times in Paul's passionate plea (5:9–13). Two of these references occur at the head of a list of vices, one when Paul is describing evil persons in the world (5:10), one when he is citing the kinds of evil persons who should be shunned by the community (5:11). Paul's *porneia* language is general. In the context of 1 Cor. 5:9–13 (cf. 5:1), it is clear that Paul considers a man's incestuous relationship with a wife of his father to be a particularly egregious form of sexual misconduct.

SEX AND EMBODIED EXISTENCE

After an interlude that functions as a kind of rhetorical digression in his argument, Paul returns to the topic of human sexuality in 6:12–20. The rhetorical digression (6:1–11) dealt with the use of the secular judicial system by Christians. It was likely that some of the more powerful Christians were using the courts to take from economically deprived Christians what little they had. This was something that Paul considered to be quite inappropriate. He argued that Christians ought to resolve their disputes among themselves rather than appealing to the "unrighteous" to make judgments about them. Indeed, said Paul, there should not have been any reason for a lawsuit in the first instance.

To illustrate what he was talking about when he took the Christians of Corinth to task for appeal to unrighteous judges, Paul employed another list of vices. The catalogue of unrighteous persons includes fornicators, idolaters, adulterers, male prostitutes, sodomites, thieves, the greedy, drunkards, revilers, and robbers. These are the kinds of people who will not inherit the kingdom of God (6:9–11). Four of the first five vices on this list of ten vices are forms of sexual immorality: fornication, adultery, male prostitution, and sodomy.[7] Within the context of his argument, it is clear that Paul is using the topos to describe the conduct of those nonbelievers who are still caught up in idolatry. With his Jewish background he was convinced that idolatry leads to various forms of sexual immorality. To make his point, Paul cites fornication, adultery, male prostitution, and sodomy as forms of behavior that one might readily attribute to nonbelievers whose lack of belief is evident in their participation in idolatrous worship. That Paul puts sexual vices at the head of his list reflects his Jewish bias about the sexual mores of pagans. The arrangement is, however, also consistent with Paul's rhetorical purpose and the literary context within which he uses the catalogue of vices. The general topic of the second rhetorical demonstration of 1 Corinthians (5:1–7:40) is human sexuality.

In 5:1–13, Paul takes the community to task for not expelling its deviant member. In 6:1–11, Paul continues to charge the community with not exercising its corporate responsibility. An important part of Paul's message in 5:1–6:11 is that the Christian community itself should be responsible and self-policing with regard to the various forms of evil in its midst. It is not only the individual who has a responsibility in this regard; the community also has its responsibilities.

Having made his point in 6:1–11, Paul returns to the topic at hand, sexual immorality (*porneia*). He begins with prostitution (6:12–20). The casual reader of 1 Corinthians might readily assume that among the troublesome conditions at Corinth was that some men in the community were employing the services of prostitutes. This is an assumption that is not warranted. Nowhere in the passage does Paul suggest that Christian men were actually visiting prostitutes. Nonetheless, he does talk about prostitution. The reason that he does so is that the moralists of his day typically used prostitution as the opening illustration in their discourse on human sexuality. Paul's first letter to the Corinthians is one that employs the rhetorical conventions of his time. When dealing with sexuality it was imperative that he treat the issue of prostitution. His Hellenistic readers would have expected nothing less, even if the use of prostitutes was not really an issue for them.

Paul begins his treatment of the classic topos with a pertinent contextualization. One of the issues that disrupted the unity of the Corinthian church was that some members of the community were acting like kings (4:8). They considered themselves to be above the law. Like several kings of old, they considered that they had unlimited license to do whatever they wanted. "Anything goes" was their motto. "All things are lawful" was, in effect, a slogan used by the philosophic moralists of Paul's time to sum up the libertarian attitude of various royal figures who did whatever they wanted to do.[8] This libertarian attitude was apparently affecting some segments of the Christian community in Corinth. Paul offers a careful critique of the slogan in two passages of his letter (6:12; 10:23–24), stating that, even though some people might think that everything whatsoever is lawful, not everything is beneficial. Some forms of conduct simply do not build up the community. Christians are called to look to the good of their neighbor, not seek their own advantage.

In a kind of *ad hominem* argument, Paul considers the freedom slogan in 6:12 as he begins his treatment of the use of prostitutes in 6:12–20. As he develops his thought, Paul uses a classic rhetorical argument, the ethos appeal. This was the tactic of offering one's own behavior as an example to be followed. Exploiting another rhetorical technique, Paul divides the question. He first considers the legitimacy of all things. While everything may be licit, in the sense that it does not contravene the law, not everything is beneficial (*ou panta sympherei*). This is an important consideration insofar as it sets before the community the idea of the common good as a norm of conduct.[9] Then Paul turns to himself. He will not allow self-proclaimed freedom to be a source of slavery. "'All things are lawful for me,'" he says, "but I will not be dominated by anything." Although everything might be permissible to him, Paul was not going to allow himself to be enslaved to anyone or anything.

Paul has a paradoxical notion of human freedom. "Whoever was called in the Lord as a slave is a freed person belonging to the Lord, just as whoever was free when called is a slave of Christ," he writes in 7:22. Paul's discussion of prostitutes is encompassed within an exposition of his paradoxical idea of human freedom. At the beginning of his exposition, he affirms that even though he has unlimited freedom, he does not intend to fall under anyone else's power (*ouk exousiasthēsomai*). At the end of his exposition, he states by way of explanation[10] that the Corinthians have been bought and paid for (6:20; cf. 7:23).[11] The allusion is to the redemption and manumission of a slave. Christians are not to become slaves of human beings; they have been redeemed by Christ and belong to him.

Having dispatched the idea that Christians might consider themselves to be completely unfettered with regard to morality with a multipronged and somewhat subtle argument, Paul turns his attention to the dualism of Hellenistic anthropology. Unlike the Semites, whose understanding of the human being was holistic, Hellenists tended to separate body from soul or spirit. With this kind of dualism, one might have argued that sexual intercourse has nothing to do with one's spirit. It is merely a bodily function and the body itself is worthless, destined to be destroyed by God. Rather than deal with the issue head-on, Paul argues with a kind of covert allusion. He cites a slogan that mentions another bodily function, namely, eating. One might argue that "food is meant for the stomach and the stomach for food" and that eventually both are to be destroyed by God (6:13).[12] This is not Paul's way of looking at things.

The apostle confronts Hellenistic dualism with his Semitic and biblical understanding of the human person (6:13-19). Embodied existence and social relationships are the key elements in this holistic anthropology. Paul develops each of these elements from a Christian point of view as he gives his own particular spin to the classic topos on prostitution. To be sure, Christians should avoid sexual immorality (*porneia*). In 5:1–13 Paul dealt with incest as a form of sexual immorality. He told the Christians of Corinth that they should ban incest from the community. Following the example of the classic topos on sexuality, Paul treats the use of prostitutes as a form of sexual immorality in 6:12-20. He tells the Corinthians that they are to flee from sexual immorality altogether (*pheugete tēn porneian*, 6:18). In the case at hand, sexual intercourse with prostitutes is the form of sexual misconduct that Paul is urging the Christians of Corinth to shun. In Paul's rhetoric it serves as an example from which the reader is expected to draw pertinent inferences.

Paul's exhortation "Shun fornication!" is simple and classic (cf. *T. Reub.* 5:5). What is particular to his exposition is the sketch of Christian anthropology in which he situates the exhortation. Why is it that

Christians should shun fornication? Because they have an embodied existence.[13] What does it mean for a human being, specifically a Christian human being, to have a body (sōma)? This is what Paul explains in 6:13–20. His understanding of embodied human existence is the ground for his exhorting the Christians of Corinth to shun sexual misconduct. Educated circles in Greco-Roman society, among whom the philosophic moralists of Stoic and Cynic persuasion were preeminent, generally held a negative view of the human body. This was not the case among Semites, and still less was it the case among Jews for whom embodied existence was the only form of human existence. God had created the human being, male and female, in the form of embodied existence (see Gen. 2:18–25). In the Semitic anthropology of which Paul is the beneficiary, body/sōma/bāśār is a reality created by God. Rudolf Bultmann spoke of the body as being objectivized, at least in the sense that the body has been created. As an "object" it has the possibility of being acted upon.

One element of Paul's Christian anthropology of the human person as embodied existence is his claim that embodied Christians are members of the body of Christ and that their bodies are for the Lord insofar as they will be raised together with the Lord Jesus. Later in his letter Paul develops each of these themes in turn. In 12:12–27 he uses the classic metaphor of the body as an illustration to show that Christians are members of the body of Christ and that, within the body of Christ, they have mutually related functions. Christians are interdependent insofar as they are members of the body of Christ. In 15:12–56 Paul explains that all who belong to Christ will be made alive with Christ at the parousia (15:20–23).

Bodily existence also implies the possibility of what people today might call interpersonal relationships. Bodily existence is, however, more than the possibility of interpersonal relationships. Bodily existence is necessarily interpersonal. It is relationship. Bodily existence means that human beings necessarily exist in solidarity with one another. There is no escaping this solidarity. It begins with the reality that each human being is in at least a biological relationship with his or her mother and father. These parents are, in turn, in a physical relationship with other human beings. Even without entering into the sophistication of modern genetics or reflecting on how each one of us is dependent on the physical work of other human beings for our food and clothing, it is clear that the reality of bodily human existence is that of a chain relationship among embodied human beings. Ancient Semites had an awareness of this when they described the human being as *bāśār*, body or flesh, into which God had breathed spirit (Gen. 2:7).

In Paul's Christian anthropology, the ultimate finality of embodied existence is its participation in the resurrection of Jesus. "The body is for the Lord, and the Lord for the body," he writes (6:13). There is solidarity between the Christian with his embodied existence and the glorified Lord with his bodily resurrection. For the benefit of Hellenists who may not fully appreciate Paul's holistic anthropology, the apostle adds, "God raised the Lord and will also raise us by his power (6:14; cf. 1 Thess. 4:14). Since the body is destined for the Lord, it is not meant for *porneia*, "fornication."

"Lord" (*Kyrios*) is Paul's favorite christological title. It draws the reader's attention to the resurrection and awaited parousia of Jesus. Paul tends to use "Christ" (*Christos*) when he wants to draw attention to the death and resurrection of Jesus. The use of the title "Christ" calls attention to the radical humanity of Jesus. In 6:15 Paul uses "Christ" to remind the Christians of Corinth that in their embodied Christian existence they are members of Christ.[14] As members of Christ, it is inconceivable that Christians should be members of a prostitute. "No way!" says Paul with his forceful *mē genoito* ("never" in the NRSV).

This calls for some reflection. Once again Paul's tradition proves useful to him. The creation stories talked about human sexuality. The Priestly narrative in Genesis 1 indicated that human sexuality was integral to God's creation of humankind: "Male and female he created them" (Gen. 1:27). The Yahwist's narrative in Genesis 2 provided an etiology for human sexuality. Human sexuality is an integral part of the human person. The human being is a relational being. Neither man nor woman was created by God to live in isolation. Their sexuality enables relationships since men and women are meant for each other. After narrating the spontaneous exclamation of praise with which the primal man greeted his partner (Gen. 2:23), the Yahwist concluded his mythic reflections on human sexuality with a solemn inference, "Therefore a man leaves his father and his mother and clings to his wife, and they become one flesh" (2:24).

The Greek Bible translates the Hebrew *bāśār* as *sarx*, normally rendered in English as "flesh." In other places in the Bible, the Septuagint renders the Hebrew *bāśār* as *sōma*, usually translated into English as "body." The same Hebrew word admits of two different translations in Greek and in English. These different words translate a single biblical notion into a different culture. Those who read Paul's argument in

1 Cor. 6:13–19 should be attentive to the fact that in this passage "body" (*sōma*) and "flesh" (*sarx*) are essentially interchangeable. If Paul uses "flesh" in 6:16, it is because *sarx* is the word that appears in the Greek Bible.

In 6:12–20 Paul's concern is with embodied existence. A man is one with his wife in embodied existence (Gen. 2:24; 1 Cor. 6:16). The Christian is not to be one in embodied existence with a prostitute. His sexual union with her would unite them in embodied existence, just as sexual union makes a man one with his wife in their mutual embodied existence. Hence, it is important that Christians marry in the Lord (7:39). Their bodies belong to the Lord; they are spiritual bodies—that is, they are embodied existence in and through which the Spirit is present and active. The Christian's embodied existence is a locus of the Spirit's activity. Embodied Christian existence allows the Christian to be the temple of the Holy Spirit (6:19).

For Paul, sexual union with a prostitute (6:15–17) is paradigmatic of sexual sin in general (6:18–20). Sexual sin relates to embodied human existence in a way that other sins do not. Thus Paul writes, "Shun sexual immorality![15] Every sin that a person commits is outside the body; but the one who sins sexually sins against the body itself" (6:18). The Christian's embodied existence is not for sexual license, an example of which is a liaison with a prostitute. One with Christ, the Christian's embodied existence is for the Lord. When Paul writes that the one who sins sexually sins against his own body (*to idion sōma*), he would have his readers think primarily of their own embodied existence. Given the thrust of Paul's argument on the nature of embodied existence and the social thrust of his parenesis, one cannot exclude from Paul's language a possible hint that sexual sin is also a sin against the body of Christ, the church.[16]

SEX AND MARRIAGE

In 6:12–20 Paul used the classic topos of prostitution as an opportunity to present foundational elements of a Christian anthropology that could provide a warrant for his exhortation, "Shun fornication!" The topos considered the matter of sexuality from the male's point of view.[17] Little attention, if any, was paid to the degradation of woman implied in a man's use of prostitutes. Paul took the occasion of his consideration of prostitution to deal with some aspects of the evil implied in the libertarian slogan "All things are lawful." This slogan was not the only buzzword to disturb the good order of the Corinthian community. Some people were saying, "It is well for a man not to touch a woman" (7:1). The ascetic attitude implied by this saying proved troublesome for some of the Christians in Corinth. So they wrote to Paul about the matter.

Some of the older translations, including the AV and the RSV, translate 7:1 as if "it is well for a man not to touch a woman" were Paul's response to a question that the Corinthians had asked. Most modern translations, however, including the NRSV, NIV, rev. NAB, NEB, NKJV, and the CEV, consider that "it is well for a man not to touch a woman" is the issue about which the Corinthians had questions. The ancient Greek manuscripts of the New Testament do not have punctuation marks, nor do they have spaces between sentences. It is only from reading the text in its context that one can decide how to punctuate a translation. Earlier generations of exegetes considered Paul to have been an unmarried sexual ascetic. Nowadays scholars are inclined to think that Paul may have been married. The natural reading of 7:1 would normally require that Paul specify the matter about which he was writing. These considerations coalesce to lead most contemporary scholars, translators, and interpreters to hold that "it is well for a man not to touch a woman" is a problematic slogan to which Paul is responding.[18] It is not Paul's answer to an unspecified problem.

In answering the Corinthians' questions about the ascetic formula in 7:1-7, Paul takes a somewhat different tack from the approach that he used in 6:12-20. In dealing with prostitution in chapter 6, Paul addressed the issue only from the point of view of the male. In dealing with the issue of asceticism in chapter 7, Paul addresses the matter from the point of view of both the man and the woman. Mutuality is the hallmark of his teaching on sex and sexual relationships.

Paul is a realist with regard to sexuality. He begins his exposition by putting it in the context of sexual misconduct (*porneia*).[19] "Because of cases of sexual immorality," he writes, "each man should have his own wife and each woman her own husband" (7:2). The word that the NRSV translates "cases of sexual immorality" is simply *porneia*, in the singular. Reading Paul's words today, we have the impression that Paul is trying to say something like "because of the human sexual libido, each man should have his own wife[20] and each woman should have her own husband."[21]

Marriage without sex is hardly an adequate way to deal with one's libido. So Paul goes on to say that "the husband should give to his wife her conjugal rights, and likewise the wife to her husband" (7:3). It is a matter of justice[22] that both husband and wife respond to the sexual needs of their partners. Within Judaism the satisfaction of her sexual needs was considered to be one of a wife's fundamental rights (Exod. 21:10). A man was expected to make his wife happy (Deut. 24:5). The Talmud links marital happiness with the enjoyment of sexual relations.[23] If a wife were to be deprived of her sexual rights, she could petition the local council to order her husband to divorce her.

With regard to sex, Paul views men and women in a remarkably similar fashion. Both men and women have to resolve the matter of their own libido. Both men and women ought to marry (7:2). Both men and women have a right to have their sexual needs satisfied by their marital partners (7:3). Paul's evenhanded parenesis continues with a third statement underlining why husbands and wives are bound to satisfy the sexual needs of their spouses: "For the wife does not have authority over her own body, but the husband does; likewise the husband does not have authority over his own body, but the wife does" (7:4). Within marriage, men have authority over their wives and women have authority over their husbands.[24] Similarity, mutuality, reciprocal consideration, and realism are the hallmarks of Paul's response to the slogan "It is well for a man not to touch a woman"—a slogan that Paul clearly considers to be out of line.

Paul's realistic attitude toward sex continues as he considers the possibility of sexual abstinence within marriage.[25] "Do not deprive one another," he writes, "except perhaps by agreement for a set time, to devote yourselves to prayer, and then come together again, so that Satan may not tempt you because of your lack of self-control" (7:5). Paul stipulates that three conditions must be fulfilled before sexual abstinence within marriage is justified. (1) There must be mutual agreement between husband and wife with regard to the abstinence. (2) Abstinence should be for a limited time only. (3) The purpose of the abstinence should be a religious one, that the partners wish to devote themselves to prayer.

Paul considers his toleration[26] of limited and mutually agreed upon sexual abstinence to be a concession,[27] the only concession that he allows. Paul's reflections on temporary abstinence within marriage derive from his Semitic and Jewish understanding of human sexuality. "There is a time for having intercourse with one's wife," says the *Testament of Naphtali*, "and a time to abstain for the purpose of prayer"

(8:8). Like Paul, the *Testament of Naphtali* indicates that prayer is an acceptable reason for abstinence[28] but that the time of abstinence should be limited. The Mishnah relates a difference of opinion between the schools of Shammai and Hillel as to the length of time during which a couple might appropriately agree to sexual abstinence (see *m. Ketub.* 5:6; cf. *t. Ned.* 5:6). The disciples of Shammai suggest that the couple may consent to two weeks of abstinence. Hillel's disciples stipulate that one week is the acceptable maximum.

The realism of Paul's attitude toward sex is apparent as he concludes his brief remark on temporary sexual abstinence by "then come together again, so that Satan may not tempt you because of your lack of self-control."[29] The reference to Satan[30] evokes Paul's apocalyptic worldview and the specter of the end-time (cf. 7:26, 29, 31). The eschaton, the approaching end-time, will color much of what Paul has to say in 7:25–38 about those who are not yet married. In 7:5 the reference to Satan simply reminds the Christians of Corinth that they live in eschatological times. In these times the temptation to turn from one's calling is ever present.

Paul alludes to his own calling in urging the Corinthians to be faithful to the gift that each of them has received from God. "I wish," he writes, "that all were as I myself am. But each has a particular gift from God, one having one kind and another a different kind" (7:7). Paul is well aware that each Christian has a particular gift from God (cf. 12:7–11). In 7:7 he seems to imply that marriage itself is a gift from God, a charism.[31] When he was writing to the Corinthians, Paul was not married (9:5). In 7:8–9 he seems to class himself among the widowers[32] and widows. As someone who seems to have had rabbinic training and who describes himself in these terms, "as to the Law, a Pharisee . . . as to righteousness under the law, blameless" (Phil. 3:5–6), it is likely that Paul would have been married at some time in his life.[33] According to Jewish tradition:

> No man may abstain from keeping the law "Be fruitful and multiply,"
> unless he already has children: according to the School of Shammai, two
> sons; according to the School of Hillel, a son and a daughter, for it is written, "Male and female he created them." . . . The duty to be fruitful and
> multiply falls on the man but not on the woman. (*m. Yebam.* 6:6; cf. *t.
> Yebam.* 9:5–6; *b. Yebam* 64b–65a)

Throughout his letter to the Corinthians, Paul consistently shows that he is a pragmatist in dealing with the variety of issues that were disturbing the good order of the community.[34] In taking issue with the kind of sexual asceticism implied by the slogan "It is well for a man not to touch a woman," Paul first addressed those who were most immediately concerned, those who were married. Then he turned his attention to those for whom nonmarriage might be a possibility, widowers and widows (vv. 8–9), those who might consider divorce (vv. 10–11), and those involved in mixed marriages (vv. 12–16). The apostle's basic advice to all of these people is that they remain as they are (7:17–24).

Citing himself as an example, Paul specifically addresses this advice to widowers and widows (7:8–9). According to Jewish tradition, the males among them would not be obliged to remarry provided that they had the expected two children. On his own authority—"I say"—Paul urges those who have lost their spouses through death to remain as they are.[35] Paul's realistic attitude toward sex (7:2–6) carries through, however, in his advice to widowers and widows: "But if they are not practicing self-control, they should marry" (7:9a). If widowers and widows cannot keep their sexual desires under control, they must marry.[36] In his explanation of why he considers this to be so, Paul specifically talks about the erotic desires of these once married people: "For it is better to marry than to be aflame with passion" (7:9b).[37] Erotic desire leads to marriage, even for widowers and widows.

Paul returns to the matter of the widow who desires to remarry at the end of chapter 7. While offering the opinion that he had voiced in 7:8, that it would be good for the widow to remain as she is, Paul affirms that once her husband has died, she is free to marry whomever she wants to marry. Should she decide to remarry, Paul encourages her to marry "in the Lord," that is, to marry another Christian.

WHAT ABOUT THE UNMARRIED?

There is one category of people whom Paul has not yet considered in his lengthy disquisition on sex. This is the category of those who have not yet been married. Paul takes up their case in 7:25–38. "Now concerning virgins," he writes, "I have no command of the Lord, but I give my opinion as one who by the Lord's mercy is trustworthy" (7:25). The unmarried are called "virgins," *tōn parthenōn*, a term that normally describes unmarried women, but is also used in the New Testament and other Hellenistic literature to designate unmarried men as well as unmarried women.[38]

With regard to the unmarried, Paul's advice is similar to that which he addressed to widows and widowers. The unmarried are encouraged to stay as they are (7:26). That those who are married should remain committed to their marriage and that those who have once married might be encouraged to remain unmarried makes a great deal of sense. It would not have made much sense for Paul, good Jew that he was and well aware of the Genesis story of the creation of man and woman as he was, to have encouraged those who were unmarried to remain unmarried were it not for his apocalyptic worldview. He was convinced that the end-time was close at hand and that the eschaton was already beginning to impinge on the Corinthians' existence. The order of things as they knew them was already beginning to pass away (7:31).

With such a radical change immediately at hand, it really made no sense for the unmarried to take a spouse and begin a family. The decisions that they are to make, Paul advises them, are to be made in the light of the impending crisis (7:26). When it comes, says Paul, things will be radically different. Even those who have wives will be as though they had none (7:29). Besides, says Paul, husbands and wives must necessarily be concerned about one another. They have every interest in pleasing their spouses and an obligation to do so. In the eschatological interim Paul would, however, encourage those who had not yet married to consider the things of the Lord who was about to appear at the parousia (7:35).

Despite his radically apocalyptic view of the impending eschaton, Paul affirms that if an unmarried man chooses to marry, he does not sin, and that if an unmarried woman chooses to marry, she does not sin (7:28). In the light of the coming of the Lord, to whom Christians should turn their expectant attention, marriage is not to be considered sinful, neither for a man nor for an unmarried woman. In this regard Paul continues to express the parity that exists in matters sexual with regard to both men and women (7:2–16, 33–34).

Before bringing his rhetorical demonstration on human sexuality to a close with an emphatic affirmation of his apostolic authority, "I too have the Spirit of God" (7:40), Paul considers one particular case of an unmarried man and one situation of an unmarried woman. The first instance is that of a man who is involved in a committed relationship with a woman. Various opinions have been advanced as to the nature of the commitment implied by the use of the pronouns "his" in v. 36 and "his own" in vv. 37 and 38, but it seems best to construe Paul's words as applying to the situation of a man who had made a commitment to marry a certain woman.[39] The NRSV translation supports this interpretation when it speaks of a man and his fiancée[40] in 7:36–38.

As is his wont in dealing with sexuality, Paul looks at the situation realistically. He writes about a man's strong passions in 7:36. His words, "so it has to be," are a concession to the reality of sexual passion. As in 7:2 and 7:9, Paul affirms that human sexual passion is a reality; erotic desire must be taken seriously. If a man has made a commitment to a woman and has strong sexual desires, then they should marry. It is not sinful for them to do so; it is really good for them to marry (7:38a).

There is, however, another possibility. It may be that a man is able to keep his sexual desire under control and that he has made a commitment within the depths of his own being. In that case, he will do well. "If someone stands firm in his resolve, being under no necessity but having his own desire under control, and has determined in his own mind to keep her as his fiancée, he will do well" (7:37).[41] Indeed, says Paul, a man who meets these conditions and "refrains from marriage will do better" (7:38) than the man who chooses to marry the woman to whom he is committed.

It is only on the occasion of the advice that he gives in 7:37–38 that Paul actually uses the comparative, "better," to describe one way of dealing with one's libido as preferable to another. Within the context of his expectation of an imminent parousia, Paul affirms that it is better for a man who is involved in a committed relationship and who can control his passions not to consummate the relationship with marriage. Otherwise the man should marry, for that is not sinful. While Paul urges social stability in the light of the coming eschaton, he also affirms that the human sexual drive is a reality that must be taken seriously.

Having written about the "engaged" man, Paul turns to the case of a widow (cf. 7:8–9). After the death of her husband, a Christian widow is free to marry. Paul reminds the widow who might contemplate remarriage that she ought to marry. She should, says Paul, marry "in the Lord" (7:39).

In his lengthy discussion of human sexuality in 1 Corinthians 7, Paul was aware that he had but a single tradition that had come from the Lord (7:10). For the rest of his parenesis Paul had to draw from his Jewish tradition and his own common sense (7:6, 12, 32, 40).[42] He did so with a spirit of apostolic confidence. The final words of his lengthy exhortation are, "I think that I too have the Spirit of God" (7:40).

NOTES

1. Paul uses the Greek word *ethnē*, "ethnics" or non-Jews (cf. 1:23; 12:2). Elsewhere in the letter he refers to *Hellēnes*, "Hellenes" or Greeks (1:22, 24; 10:32; 12:13). The latter term identifies them by their culture; the former as non-Jews, the "nations," as distinct from "the people [of Israel]" in Paul's biblical tradition.

2. See *m. Sanh.* 7:4: "These are they that are to be stoned: he that has connection with his mother, his father's wife, his daughter-in-law, a male, or a beast. . . ."

3. See *m. Sanh.* 7:4. In effect, a man who has an incestuous relationship with his own mother has violated at least two commandments. The rabbinic tradition considers that a single act of sexual intercourse may indeed violate several commandments. The tractate *Keritot* suggests that one act of incestuous intercourse may violate up to seven commandments (3:5–6).

4. See Lev. 18:3, 24. The *Sipra* on Lev. 18:3 interprets the reference to the inhabitants of Egypt and Canaan to mean that Gentiles generally participate in the incestuous practices described in Leviticus 18. Cf. *Sipra* 9:8 (85c–d); 13:8, 10 (85a). See also O. Larry Yarbrough, *Not Like the Gentiles: Marriage Rules in the Letters of Paul*, SBLDS 80 (Atlanta: Scholars Press, 1985), 18–19.

5. See Adela Yarbro Collins, "The Function of 'Excommunication' in Paul," *HTR* 73 (1980): 251–63; cf. Dale B. Martin, *The Corinthian Body* (New Haven/London: Yale University Press, 1995), 168–74. For Martin, "the pneuma that needs to be saved is both the pneuma of the man and that of the church" (p. 174).

6. See chap. 5 above.

7. On the meaning of these terms, see above, pp. 80–92.

8. See R. F. Collins, *First Corinthians*, SacPag 7 (Collegeville, Minn.: Liturgical Press, 1999), 240–41, 243.

9. In an important study of the rhetoric of 1 Corinthians, Margaret Mitchell has drawn attention to the significance of Paul's argument from advantage in the letter. "Beneficial" (*sympherei*) is a "buzzword" in this argument. See M. M. Mitchell, *Paul and the Rhetoric of Reconciliation: An Exegetical Investigation of the Language and Composition of 1 Corinthians* (Louisville: Westminster/John Knox, 1992), 25–38.

10. Note the explanatory "for" (*gar*).

11. See Ceslas Spicq, "*agorazō*, to buy," *EDNT* 1:26–28.

12. As he wrote to the Corinthians, this approach might have had more than incidental value. In chapters 8–10 Paul will deal with the issue of food that has been offered to idols.

13. See Martin, *Corinthian Body*, 174–79.

14. The allusion to redemption in 6:20 suggests that it is through the death of Jesus that Christians have become "members of Christ" (cf. 1:30).

15. The NRSV translates the *porneia* of 6:18 as "fornication." The Greek term, as has been noted above (pp. 80–83), has a wide semantic range that can be summed up under the rubric of "sexual immorality."

16. On the church as the body of Christ, see 10:17; 12:12–26. Cf. 8:12,

where Paul argues that a sin against a member of the Christian family is also a sin against Christ.

17. It can be argued that Paul had rabbinic training. Rabbinic texts on human sexuality are generally androcentric, as is Paul's exposition on prostitution. Rabbinic law did not address the issue of men using prostitutes to satisfy their sexual urges. It did, however, prohibit Jewish women from serving as prostitutes (*b. Sanh.* 82a).

18. See, e.g., Wolfgang Schrage, "Zur Frontstellung der paulinischen Ehebewertung in 1 Kor 7:1–7," *ZNW* 67 (1976): 214–34.

19. On the importance of controlling the *yēṣer hārāʿ*, "evil desire," in Judaism, see Michael Satlow, *Tasting the Dish: Rabbinic Rhetorics of Sexuality*, Brown Judaic Studies 303 (Atlanta: Scholars Press, 1995), 158–69.

20. Cf. 1 Thess. 4:4 and above, pp. 103–4.

21. Paul would have been unaware that some human beings have a same-sex orientation. See above, p. 88.

22. Paul uses the verb *opheilō*, which means "to owe, to have to, to be obligated." It is commonly used of an obligation to pay money, debts, or taxes. See Michael Wolter, "*opheilē*," *EDNT* 2:550; "*opheilō*," *EDNT* 2:550–52.

23. Cf. *b. Pes.* 72b, which says "there is the happiness of her marital intercourse [ʿōnah]."

24. See Gerhard Schneider, "*exousiazō*," *EDNT* 2:12. Within the Hellenistic world, Antipater wrote that husband and wife "not only share a partnership of property, and children . . . , but they also share their bodies" (*SVF* 2.355.12–18).

25. In the first letter to the Corinthians, Paul frequently interrupts his main line of argumentation to address a particular issue. See, e.g., 7:11, 15, 21, 28, 39b; 10:28–29, etc.

26. Paul explicitly states that it is "not a command" (*ou kat' epitagēn*) in 7:6.

27. The demonstrative pronoun, "this" (*touto*) in 7:6 refers to the immediately preceding sentence, v. 5, not to the teaching on sexuality set forth in vv. 2–4. Chrys Caragounis has suggested that Paul is well aware that he has delved into the most personal aspects of the Corinthians' lives in 7:2–5, and so offers them an apology. Caragounis's paraphrase of v. 6 is "Pardon me, for intruding; I just wanted to help. I have only given an advice, not a command!" See C. C. Caragounis, "'Fornication' and 'Concession'? Interpreting 1 Cor 7,1–7," in *The Corinthian Correspondence*, ed. Reimund Bieringer, BETL 125 (Louvain: University Press/Peeters, 1996), 543–59, esp. 558.

28. A modern analogue might well be a husband or wife going on a religious retreat apart from their spouse.

29. "Lack of self-control" is the NRSV translation of the Greek word *akrasian.* This is the only time that Paul uses the expression "lack of self-control." He uses its opposite, "self-control" (*egkrateia*), only once, in a list of virtues (Gal. 5:23). The antonym is often found in Hellenistic catalogues of virtues, where it stands in opposition to various forms of sexual immorality. A modern Greek commentator, Konstantinos Nicolaou Papadopoulos has suggested that in 7:5 *akrasian* means incontinence rather than lack of self-control (*Deltion Biblikon Meleton* 1 [1979]: 135–37).

30. Interestingly, the only two references to Satan in 1 Corinthians are to be found in passages dealing with sexual issues, 5:5 and 7:5.

31. Charism (*charisma*) is a new word. It is clearly attested for the first time in Greek literature in 1 Corinthians, where Paul uses the term seven times (1:7; 7:7; 12:4, 9, 28, 30, 31).

32. The Greek term used by Paul is *agamois*, literally, "the unmarried." The comprehensive term includes three categories of people: those who have never been married, those who have been married and who divorced, and those who have married but their spouses have died. Joined to "widows" (*chērais*) in 7:8, the term *agamois* denotes men in the third category, widowers.

33. Toward the end of the second century Clement of Alexandria had already expressed the view that Paul had been married.

34. See n. 25 above, p. 126.

35. Paul's language is terse. He writes *kalon autois ean meinōsin hōs kagō*, literally, "well for them if they remain as even I." The emphasis is on "remaining" as they are; not specifically remaining "unmarried."

36. Paul uses an imperative, *gamēsatōsan*; cf. 7:36.

37. The King James Version of Paul's words is commonly cited as a bon mot, "it is better to marry than to burn." See also the rev. NAB's "be on fire." This translation is ambivalent and often gives rise to a discussion as to whether Paul meant to imply that widowers and widows who cannot control their sexual desires will burn in hell if they do not marry. Paul, however, uses the verb "to burn" (*pyroomai*) only in a metaphorical sense. In Hellenistic literature it is used with the meaning "be on fire with passion." This understanding is reflected in many contemporary versions of Paul's letter (NRSV, RSV, REB, NIV, CEV). The translation of the JB, "it is better to be married than to be tortured," exceeds the limits of hyperbolic metaphor. See Roy Bowen Ward, "Musonius and Paul on Marriage," *NTS* 36 (1990): 281–89, esp. 284.

38. That Paul uses a formulaic "Now concerning virgins" (*peri de tōn parthenōn*) does not necessarily indicate that the Corinthians had specifically written to him about the case of those who were not married. The formula merely means that Paul is moving on to a new topic, whether or not it was one about which the Corinthians had specifically asked for advice.

39. See Collins, *First Corinthians*, 299, 301–2.

40. That is, *tēn parthenon autou*, literally, "his virgin," in 7:36. The same translation appears in vv. 37 and 38.

41. In 7:37 Paul twice writes about the "heart" (*kardia*), a word that, in his Semitic anthropology, suggests the very core of the human being. The NRSV translation obscures this focus when it translates *hestēken en tę kardią* as "stands firm in his resolve" and *kekriken en tę kardią* as "determined in his own mind."

42. Much of what Paul has to say is consistent with the advice offered by Hellenistic moralists. See Will Deming, *Paul on Marriage and Celibacy: The Hellenistic Background of 1 Corinthians 7*, SNTSMS 83 (Cambridge: Cambridge University Press, 1995).

8

Pleading with the Saints in Rome

AUL'S LETTER TO "ALL GOD'S BELOVED IN ROME, who are called to be saints" is unique within the New Testament. It is the only one of Paul's seven authentic letters that is not addressed to a "church." Paul's letters to the Corinthians, the Galatians, the Philippians, the Thessalonians, and those who gathered in Philemon's house were addressed to communities that the apostle had evangelized. The letter to the Romans was written to a group of Christians whom he had not yet visited (1:13; 15:22). To be sure, Paul knew many members of the community (see 16:3–16), but he had not yet visited them in Rome. Nor had the apostle been to the imperial capital.

He wrote his letter to God's beloved in Rome as a letter of introduction, to prepare the way for his visit to the city as he made his way toward Spain. Since the letter is one of introduction, it is not as personal as most of Paul's other letters. When he wrote to the Thessalonians, Paul had information about the community from Timothy, who had just returned from a visit to the Macedonian community (1 Thess. 3:6). When he wrote to the Corinthians, Paul had information about the community from Chloe's people (1 Cor. 1:11), from Stephanas, Fortunatus, and Achaicus (1 Cor. 16:17), as well as from the letter that the Corinthians had sent to him (1 Cor. 7:1). Paul's letter to the Philippians is filled with the affection that he had for those who had supported him in his mission (Phil. 4:14–18). The letter to the Galatians burns with passion as Paul responds to communities[1] that were in danger of turning from the gospel that he had preached (Gal. 1:6–9). In contrast to these earlier letters, Paul's letter to the Romans seems to be virtually a dispassionate treatise in which the argument is carefully developed point by point. The missive has sometimes been described as a letter essay in which Paul treats the "Jewish question."[2] The thesis of at least the first part of the letter is expressed in 1:17: "For in it [the gospel] the righteousness of God is revealed through faith for faith; as it is written, 'The one who is righteous will live by faith.'"

GENTILES AND JEWS

With regard to righteousness Paul affirms that no distinction is to be made between Gentile and Jew (3:21–31). All people "have sinned and fall short of the glory of God" (3:23). All men and women are "justified by his grace as a gift through the redemption that is in Christ Jesus" (3:24). To establish that all people are sinners and stand in need of the gift of justification, Paul addresses himself to the Jewish Christians in the Roman community. He begins by developing a panorama that illustrates the ungodliness and wickedness of those who suppress the truth by their idolatry (1:18). Since God has revealed himself through creation (1:19–20), these people should have known better. They who claimed to be wise chose to become fools. They exchanged the glory of God for the worship of idols, images of mere creatures (1:22–23).

From this portrayal of the Gentiles as "foolish" idol worshipers (1:18–23), Paul draws a strong inference. "Therefore," he writes, "God gave them up in the lusts of their hearts to impurity, to the degrading of their bodies among themselves, because they exchanged the truth about God for a lie and worshiped and served the creature rather than the Creator, who is blessed forever" (1:24–25).[3]

Paul is not content with merely stating that God gave the Gentiles up to their impure lusts. He portrays this within the context of the revelation of God's wrath from heaven. The wrath of God is a topic that appears more often in the letter to the Romans than in any other letter.[4] The wrath of God is an eschatological notion. God's wrath will be fully revealed on the Day of the Lord (cf. 2:5).[5] The wrath of God is, however, also being revealed in the present activity of God.[6] God's wrath is the expression of his judgment on human sin.

The notion of God's wrath is anthropopathic. God is described as an angry person wreaking vengeance on those who have done wrong. It is a biblical way of describing the reality of evil finding retribution in the evil that it entails. Evil has its own "reward," the evil that accrues to the evildoer. Biblical and other Jewish writings often use the anthro-pomorphic image of God as judge to portray the idea that evil has its own retribution and that good has its own reward. A classic case is Exod. 20:5b–6 (par. Deut. 5:9b–10), "I the Lord your God am a jealous God, punishing children for the iniquity of parents, to the third and the fourth generation of those who reject me, but showing steadfast love to the thousandth generation of those who love me and keep my com-mandments."

What the biblical authors portrayed in judicial imagery is common-place in human experience. The social and genetic sciences explore the reality of an alcoholic parent leaving the legacy of a dysfunctional fam-ily to his or her children. Child molesters are often those who have been themselves abused as children, and so forth. Jeremiah and Ezekiel cite the proverb about children's teeth being set on edge when parents eat sour grapes as a colorful expression of this bit of human wisdom (Jer. 31:29–30; Ezek. 18:2–3). The prophets offer a theological critique of the image (Jer. 31:30; Ezek. 18:3), but it remains a fact of human experience that evil is like a cancer on the human being and on humankind. Sin and evil have their one inherent "reward."

"'Wrath'" says John A. T. Robinson, "is the process of inevitable ret-ribution which comes into operation when God's laws are broken. It contains the idea of what happens in the life of a man or society when moral control is loosened. It is what takes over if the situation is allowed to rip."[7] Because of their sin, God releases sinners to the almost inevitable consequences of their evildoing. God's wrath does not fall upon these evildoers because of their evil; rather, their evil is the consequence of God's wrath.

In graphic detail Paul describes what happens to Gentiles as a result of their idol worship. "Their women," he writes, "exchanged natural intercourse for unnatural, and in the same way also the men, giving up natural intercourse with women, were consumed with passion for one another. Men committed shameless acts with men and received in their own persons the due penalty for their error" (1:26b–27). For the apostle, the homoerotic activity of Gentiles is proof positive of their moral perversity, itself the result of their rejection of the truth.

As if this description were not enough to illustrate the degradation to which Gentile men and women had fallen as a consequence of their idolatry, Paul adds a long list of other vices to which the Gentiles had succumbed.

Since they did not see fit to acknowledge God, God gave them up to a debased mind and to things that should not be done. They were filled with every kind of wickedness, evil, covetousness, malice. Full of envy, murder, strife, deceit, craftiness, they are gossips, slanderers, God-haters, insolent, haughty, boastful, inventors of evil, rebellious toward parents, foolish, faithless, heartless, ruthless. (1:28–31)

This list of twenty-one vices is the longest of Paul's catalogues of vices, but it contains no mention whatsoever of sexual impropriety. The description of lesbian and homosexual activity in 1:26–27 suffices to castigate the Gentiles as people who were guilty of sexual immorality.

Paul concludes his portrayal of the Gentiles as a group of totally corrupt individuals with a telling statement. "They know God's decree, that those who practice such things deserve to die—yet they not only do them but even applaud others who practice them" (1:32). There is no escaping the fact that Paul paints the Gentiles as thoroughly immoral. One can almost hear the apostle's Jewish readership responding to his rhetoric and applauding his description of Hellenes as people who are simply no good at all.

Then comes the zinger. To his description of the rampant immorality of the Gentiles, Paul adds a poignant statement about Jews. "You have no excuse," he writes, "whoever you are . . . because you, the judge, are doing the very same things" (2:1). Using a less impassioned and more reasoned fashion of writing than he had employed in his vivid description of the Gentiles, Paul then portrays the sinfulness of Jews, to whom the law had been given (2:2–3:20).[8]

Having completed his diptych on the sinfulness of humanity,[9] Paul concludes that the whole world is held accountable to God (3:19) since all have sinned (3:23). Similar in their sinfulness, all people, Jew and Gentile alike, are justified by the gift of God through faith (3:21–31). Similar in their sin, Jew and Gentile are in a position of parity with regard to the gift of justification.

THE DIVINE JUDGE

If one is to understand what Paul has to say about lesbian and homosexual activity in 1:26–27, one must appreciate Paul's words within the context of the argument that Paul develops in 1:16–3:31. Paul's overall rhetorical argument is very powerful. To illustrate that all people are sinners, Paul begins by appealing to a well-known Jewish bias.

Gentiles are given over to idolatry and sexual immorality. Their deviant sexual behavior is a consequence of their worship of idols.

In times past great Jewish prophets had railed against the worship of Baal, with its fertility cult and its sacred prostitutes, both male and female.[10] The Wisdom of Solomon attributes the origin of sexual immorality to idolatry.[11] "The idea of making idols was the beginning of fornication (*porneia*), and the invention of them was the corruption of life" (Wis. 14:12).[12] Paul's contemporary Philo of Alexandria and other Jews considered that sexual immorality was characteristic of the Gentiles. Sexual immorality was one of the things that distinguished the ethos of Gentiles from that of the Jews.

In portraying the Gentiles as totally immoral, Paul does not stop with a generic description of their sexual immorality (1:24). He illustrates the sexual immorality of the Gentiles with a graphic description of lesbian and homosexual activity. From a Jewish perspective lesbianism and homosexual intercourse were among the worst forms of sexual immorality. Jews considered that procreation was one of the most important values in human sexual intercourse.[13] That lesbian and homosexual intercourse was not open to procreation only added to its deviancy.

Paul's caricature of the sexual immorality of Gentiles was intended to evoke a passionate response from his Jewish Christian readership. Paul could then exploit their response to lead them to a judgment about their own sinfulness. What Paul intends to accomplish with his rhetoric in 1:16–3:31 must be taken fully into account when one reads what he has to say about lesbianism and homosexuality in 1:26–27.

Homoerotic activity is but one among the twenty-two vices that are to be found among those who have rejected the worship of the one true God for idol-worship. Lest his Jewish Christian readers gloat over the fact that Gentiles are so thoroughly corrupt, Paul reminds them that they too are accountable for the kinds of reprehensible behavior summarized in his litany of vices.

What, then, does Paul have to say about lesbianism and homosexuality? The apostle clearly presents homoerotic activity as the consequence of human beings' rejecting the Creator and pursuing the worship of idols. In the vice catalogues of 1 Cor. 5:10–11; 6:9–10; and Gal. 5:19–21, Paul had closely linked idolatry with sexual immorality. The sin of idolatry appears alongside various forms of sexual immorality. In his letter to the Romans, Paul goes beyond what he has suggested in the vice lists. In Rom. 1:18–32, idolatry is presented as the root sin. Sexual immorality and the other vices that Paul mentions are presented as the consequence of idolatry.

Paul uses the image of the judge who metes out a penalty for a crime. For Paul, God is the judge. Three times Paul says that "God gave them up" (*paredōken autous ho theos*, vv. 24, 26, 28).[14] The image is that of the judge who hands a convict over to the bailiff for punishment. The verb used by Paul (*paradidōmi*) frequently appears in classical and Hellenistic Greek as well as in the New Testament[15] with precise juridic meaning.[16] Within a judicial process, the verb means "to hand over for judgment or punishment."

Paul continues to exploit the judicial imagery in v. 27 when he writes about those men who participate in homoerotic activity as receiving a "due penalty" for their error. Their error (*planē*) is not a simple "mistake." It is a matter of a perverse and crafty deception. The word "penalty" (*tēn antimisthian*) suggests a penal recompense.[17] Paul says that the penalty that God has meted out is appropriate, even mandatory. He describes the penalty as a "due" (*hēn edei*) penalty. The use of judicial language continues until the end of the pericope. In v. 32 Paul writes of God's "decree" (*dikaiōma*), a technical term that means ordinance or decree but that often means "judgment, punishment, or penalty" in a judicial context. Finally, Paul states that the perpetrators of the evils of which he writes "deserve to die" (*axioi thanatou*). The adjective has a strictly legal sense. Evildoers deserve the death penalty.

The crime about which Paul is writing is the idolaters' refusal to acknowledge God (vv. 19–23). In consequence of this crime, an appropriate penalty is to be meted out. In this way God's wrath is made manifest (1:18). Having described the crime in graphic detail, Paul offers the judicial sentence. He does so in three parallel scenes that describe God's wrath at work in the world (vv. 24–25, 26–27, 28–32). Each scene links the punishment to the crime. The first scene opens with an inferential "therefore." The second is introduced by "for this reason." The third begins "since they did not see fit to acknowledge God."

God is first presented as exercising his judicial function by handing the idolaters over to the lusts of their hearts for impurity[18] with the result that they are degraded as persons (vv. 24–25).[19] Their bodily degradation symbolizes their personal degradation. Then (vv. 26–27) God is presented as exercising his judicial function by handing the idolaters over to their degrading passions with the result that they engage in homoerotic activity.[20] In these scenes lust and degrading passion are presented as powerful and almost demonic forces which serve as instruments of divine vengeance. To appreciate Paul's imagery properly, one should not forget that in the ancient world, and all too often in the modern world as well, the rape of a male by a male was a degrading form of subjection sometimes inflicted on prisoners taken captive in war. Recent conflicts in the former Yugoslavia have resulted in many stories of the raping of women being used to terrorize and inflict punishment on the civilian population.

In the third scene (vv. 28–32), God is presented as exercising his judicial function by handing over the idolaters to all forms of wickedness. Paul would have his readers understand that the rejection of God expressed in idolatry is the root sin; all forms of wickedness are its consequence. Paul's language is anthropomorphic. God is presented as acting in the manner of a human judge, meting out the severest form of punishment for the most egregious of crimes.[21]

LESBIANS AND HOMOSEXUALS

The second punishment is lesbian[22] and gay activity (1:26–27). Why does Paul present homoerotic behavior in this way? The answer must be sought as one attempts to understand Paul's writing about human sexuality.

That homosexual activity took place in the Greco-Roman world is a well-known fact.[23] Despite the occasional plea of one or another moralist, homosexuality was considered to be neither immoral nor odd. Writings such as Plato's *Symposium* and Plutarch's *Lycurgus* suggest that homoerotic activity was fairly common and well regarded in Hellenistic culture. Gods and emperors engaged in homosexual activity.[24] In some circles, where the beauty of the male form was well regarded, it was considered to be a component of cultured education for a grown man to have homoerotic activities with a youth. That women on Lesbos engaged in sexual activities with other women was known long before Lucian wrote about it in the fifth *Dialogue of the Courtesans* (second century C.E.).

Jewish authors were well aware of this activity. Philo went so far as to claim that in many nations prizes were awarded for licentiousness and effeminacy (*akrasias kai malakias athla*) (*Special Laws* 3.40). Hellenistic Jewish writers considered that Gentiles participated in homoerotic activity while Jews did not. Homoerotic activity had long been banned by the Torah[25] and frowned upon in other biblical texts.[26] The difference between Gentiles and Jews with regard to this kind of behavior was something that distinguished a Jewish culture from a Gentile culture. "We are distinct," wrote the author of the *Letter of Aristeas,* "from all other men. The majority of other men defile themselves in their relationships, thereby committing a serious offense, and lands and whole cities take pride in it: they not only procure the males; they also defile mothers and daughters. We are quite separated from these practices" (*Ep. Arist.* 151–52). According to the *Sibylline Oracles,* after God has destroyed the Macedonian kingdom, there will come the beginning of another kingdom:

> They will also oppress mortals. But those men will have a great fall when they launch on a course of unjust haughtiness. Immediately compulsion to impiety will come upon these men. Male will have intercourse with male and they will set up boys in houses of ill-fame and in those days there will be a great affliction among men and it will throw everything into confusion. (*Sib. Or.* 3:182–87).[27]

For these authors, as for Paul, homoerotic activity was a "Gentile thing." It was not to occur among God's own people.

Paul describes homosexual activity among men as a "shameless act" (*aschēmosynēn,* 1:27). The abstract term, used elsewhere in the New Testament only in Rev. 16:15, denotes a lack of proper shame or form. Hence, it connotes something that is dishonorable or shameful. For a Hellenistic Jewish author familiar with the Greek Bible as was Paul, the term surely evoked the sexual transgressions of Gentiles. All but a handful of the biblical uses of *aschēmosynē* are in Leviticus 18 and 20, where the term identifies various sexual transgressions committed by the Egyptians but not to be committed by Israel when it entered the promised land. Those who committed such abominations were to be cut off from the people.

Paul's thoughts on the close connection between idolatry and homoerotic intercourse are echoed in the writings of Philo, the Jewish philosopher who was Paul's contemporary:

> Incapable of bearing such satiety, plunging like cattle, they threw off from their necks the law of nature and applied themselves to deep drinking of strong liquor and dainty feeding and forbidden forms of intercourse. Not only in their mad lust for women did they violate the marriages of their neighbors, but also men mounted males without respect for the sex nature which the active partner shares with the passive; and so when they tried to beget children they were discovered to be incapable of any but a sterile seed. Yet the discovery availed them not, so

much stronger was the force of the lust which mastered them. Then, as little by little they accustomed those who were by nature men to submit to play the part of women, they saddled them with the formidable curse of a female disease. For not only did they emasculate their bodies by luxury and voluptuousness but they worked a further degeneration in their souls and, as far as in them lay, were corrupting the whole of mankind. (*Abraham* 135–36)

In the *Special Laws* Philo rails against male homosexuality. In a description of the wicked man, he portrays the wicked man as one who "forces the male type of nature to debase and convert itself into the feminine form, just to indulge a polluted and accursed passion" (*Special Laws* 2.50). In a description of male homosexuality, Philo writes about the "transformation of the male nature to the female" (3.37). He derides the passive partner in homoerotic sexual activity as a "man-woman" (*androgynos*) (3.38, 40).[28]

The Jewish historian Flavius Josephus, another contemporary of Paul, states that the laws of the Jews are a characteristic feature of their nation.

What are our laws about marriage? That law owns no other mixture of sexes but that which nature hath appointed, of a man with his wife, and that this be used only for the procreation of children. But it abhors the mixture of a male with a male; and if any one do that, death is his punishment. (*Against Apion* 2.25 §199).[29]

In these passages Philo and Josephus, a pair of well-known Hellenistic Jewish writers, write only about homoerotic activity between males. In other respects what they write about homoeroticism—especially Philo, who has more to say on the subject than Josephus—is quite similar to what Paul has to say about lesbian and homosexual activity. Paul, Philo, and Josephus speak about "nature" (*physis*) in regard to homoerotic activity. That these Hellenistic Jewish writers speak of "nature" in writing about human sexuality brings their discourse into dialogue with that of the philosophic moralists, who also spoke about "nature" when dealing with sex.[30] Paul writes in 1:26–27 about women who engage in a form of sexual activity that is contrary to nature (*para physin*).[31] Philo writes about the male type of nature (*ton arrena tēs physeōs*) (*Special Laws* 2.50). Philo also writes about those who recklessly reject the law of nature (*ton tēs physeōs nomon*) (*Abraham* 135)[32] and says that men who engage in homosexual intercourse are participating in a form of intercourse forbidden by all laws (*eknomōtatous*), presumably including the law of nature.

The *pathos* appeal of Paul's rhetoric is such that he cannot say why he considers lesbian and homosexual intercourse to be contrary to nature.[33] For a Jewish Christian readership there would be no need for him to explain why he believes that homoerotic intercourse is contrary to nature. Paul's appeal need only capitalize on the common Jewish consensus in order to confirm in his readers the conviction that Gentiles are indeed sinners.

The purpose of Philo and Josephus in writing about homoerotic activity is quite different from that of Paul. The philosopher wants to show that homoerotic activity is contrary to nature and forbidden by law. The historian is concerned to demonstrate that Jews, his own people, are different from Greeks. From these respective perspectives Paul's contemporaries describe homosexual intercourse as violating the law of separation between the sexes. Homosexual intercourse turns a male into a female.[34] This is one reason why homoerotic activity among men is wrong and contrary to nature.

Philo suggests a second reason why he considers homoerotic activity to be contrary to nature and unlawful. He writes about the use of the "organs of generation" in a manner that is not seasonable (*peri panta akaireuomenos . . . ta gennētika*) (*Special Laws* 2.49). In a metaphorical description of the relationship between the active and passive partners in homosexual intercourse, Philo says, "Like a bad husbandman he lets the deep-soiled and fruitful fields lie sterile, by taking steps to keep them from bearing, while he spends his labor night and day on soil from which no growth at all can be expected" (ibid. 3.39). He speaks of "destroying the means of procreation" (*diaphtheirōn tas gonas*) (ibid.). In his treatise *On Abraham*, Philo explains that homosexual intercourse leads to sterility. "So," he writes, "when they tried to beget children they were discovered to be incapable of any but a sterile seed" (135). In effect, Philo holds that homosexual intercourse renders God's creative blessing void and makes a man incapable of obeying the command to be fruitful and multiply (Gen. 1:28), a responsibility that is particularly incumbent on males, according to Jewish tradition (see *m. Yebam.* 6:6).

Paul does not offer either of these explanations or any other as to why he believes homoerotic intercourse to be so abhorrent. It may well be that he simply shared the views of his contemporaries that homosexual intercourse turned males into females and therefore violated the order created by God who had created them "male and female." Paul's initial and comprehensive statement about the impurity (*akatharsian*) of idolaters in 1:24 is encompassed within a relatively long exposition on the Creator God (1:18–25).

In addition to what the three Hellenistic Jewish writers have to say about nature and homoerotic intercourse and the fact that all three of them attribute homosexuality to Gentiles, Paul and Philo share the view that homoerotic activity stems from lust. Paul writes about the "lusts of their hearts" (*tais epithymiais tōn kardiōn*, 1:24) and "degrading passions" (*pathē atimias*, 1:26). He says that men who participate in homoerotic activity are "consumed with passion" (*exekauthēsan en tē orexei*).[35] Philo writes about lust (*oistrous*, "insane passion") and "a polluted and accursed passion" (*memiasmenō kai eparatō pathei*) (*Special Laws* 2.50). Elsewhere Philo says that the sexual partners in homoerotic activity are conquered by "the force of lust" (*biaioteras epithymias*) (*Abraham* 135) and that those who engage in homoerotic activity are under the influence of passion (*orgōntas*) (ibid. 137). Philo also speaks about the pursuit of unnatural pleasure (*para physin hēdonēn*) (*Special Laws* 3.39). Philo and Paul use the word "lust" (*epithymia*) in their discourse about homoerotic activity. They agree that homoerotic activity stems from deep-seated and misplaced passion.

Paul and Philo also agree in their conviction that homoerotic activity is characteristic of Gentiles, who do not believe in the one God, Creator of all things; that it is contrary to nature; and that it stems from lust. Furthermore, both authors agree that homoerotic activity profoundly affects the human body for the worse. Philo, whose anthropology is more open to Hellenistic philosophy than Paul's, writes about the degeneration of body and soul that comes with homoerotic activity: "Not only did they emasculate their bodies by luxury and voluptuousness but they worked a further degeneration in their souls[36] and, as far as in them lay, were corrupting the whole of mankind" (*Abraham* 136).

That Paul and Philo agree that homoerotic activity profoundly affects the human body is an important feature in their common assessment of the evil of homoerotic activity. In their Semitic and Jewish anthropology, the human person is an embodied person. "Body" (*sōma/bāśār*) serves as a cipher for a whole range of ideas that we moderns might sum up under the rubric of "person."[37] In the biblical understanding of the human person to which both Paul and Philo are heir, the human being does not have a body. He or she is body. The word suggests that a person is a being in the world, that he or she shares some commonality with other human beings, even some commonality with animate creatures. Together they share bodily existence. A modern philosopher might say that the body is the modality of human presence in the world, that the body is potentiality for communication and interaction, that the body is the possibility of relationships. All of these ideas, minus their contemporary philosophical trappings, are present in the Hellenistic Jewish idea of the "body."

"Body" evokes vitality. As body, the human person is alive and active. As body, the human person grows and develops as he or she interacts. As body, the human person ages and eventually dies. "Body" symbolizes transitoriness and mortality.

From a theological point of view, "body" speaks of the human person in its distinction from God. God alone lives from age to age; the human person lives in a single age. God is spirit; the human person is body. "Spirit" evokes the power of God, most especially God's creative power.[38] As "body" the human person is a creature; God is the creator. God has created the human person in his or her relationality; God has created the human person in his or her individuality. Notions of social relationships and creaturehood are never far removed from the Hellenistic Jewish idea of "body."

Paul's Jewish perspective on the "body" explains much of what he has to say about homoerotic activity in Romans 1. Gentiles who do not acknowledge God simply do not understand human existence as Jews do. They do not acknowledge and respect the order of God's creation as Jews do. They do not understand that the human person has been created as "body," distinct and social. Separating soul from body as they do,[39] they do not comprehend that bodily sexual activity affects the human person to the very core of his or her being (see 1 Cor. 6:18). A Hellenistic Greek might say that sexual activity affects only the body, not the soul or the spirit of the person. A Hellenistic Jew could not say something as naive as that.

Paul shared a basic understanding of the human being as embodied existence with his biblical forebears and his Jewish contemporaries. He also shared with them the idea that homoerotic activity was something that Gentiles engaged in but God's people did not. With other Jewish authors Paul shared the idea that homoerotic activity was due to the powerful force of lust and that somehow it was contrary to nature.

What Paul writes about homoerotic activity in Rom. 1:24–27 differs from what his contemporaries have written on the subject in two significant respects. On the one hand, Paul does not link homoerotic activity and bestiality. Apparently inspired by Lev. 18:22–23, which listed the prohibition of bestiality immediately after the ban on homosexual intercourse, extant rabbinic texts speak first about homoerotic activity and then about bestiality.[40] Philo has much to say about bestiality, attributing it to lust and frantic passion (*Special Laws* 3.43–50) but Paul does not write about bestiality.

On the other hand, Paul writes about lesbian activity as well as homoerotic activity among males. The biblical prohibition (Lev. 18:22) addresses only homosexual activity among men; it is silent about same-sex activity on the part of women.[41] Rabbinic sources hardly mention lesbian activity.[42] There is a single reference in tannaitic literature (see *Sipra* Lev. 9:8) and only a few mentions in the talmudic literature (see *t. Soṭa* 5:7; *y. Giṭ.* 8:10, 49c; *b. Yebam.* 76a). In fact, references to lesbian activity are rarely found in ancient literature.[43] Paul, however, juxtaposes what he has to say about lesbian activity with what he writes about homosexual activity among men. This is a departure from what one would expect, but it is in keeping with Paul's view of human sexuality. For the apostle similar norms are to be followed and similar responsibilities are to be borne by both women and men in regard to sex. He made that point very clearly in writing to the Corinthians (1 Corinthians 7). In Rom. 1:26–27 Paul makes the point again with regard to a rather different form of human sexual activity.

Words of a Wise Man

Much of what Paul has to say in Rom. 1:18–32 is similar to what was written by an anonymous Jewish sage in the Wisdom of Solomon (see chapters 11–15). "All people, writes the author, "who were ignorant of God were foolish by nature and they were unable from the good things that are seen to know the one who exists" (Wis. 13:1). Those foolish persons went the way of idolatry, as a result of which God punished them. "In return for their foolish and wicked thoughts, which led them astray to worship irrational serpents and worthless animals," wrote the wise man, "you sent upon them a multitude of irrational creatures to punish them, so that they might learn that one is punished by the very things by which one sins" (Wis. 11:15–16).

The sage was convinced that various moral disorders were the consequence of idolatry. He used a catalogue of vices to make his point (Wis. 14:23–26, 28–29). The wise man made it very clear that the evils that he cited stemmed from idolatry. "For the worship of idols not to be named is the beginning and cause and end of every evil" (14:27). For this author, idolatry goes hand in hand with deception. "It was not enough for them to err about the knowledge of God, but though living in great strife due to ignorance, they call such great evils peace" (14:22).[44] Paul concluded that those who practiced such evils as he had listed "deserve to die" (1:32). In similar fashion the sage had written about God punishing "those deserving of death" (12:20).[45]

The author of the book of Wisdom did not single out gay and lesbian activity for particular mention, but he clearly attributed the evil of sexual immorality to the worship of idols. "The idea of making idols was the beginning of fornication (*archē . . . porneias*)," he stated (Wis. 14:12) Some verses later he wrote, "they [idolaters] no longer keep either their lives or their marriages pure, but they . . . grieve one another by adultery" (14:24). As he continued his vice list, the sage cited sexual perversion, disorder in marriages, adultery, and debauchery among the evils that have come about as the result of idolatry (14:26).

Paul attributed the evils that humans commit to their debased mind (v. 28) and their sexual misconduct to the lusts of their hearts (v. 24) and their degrading passions (v. 26). Lust and passion appear to be almost demonic powers at work in the lives of those who do not acknowledge God. God turns idolaters over to these malevolent forces. Lust and passion are the means that God uses to punish those who do not acknowledge him. Divine retribution takes the form of idolaters suffering in their own bodies, by means of which they engage in various forms of sexual immorality.

The author of Wisdom also portrayed God as a judge[46] who hands idolaters over to hostile powers with the result that idolaters suffer from the disorder of their own sin: "You sent upon them a multitude of irrational creatures to punish them, so that they might learn that one is punished by the very things by which one sins" (11:15b–16). In Wisdom, the plagues of creatures serve to inflict punishment on idolaters. In Romans the bondage of lust is the instrument of divine vengeance.

A HERMENEUTICAL NOTE

Apart from the brief mentions of homosexuality in the vice catalogues of 1 Cor. 6:9–10 and 1 Tim. 1:9–10, Rom. 1:26–27 is the only passage in the New Testament that explicitly and at some length speaks about homoeroticism. In his letter to the Romans, Paul is not attempting to give a teaching on homoeroticism. Rather, he is reflecting the common opinion of his times on the nature of homosexual activity.[47] His discourse, although situated within a theological framework, is comparable to that of his Hellenistic Jewish contemporaries and the philosophic moralists. To a large extent that discourse is dominated by the Stoic idea of "nature," an idea that Jewish authors would use but only insofar as they deemed nature to have been created by God.

All statements made by human beings, including those written by inspired biblical authors, are limited by the worldview of those who wrote them. Paul shares with his contemporaries the idea that by nature and by creation there are men and women. He would not have known, as do moderns, that there are individual men and women who have an inclination toward the same sex, whether that attraction be genetically or culturally induced. The way in which Paul writes about homoerotic activity indicates that he has in mind women who willingly forgo their sexual attraction for men in order to participate in lesbian activity with other women. Similarly he writes about men who abandoned natural intercourse with women to pursue homoerotic activity with men. Paul's language, "exchanged natural intercourse" and "giving up natural intercourse," indicates that he is thinking of those who willingly forgo their natural sexual activity in order to participate in same-sex sexual activity. His verbs, "exchange" (*metēllaxan*) for women and "giving up" (*aphentes*) for men, suggests an element of free will and deliberate choice that may not be present in those who are naturally attracted to members of their own sex.

To say that Paul did not intend to speak of those who were naturally attracted to members of their own sex goes beyond the evidence of his words. A person of his own times, he would not have known that some people are naturally attracted in a sexual way to members of their own gender. Paul deemed homoerotic activity to be contrary to God's creative intention for humankind and an expression of God's wrath on idolatrous humanity. How Paul's views bear on the formation of contemporary moral norms and the Christian conscience is a matter that goes beyond the interpretation of the Pauline text.[48]

NOTES

1. That is, the churches of Galatia; see Gal. 1:2.
2. Other scholars have described Romans as Paul's last will and testament.

3. The doxology, with its responsive "Amen," stems from the apostle's Pharisaic heritage and his rabbinic training.

4. One-third of the occurrences of the "wrath of God" in the New Testament are in Romans (12 of 36 instances). Among the other authentic Pauline letters, 1 Thessalonians speaks of God's wrath (1:10; 2:16; 5:9). In the Deutero-Pauline literature the motif occurs in Ephesians (2:3; 4:31; 5:6), and Colossians (3:6, 8). After Romans, the theme is most often taken up in the book of Revelation.

5. See also 2:8; 5:9; 1 Thess. 1:10; 5:9; cf. Rom 3:5; 4:15; 9:22.

6. Although some authors maintain that the revelation of God's wrath mentioned in 1:18 refers to the future, eschatological manifestation of divine judgment, the parallelism between 1:17a and 1:18a strongly suggests that Paul is writing in 1:18 about the present manifestation of God's wrath.

7. J. A. T. Robinson, *Wrestling with Romans* (Philadelphia: Fortress, 1979), 18.

8. The use of the catalogue of vices in 1:29–31 is less emotive than the description of homoerotic activity in 1:26–27. In 2:1–3:31 Paul develops a logical argument to show how Jews are also sinners. This is the rhetorical argument from *logos*. Not all the elements of an argument that appeared "logical" to a Hellenistic reader may appear logical to a contemporary reader.

9. The social world of Paul, a first-century Jew, is relatively simple. It consists of Jews and Gentiles, the people and the nations.

10. Male prostitutes are mentioned in 1 Kgs. 14:24; 15:12; 22:46; 2 Kgs. 23:6–7; and Deut. 23:17. Female prostitutes are cited in Hos. 4:14; Gen. 38:21–22; and Deut. 23:17. See John Day, "Baal," *ABD* 1:545–49; and Joseph P. Healey, "Fertility Cults," *ABD* 2:791–93.

11. On idolatry as the source of all evils, see also *Ep. Arist.* 132–38; *Sib. Or.* 3:8–45; Josephus, *Against Apion* 2.34–36 §§236–54; *T. Naph.* 3:3–5; Philo, *Special Laws* 1.13–31.

12. See *T. Reub.* 4:6; *T. Sim.* 5:3; *Sipre Deut.* 171; *Sipra Lev.* 13:7.

13. See Josephus, *Against Apion* 2.25 §199. Commenting on rabbinic literature, Michael Satlow writes of "the concentration by Palestinian rabbis on marriage and procreation" and of procreation as "the goal of sex" (*Tasting the Dish: Rabbinic Rhetorics of Sexuality,* Brown Judaic Studies 303 [Atlanta: Scholars Press, 1995], 324).

14. The threefold use of "God gave them up" may correspond to the threefold use of "exchange" in vv. 23, 25, and 26. If so, the triadic pairing suggests the vicious circle of human sin. See James D. G. Dunn, *Romans 1–8,* WBC 38A (Dallas, Tex.: Word, 1988), 53.

15. See Matt. 5:25; 10:17, 19; 24:9; 27:2; Mark 13:9, 11; 15:1; Luke 12:58; 20:20; 21:12; 24:20; John 18:30, 35; Acts 8:3; 12:4; 21:11; 22:4; 27:1; 28:17.

16. See Ceslas Spicq, "*paradidōmi*," *TLNT* 3:13–23, esp. 23. Spicq cites several papyri that illustrate the judicial use of the term. In the New Testament the verb is also used in another technical sense, namely, when it denotes the rabbinic-like process of faithfully handing down traditions.

17. Herbert Preisker, "*misthos, ktl.,*" *TDNT* 4:695–706, esp. 702.

18. Impurity appears on Pauline vice lists in 2 Cor. 12:21 and Gal. 5:19; cf. Eph. 5:3, 5; Col. 3:5. The term *akatharsia*, "impurity," denotes sexual impurity in such extrabiblical texts as *1 Enoch* 10:11; *T. Jud.* 14:5; *T. Jos.* 4:6.

19. Paul's words in this regard are echoed in Eph. 4:17–24. Ephesians lacks, however, Paul's judicial frame of reference. On the other hand, it adds a christological perspective that is absent from Rom. 1:18–32.

20. Robin Scroggs holds that v. 27 specifically concerns pederasty, but this narrow interpretation is not justified by the context in which Paul parallels lesbian activity among women with homoerotic activity among men (*The New Testament and Homosexuality: Contextual Background for Contemporary Debate* [Philadelphia: Fortress, 1983], 115).

21. In the Decalogue, the classic formulation of Judeo-Christian morality, the prohibition of idolatry comes before any other prohibition. It is not one among many sins; it is the sin from which all others flow.

22. *Pace* Peter J. Tomson, *Paul and the Jewish Law: Halakha in the Letters of the Apostle to the Gentiles*, CRINT 3/1 (Assen: Van Gorcum; Minneapolis: Fortress, 1990), 94 n. 157, v. 26 describes lesbian activity, not some form of unnatural intercourse between women and men. See Richard B. Hays, "Relations Natural and Unnatural: A Response to John Boswell's Exegesis of Romans 1," *Journal of Religious Ethics* 14 (1986): 184–215.

23. See Wilhelm Kroll, "Kinaidos," *Paulys Real-Encylopädie der classischen Altertumwissenschaft* (Stuttgart: Metzler; Munich: Druckenmüller, 1921), 459–62; idem, "Knabenliebe," ibid., 897–906; idem, "Römische Erotik," *Zeitschrift für Sexualwissenschaft und Sexualpolitik* 17 (1930–31): 145–78; Hans Licht [= Paul Brandt], *Sexual Life in Ancient Greece* (London: Routledge & Kegan Paul, 1932; reprint, New York: AMS, 1974), 411–98. See above, pp. 90–92.

24. See, for example, the legend of Zeus's attraction for Ganymede and the tales of Nero's seduction of young boys.

25. Lev. 18:22; 20:13. See prohibitions 350–52 among the 613 commandments of the law.

26. 1 Kgs. 14:24; 15:12; 22:46; 2 Kgs. 23:7.

27. Cf. *Sib. Or.* 3.594–600, "Greatly, surpassing all men, they are mindful of holy wedlock, and they do not engage in impious intercourse with male children, as do Phoenicians, Egyptians, and Romans, spacious Greece and many nations of others, Persians and Galatians and all Asia, transgressing the holy law of immortal God, which they transgressed."

28. In Colson's LCL translation of Philo's *Special Laws, androgynos* is rendered as "man-woman" in 3.38 and as "hybrid of man and woman" in 3.40.

29. Similarly Philo writes that "these persons are rightly judged worthy of death" (*Special Laws* 3.38).

30. Use of the term "nature" evokes Stoic ideas about the law of nature. See James B. DeYoung, "The Meaning of 'Nature' in Romans 1 and Its Implications for Biblical Proscriptions of Homosexual Behavior," *JETS* 31 (1988): 429–41.

31. In most contexts, the Greek phrase *para physin* would be translated "contrary to nature." Philo uses the expression *para physin* in a discussion of homoerotic activity in *Special Laws* 3.39, as does Josephus in *Against Apion* 2.38 §§273, 275. See also Philo, *Abraham* 137; *Special Laws* 2.50; *T. Naph.* 3:4–5; Pseudo-Phocylides 190–91. In the NRSV translation of 1:26, the Greek phrase (*eis*) *tēn para physin* is reflected in the words "for unnatural."

32. With reference to Philo's *Abraham* 135, Helmut Koester notes that "very typical is the emphasis on sexual aberrations as a violation of natural law." See H. Koester, *"physis, ktl.," TDNT* 9:251–77, esp. 269.

33. Hellenistic rhetoricians distinguish among three forms of rhetorical argument: the argument from the prestige of the rhetor (*ethos*), the argument that is based on an appeal to the audience (*pathos*), and the argument that is based on reason (*logos*). An argument that is intended to elicit an emotional response from the audience would be weakened were it to be "complicated" with explanations and syllogistic arguments.

34. This theme is developed in great detail by Philo in *Special Laws* 3.37–42.

35. Paul's use of *orexis* to connote homoerotic passion is unique in the New Testament. Elsewhere, however, he does write about being "inflamed with passion" (*pyrousthai*, 1 Cor. 7:9; cf. Sir. 23:16).

36. The Greek is *ou monon ta sōmata malakotēti kai thrypsei gynaikountes, alla kai tas psychas agennesteras apergazomenoi.* Translated rather literally these words mean "not only did they make their bodies female by 'male prostitution' and voluptuousness but they also hindered their lower born souls." Philo's *malakotēti* ("luxury" in the Loeb edition) is akin to Paul's *malakoi* (1 Cor. 6:9), which the NRSV renders as "male prostitution." See the discussion above, pp. 86–90.

37. Thus, Eduard Schweizer in *TDNT* 7:1045, who writes: "In translation of *basar* it [*sōma*] replaces *sarx* about one out of seven times. This is especially so when what is in view is neither man's transitoriness nor his flesh as distinct from his bones but bodily man in his totality." Writing of the related adverb, "bodily" (*sōmatikōs*), Ceslas Spicq says, "it would probably be better to translate 'personally' in the only three papyri in which it is attested" (see Spicq, *"sōmatikōs," TLNT* 3:358). See further E. Schweizer and Friedrich Baumgärtel, *"sōma, ktl.," TDNT* 7:1024–94; E. Schweizer, *"sōma," EDNT* 3:321–25; Rudolf Bultmann, *Theology of the New Testament* (New York: Scribner's, 1951), 1:191–203; Robert Jewett, *Paul's Anthropological Terms: A Study of their Use in Conflict Settings,* AGJU 10 (Leiden: Brill, 1971), 201–304.

38. In Paul's theology of the resurrection of the body, the body must be "inspirited" so that it is able to live the resurrected, "spiritual" life (see 1 Cor. 15:35–50; see also Ezekiel's vision of the dry bones in chapter 37). Paul views the resurrection of the body as a new creation.

39. See Schweizer, *"sōma,"* 3:322.

40. See Satlow, *Tasting the Dish,* 201–3. Within the collection of the 613 commandments, prohibitions 348 and 349 ban bestiality committed by a man and by a woman, respectively. Prohibitions 350–52 ban homosexuality among males, particularly with one's father (cf. Lev. 18:7) or one's uncle (cf. Lev. 18:14) as a partner.

41. Cf. Halvor Moxnes, who writes, "In a significant departure from the almost complete silence on female homosexuality in antiquity, Paul also speaks of women breaking with sex roles," in *The Social World of Formative Christianity and Judaism: Essays in Tribute to Howard Clark Kee,* ed. Jacob Neusner et al. (Philadelphia: Fortress Press, 1988), 207–18, esp. 213.

42. See Satlow, *Tasting the Dish,* 188–92.

43. For some examples, see Joseph A. Fitzmyer, *Romans,* AB 33 (New York: Doubleday, 1993), 286.

44. See also Wis. 12:24: "they went far astray on the paths of error" (*tōn planēs hodōn makroteron*). "Error" (*planēs*) is the very word used by Paul in 1:27. The related verb, "to go astray" (*planaō*), used by the sage in Wis. 12:24, recurs in 13:6 as he begins to describe the error of those who go astray. See also Wis. 13:6–9; cf. 14:22.

45. On human mortality, see also Wis. 15:3, 8–9.

46. Judicial language—"judge," "judgment," "punish," "condemnation," and so forth—is sprinkled throughout Wisdom 11–15.

47. Cf. Bernadette J. Brooten, *Love Between Women: Early Christian Responses to Female Homoeroticism* (Chicago: University of Chicago Press, 1996), 215–302.

48. See Gerald T. Sheppard, "The Use of Scripture within the Christian Ethical Debate Concerning Same-Sex Oriented Persons," *USQR* 40 (1985): 13–35; Hays, "Relations Natural and Unnatural"; Raymond E. Brown, *An Introduction to the New Testament,* ABRL (New York: Doubleday, 1997), 530.

9

Revisionist Paul

T HE LETTERS THAT PAUL WROTE to Christians living in the provin-
cial capitals of Macedonia and Achaia and that which he wrote
to Christians living in the imperial capital itself contain much
of what the New Testament has explicitly to say about human sexuality. Later texts that bear the apostle's name are remarkably devoid of
any explicit teaching on sexuality and have little to say by way of
moral exhortation with regard to sex. Exceptions are the lists of vices
scattered throughout the Pauline pseudepigrapha (Eph. 4:31; 5:3–5;
Col. 3:5–8; 1 Tim. 1:9–10; 2 Tim. 3:2–4; Titus 3:3).[1]

EPHESIANS 4:17–24

Apart from its vice lists in chapters 4 and 5, the Epistle to the Ephesians contains two passages that are pertinent to a study of sexual
ethics and the New Testament, 4:17–24 and 5:22–33. To a great extent
Eph. 4:17–24 echoes Rom. 1:18–32. Particularly striking are the similarities between 4:17c–18a and Rom. 1:21 and between 4:19 and Rom.
1:24. Eph. 4:17–24 is, nonetheless, so dependent on Col. 3:5–11 that
the pericope must have been a revision of the Colossians passage that
was made for the benefit of a different Christian readership.[2] Col.
3:5–11 describes the earthly way of life that must be put to death. It
features two lists of vices. The first, Col. 3:5, highlights a variety of
sexual transgressions, specifically, fornication, impurity, passion, and
evil desire, and connects these with greed "which is idolatry."[3] "On

147

account of these," says the author (3:6), "the wrath of God is coming on those who are disobedient."

The second list, Col. 3:8, features five vices that pertain to anti-social attitudes and behavior. These vices illustrate an old way of life that must be stripped off. Contrasting with the old way of life is a new way of life with which God's chosen people must be clothed. To characterize the new way of life, the author of Colossians speaks of forgiveness, love, and peace (3:13–15), in addition to the virtues of compassion, kindness, humility, meekness, and patience, which are listed in 3:12. What the author has given us is a version of the two ways, a familiar topos in Jewish writings,[4] employed in a then-now parenetic pattern.

The reviser responsible for Eph. 4:17–24 used the vice list that he found in Col. 3:5. He has written an exposition in two parts. The first part is an exhortation that Christians not live as Gentiles live (4:17–19). It is this section that is most reminiscent of Rom. 1:18–32, with its references to the darkened minds, the futility, and the ignorance of the Gentiles. To characterize the behavioral consequences of this ignorance, the author of Ephesians says that Gentiles "have lost all sensitivity and have abandoned[5] themselves to licentiousness, greedy to practice every kind of impurity" (4:19). This characterization takes over two vices, impurity and greed, from the list of vices in Col. 3:5, adding to them the vice of licentiousness (*aselgeia*).

The vice of sexual debauchery, licentiousness, about which Plato had written and Demosthenes had railed, had appeared in a list of vices in 2 Cor. 12:21 and Gal. 5:19. Using familiar imagery of conduct that belongs to the night and is therefore not appropriate for Christians who are children of the day (see 1 Thess. 5:4–8; cf. Eph. 5:8–14), Paul had used the expression "debauchery and licentiousness" (*koitais*[6] *kai aselgeiais*) in Rom. 13:13. Together with greed, a vice that Jews typically associated with Gentiles, the sexual vices of licentiousness and impurity are cited as examples of the Gentiles' way of life, which is no longer to be lived by the Christians of Ephesus (4:17–20). As Paul does in Rom. 1:24–27, the author of Ephesians singles out sexual misbehavior as characteristic of those who are alienated from God by reason of their ignorance.

The way of life to be practiced by those who have learned Christ ought to be different from that of the Gentiles, who are ignorant of God (4:20). Those who know Christ are to put off the old self and be renewed in spirit. The second part of the author's parenesis (4:21–24) describes a way of life that is appropriate for Christians. Using various motifs from baptismal catechesis, the author portrays "the new self (*ton kainon anthrōpon*), created according to the likeness of God in true righteousness and holiness" (4:24). The new self has put away the old self (*ton palaion anthrōpon*) with its lust arising from deception.[7]

That Christology is the basis for the moral exhortation of the Epistle to the Ephesians[8] is clearly to be seen on any reading of Eph. 4:17–24. The author introduces his parenesis by saying, "this I affirm and insist on in the Lord" (4:17). Then, in the transition between the two parts of his exhortation, he writes: "This is not the way you learned Christ! For surely you have heard about him and were taught in him, as truth is in Jesus" (4:20–21). The author does not provide his readers with an epistemology that allows for one's mind to appreciate how knowledge of Christ and being taught in him leads to the conviction that licentiousness, impurity, and lust are characteristic of the old self and are to be put off by those who would put on a new self. Parenesis does not offer explanations; it offers challenge. The challenge of 4:17-24 is the necessity of putting off the old self with its licentiousness, impurity, and lust so that one can put on a new self in Christ Jesus.

EPHESIANS 5:3–5

The author of the Epistle to the Ephesians makes further use of the Colossians list of vices in another hortatory unit, 5:3–5. Three of the six vices of Col. 3:5—fornication, impurity, and greed—recur in Eph. 5:3 when the author writes "but fornication and impurity of any kind, or greed must not even be mentioned among you, as is proper among saints." The passage begins with an adversative "but" (*de*), which contrasts the life of love to which the Christian is called as a result of having been loved by God and his Christ (Eph. 5:1–2) with a life of fornication, impurity, and greed. So far removed from the Christian should these vices be that they should not even be a topic of conversation[9] within the Christian community.

The author of the Epistle to the Colossians had characterized the Colossians' former way of life as one corrupted by vices of various sorts, among which the sexual vices are given prominent mention. The author of Ephesians cites these vices not so much to describe the Ephesians' previous way of life as to characterize the life of those who have not been called to be God's holy people. He capitalizes on a synchronic rather than a diachronic contrast. Rather than use the then-now schema of Colossians,[10] the author of Ephesians uses a kind of outsider-insider or them-us schema. This is in keeping with the nature of the epistle, which is almost a treatise on ecclesiology. Its contents, though largely dependent on Colossians, are presented in a more reflective and abstract fashion than are the more personal descriptions and exhortations found in Colossians.

The author of the Epistle to the Ephesians likes groups of threes. In Eph. 5:3–5, so heavily dependent on the list of 5 + 1 vices in Col. 3:5, the author gives three lists, each of which consists of three vices, fornication, impurity, and greed (v. 3), obscene, silly, and vulgar talk (v. 4), and fornication, impurity, and greed (+ idolatry, v. 5). In the first triad the author speaks not simply of impurity (*akatharsia*) but of impurity of every sort (*akatharsia pasa*). He wants his audience to avoid a minimalist reading of his exhortation.

"Greed" (*pleonexia*) is one of the most frequently mentioned vices in the various New Testament catalogues,[11] but one must ask if it was the sin of avarice that the author had in mind when he put together the triad of vices that appear in Eph. 5:3, 5. To be sure, the philosophic moralists knew greed to be one of the most cancerous of vices. "Greed," wrote Menander, "is a very great evil for humans; for those who wish to have their neighbors' goods often fail and are vanquished" (*Florilegium* 10.3).

Plutarch, however, associates greed with debauchery, soft living, and luxury (*Agis* 3.1; 10.3), and Jewish writings link desire for another person's goods with desire for another person's wife. Philo associates greed with licentiousness (*akolasia*, a word not used in the New Testament) and contrasts the two vices with self-control (*egkrateia*) (see *Special Laws* 1.173). Within the New Testament greed is often associated with carnal disorders.[12] Paul uses the related verb "exploit" (*pleonekteō*) in the context of his discussion of adultery in 1 Thess. 4:6.[13] Coveting a woman,[14] the most important of a neighbor's possessions, was banned by the tenth commandment (Exod. 20:17).[15] *The Testament of the Twelve Patriarchs* and various Qumran texts link covetousness with sexual immorality (see *T. Levi* 14:6–7; *T. Jud.* 18:2; 1QS 4:9, 10; CD 4:17). With this as a frame of reference, it is likely that the author of Ephesians had desire for another man's wife in mind when he joined "greed," that is, illicit desire, to fornication and impurity in 5:3 and 5:5.[16]

In 5:5 the author of the Epistle to the Ephesians creates an *inclusio* forming 5:3–5 as a distinct subunit within a larger exhortation. Eph. 5:5 repeats the three vices of 5:3, using personal nouns to identify those who practice the three vices rather than using the abstract nouns that he had used in 5:3. He adds to his description an interpretive remark, "that is, an idolater." The idea that anyone who submits to excessive and illicit sexual desire is an idolater is a notion that the author of Ephesians has taken over from Col. 3:5. The idea is, however, one that is found in Rom. 1:18–32 and is suggested in many of the New Testament's catalogues of vices.[17] For these New Testament authors the sin of idolatry manifests itself in various forms of sexual disorders.

Between the two triads that speak of fornication, impurity, and illicit desire, the author of Ephesians has inserted a third triad—obscene, silly, and vulgar talk (5:4). Control of the tongue is a well-known topos in the writings of the philosophic moralists. Within the New Testament this concern is most graphically expressed in Jas. 3:1–12 (cf. Col. 3:8–9; 4:6), but it is of no little concern to the author of Ephesians as well (cf. 4:15, 29, 31). The three kinds of speech cited in 5:4 are identified by words that do not otherwise appear in the New Testament, "obscene" (*aischrotēs*), "silly" (*mōrologia*), and "vulgar" (*eutrapelia*) talk. In 4:29 the author had encouraged Christians to ban every sort of evil talk (*pas logos sapros*) from their mouths. Now he specifies that obscene, silly, and vulgar talk are to be excluded. Although they do not occur elsewhere in the New Testament, it would seem that the three nouns identify various forms of sexually offensive speech.

"Obscene" talk is foul language.[18] "Vulgar" talk is identified by the word *eutrapelia*, which connotes witty speech. Yet even Aristotle was aware that not all witticisms were appropriate. He writes of the follies of youth that "they are fond of laughter, and therefore witty (*eutrapeloi*); for wit (*eutrapelia*) is cultured insolence" (*Rhetoric* 2.12.12). The witticism to which the author of 5:4 refers may be ribaldry[19]—hence, the translation "vulgar talk." "Silly" talk was a kind of foolish talk that even Aristotle identified as inappropriate. Sandwiched between "obscene" and "vulgar" language, "silly talk" must connote some form of inappropriate talk about sex.[20] The fact that this triad on inappropriate talk is enveloped between two triads that explicitly mention inappropriate sexual conduct confirms the fact that the topic of v. 4 is inappropriate sexual language.

To make his point, the author employs the rhetorical device of repetition. It is not necessary to distinguish adequately the meaning of one of his terms from another. Like Paul before him, the author makes use of three more or less synonymous terms to drive home a single point. Obscenities and dirty jokes are simply out of place in the life of a Christian whose tongue ought to be employed for thanksgiving. The author's Greek language makes it possible for him to make his point more forcefully than is apparent in an English translation of the text. His Greek text uses a clever play on words to contrast ribald speech (*eutrapelia*) with thanksgiving (*eucharistia*). The author of the Epistle to the Ephesians shares with the Hellenistic moralists and some of the other late New Testament authors a concern for the proper use of the tongue, but his is the only text in the New Testament that makes dirty jokes and obscene talk a specific concern in his moral exhortation.

The fact that v. 4 specifically mentions that sexual obscenities are really out of place in the life of a Christian may shed some light on what the author had to say in 5:3. He had said that fornication, impurity of any kind, and illicit desire were not even to be mentioned within the community. The exhortation is not to be taken literally. As the epistle is being read to the community, its members will hear about fornication, impurity, and illicit desire not once but twice (vv. 3, 5). Exhorting the members of the community not to even mention fornication, impurity, and illicit desire, as he does in v. 3, the author is not only imaginatively encouraging them to avoid this kind of activity; he is also telling them not to speak lightly or in jest about such things. Christians are to shun fornication, impurity, and illicit desire, not only in their acts (v. 5) but also in their speech (v. 3). Sexually explicit language and sexual innuendo simply do not build up the community as the speech of a Christian should do (4:29).

Within the context of its dominant ecclesiological theme, the epistle's moral exhortation is essentially a holiness ethic.[21] The author summons Christians to live as God's holy people (cf. 1:1). To motivate Christians to avoid fornication, impurity, and illicit desire the author states that this kind of conduct and this kind of talk are simply not fitting among God's holy people. His language is reminiscent not only of the philosophic moralists who wrote about what is fitting (*prepei, prepon estin*) but also of the biblical and later rabbinic idiom that spoke of behavior that is not fitting in Israel. In Eph. 5:3–5 the author's concern is for what is fitting for God's holy people, what is "proper among saints" (*prepei hagiois*, v. 3). Sexual misconduct and loose talk about sex are simply not appropriate for God's holy people.

The author adds to his community-oriented ecclesial motivation, an element of eschatological motivation. Those who are involved in sexual misconduct do not have any inheritance in the kingdom of God (v. 5). Instead, the wrath of God is to come on them (v. 6). The themes are familiar. Exclusion from the kingdom of God was the motivation used by Paul in urging the Corinthians to avoid the ten vices mentioned in 1 Cor 6:9–10, the first five of which were forms of sexual misconduct.[22] That God's wrath is manifest in the sexual depravity of those who commit idolatry was the overarching theme of Rom. 1:18–32. Presumably the author of Ephesians has taken the motivational motif of the wrath of God over from Col. 3:6.[23] The theme was, however, an important feature of Paul's apocalyptic worldview.[24] He often wrote about the wrath of God[25] in his correspondence with the Christians of Thessalonica and the holy ones in Rome.

EPHESIANS 5:22–33

One readily identifiable feature of the Paulinist's parenesis is his incorporation of a christianized household code into the epistle (5:22–6:9). As had been the case with 4:17–24 and 5:3–5, the Paulinist is dependent on the earlier Epistle to the Colossians. The earlier text also featured the use of a christianized household code (Col. 3:18–4:1). The revision that is to be found in Eph. 5:22–6:9 is developed in a much more sophisticated theological fashion than the relatively simple version found in Colossians. The Paulinist author of the Epistle to the Ephesians has brought many of his particular christological and ecclesiological insights to bear upon his revised version of the traditional topos. This is nowhere more evident than in Eph. 5:22–33, where the author writes about the relationship between husbands and wives.

The household codes in Col. 3:18–4:1 and Eph. 5:22–6:9 share a neatly balanced structure in which the three relationships that defined the Greco-Roman household are set out in parallel statements. The defining relationships are those between man and wife (5:22–33; Col. 3:18–19), parent and child (6:1–4; Col. 3:20–21), slave and master (6:5–9; Col. 3:22–4:1). In describing these relationships the code first sets out the ethical responsibility of the socially inferior member of the relationship. Wives, children, and slaves are exhorted to be subject to husbands, parents, and masters, respectively. Within each pairing, the code then speaks of the responsibility of the socially superior per-

son toward the socially inferior person. Husbands are exhorted to love
their wives. Fathers are encouraged not to provoke their children.[26]
Masters are urged to treat their slaves justly. That the code speaks as
matter-of-factly as it does about masters and their slaves is an indication that the topos itself is conditioned by time and culture. In the
form in which it appears in Ephesians and Colossians, the household
code is a plea for social order within the Christian household as it
made its way in the Greco-Roman world of the late first century C.E.

Eph. 5:22–33 has nothing explicit to say about the role of sexuality
within marriage,[27] but it does provide the reader, both ancient and
modern, with some ideas that are pertinent to a Christian understanding of marriage.[28] These elements are lacking in the two verses of
Colossians addressed to wives and husbands. In Colossians' version of
the household code wives are urged to be subject to their husbands "as
is fitting in the Lord" (Col. 3:18). Husbands are exhorted to love their
wives and never treat them harshly (Col. 3:19); that is, they are not to
become bitter toward their wives.[29] Among the notions that the author
of Ephesians advances is the ecclesial dimension of marriage. From his
perspective the husband–wife relationship is not only the nuclear cell
of society, it is also integral to the life of the church itself. A related
idea is that the love that husbands are to extend to their wives should
reflect the love that Christ has for the church.

In 5:31, the author of Ephesians quotes the Yahwist's adage, "for this
reason a man will leave his father and mother and be joined to his wife,
and the two will become one flesh" (Gen. 2:24). The biblical verse is
also cited in Matt. 19:5 and Mark 10:7–8. In abbreviated form it appears
in 1 Cor. 6:16. The two-in-one flesh of which the Yahwist wrote
bespeaks the intimacy of life and the strength of the bond that joins
husband to wife, but it also evokes their physical relationship, the joining of their flesh in sexual intercourse. A philosophic moralist might
have used the words of a well-known sage to support his parenesis. By
citing Gen. 2:24, the author of Ephesians focuses his vision of marriage
within the age-old Judeo-Christian tradition. His use of that particular
scripture serves to remind his readers that physical sexual union is
integral to the marital relationship.

"MARRIED ONLY ONCE"

The three so-called Pastoral Epistles, two to Timothy and one to Titus,
clearly stand within the Pauline tradition. The oldest of the three may

well be the Epistle to Titus. It begins with an epistolary *intitulatio,* which presents a richly hued portrayal of the apostle Paul (Titus 1:1–3). Paul's ministry is located "in due time," at the opportune moment, within a temporal perspective that starts before the ages began and ends with hope of eternal life. From a literary point of view the presentation of Paul in Titus 1:1-3 serves as a foreword to the three-item epistolary collection. From a rhetorical standpoint, it provides a theological warrant for the parenesis of the Epistle to Titus, eventually as a warrant for the parenesis of 1–2 Timothy as well.

For the most part the Pastoral Epistles are concerned with church order. They describe the qualities that one would like to see in those called to the ministry of overseer/bishop,[30] elder/presbyter, and servant/deacon within the church. The overseer and elder—apparently these two terms designate one and the same office holder in the Pastorals[31]—is to be "married only once" (Titus 1:6). A similar expectation is set out for overseers in 1 Tim. 3:2 and for servants in 1 Tim. 3:12. A senior citizen who is to be enrolled as a "widow" must likewise have been "married only once" (1 Tim. 5:9).

In each instance the phrase "married only once" occurs in a brief description of the would-be elder, overseer, servant, or widow as a good family person. The technical phrase is, literally, "the husband of one wife" for men and "the wife of one husband" for women. It presupposes that those who are recognized as being capable of exercising these respective functions within the church have been married. It does not, however, so much set forth the requirement that they be married, as an expectation that they be faithful to a single spouse.

What sort of fidelity does the phrase envision?[32] This is a difficult question for a contemporary person to answer, yet the answer must have been obvious to the readers of the Pastorals since the phrase is repeated four times and never explained. The phrase excludes polygamy and polyandry, but the prohibition of bigamy would seem not to have been the reason why officeholders were to have but one wife and enrolled widows to have had but one husband. Nothing suggests that polygamy or polyandry were issues for first-century Christians.

The technical phrase implies marital fidelity and the avoidance of sexual immorality. That a Christian would shun sexual immorality and refrain from adultery was a given in the Pauline communities of the first century. Why then specify that elders, overseers, and servants have but one wife and that enrolled widows have had but one husband? The situation of the widow might provide a clue to the meaning of the technical phrase. A woman who is to be enrolled in the order of widows must be a woman who is no longer married. Having arrived at the age of sixty, those who look upon her know that she has had only one husband. The widow who is qualified for enrollment as a widow is one who did not remarry after the death of her husband. It is likely that the phrase "married only once," as this NRSV translation implies, means that the would-be officeholder is a person who, should his wife have died or he be divorced, would not have remarried.[33]

For the officeholder and the enrolled widow to have but one spouse in their lifetimes would have been counter-cultural in the first-century Roman Empire. Both the *lex Julia* of 18 B.C.E. and the *lex Papia Poppaea* of 9 C.E. strongly encouraged widows and unmarried men to get married. The expectation that within the church male officeholders and older women who were to be enrolled among the widows should have married and raised a family is likewise a rejection of that skewed asceticism that held that it was good for a man not to touch a woman.

A NOTE ON MARRIAGE

The situation in which the Pastoral Epistles were written was one in which the pastor[34] had to deal with people who forbade marriage and required abstinence from some foods (1 Tim. 4:3). A similar problem, at least with regard to sex and marriage, had confronted the church of Corinth (1 Cor. 7:1). A century later, the *Acts of Paul and Thecla* would portray Paul as preaching "the word of God concerning continence and resurrection" (5). In his preaching, Paul was to have offered as an interpretation of "Blessed are the pure in heart" (Matt. 5:8), "Blessed are the continent, for to them will God speak. Blessed are they who have renounced this world, for they shall be well pleasing unto God. Blessed are they who have wives as if they had them not, for they shall inherit God" (ibid. 5). Later in this apocryphal late-second-century text, Paul is presented as a model of prayer and fasting (cf. *Acts of Paul and Thecla* 23).

The situation to which 1 Tim. 4:3 refers is similar to that of mid-first-century Corinth and late-second-century Asia Minor. It is almost impossible to identify the source of the pastor's problem with any certainty. Most likely it arose from a kind of asceticism that was soon to be identified with various Gnosticizing movements[35] in the Mediterranean basin. The pastor has harsh words for those who are the source of the problem. He characterizes them as belonging to an apocalyptic movement that paid attention to deceitful spirits and the teachings of demons (1 Tim. 4:1). Those who propose such teaching are liars whose consciences are seared with a hot iron (1 Tim. 4:2).

Obviously the pastor has no tolerance for those who would forbid marriage and mandate dietary asceticism. Nonetheless, he does offer a brief theological critique of their position (1 Tim. 4:3–5). He reminds his flock that everything that God had created, including the distinction between the sexes, was good, indeed very good (Genesis 1). Faithful Christians should give thanks to God for the gifts of creation.

In encouraging the putative Timothy to take a bit of wine for the sake of his stomach and because of his ailments (1 Tim. 5:23), the pastor rejects the abstinence proposed by the false teachers. His words about women (1 Tim. 2:9–15), typical of the era, extol the feminine virtue of "modesty." The pastor concludes his statement on women with a word of encouragement, "she will be saved through childbearing, providing they continue in faith and love and holiness, with modesty" (1 Tim. 2:15). Luke Timothy Johnson suggests that the exceptive clause defines women's role domestically.[36] In fact it describes the quality of their lives in terms of their Christian commitment, faith, love, and holiness, and their feminine virtue, modesty.

That the verb in the exceptive clause is in the plural and the verb in the first part of the verse is in the singular constitutes part of the difficulty of understanding what the pastor meant when he wrote "she will be saved through childbearing."[37] The most plausible interpretation of the text is that the pastor is affirming that a woman's salvation is assured through her engagement in family life, rather than in any Gnosticizing attempt to attain salvation by avoiding marriage and childbearing. The mere fact of bearing children is, however, not an automatic ticket for salvation. The woman who seeks salvation must lead a Christian life and have the appropriate social virtues.

The pastor's use of household codes and his emphasis on family life and the social virtues suggest that the most likely reading of 1 Tim. 2:15 is one that encourages women to marry and raise a family.[38] In similar fashion, far from avoiding marriage altogether or abstaining from sex within marriage, church leaders were expected to be recognized as good individuals with wife and family. Their ability to run their own households was an indication of their ability to lead the household of the church.[39] "If someone does not know how to manage his own household, how can he take care of God's church?" asks the author of 1 Tim. 3:5.

ADVICE FOR YOUNG PEOPLE

In contrast to older widows, whose single marriage was considered to be meritorious and a condition for her being enrolled among the widows, younger widows are urged to marry, have children, and be competent managers of their own households (1 Tim. 5:14). One of the reasons why young widows are encouraged to marry is their sexual passion. "When their sensual desires alienate them from Christ," writes the pastor, "they want to marry" (1 Tim. 5:11). The intensive form of the verb, "to have sensual desires" (*katastrēniaō*[40]) presumes that the young woman has strong sexual needs. Her desires may alienate her from Christ. It is difficult to understand what the pastor means when he speaks of a young widow's strong sexual desires alienating her from Christ.[41] He relates this to her desire to remarry. A young widow's second marriage might alienate her from Christ insofar as it would not have been well regarded in a society that highly esteemed young, chaste widows.[42] This would have given non-Christians opportunity to revile the church, the household of God (1 Tim. 4:14). Alternatively, it may be that a young widow's desire to marry might lead her to marry a non-Christian (cf. 1 Cor. 7:39) and all too quickly worship the gods of her husband rather than remain committed in her fidelity to Christ.[43] Given the strength of her passion, the realistic pastor counsels a young widow to remarry (cf. 1 Cor. 7:9) and raise a family.

According to the household code of Titus 2:1–6, it was the responsibility of the older women to encourage young women to love their husbands and their children, to be self-controlled (*sōphronas*[44]) and chaste (*hagnas*[45]). In the context of this household code, suggests Jerome Quinn, the young woman's chastity implies a young wife's fidelity to her husband.[46]

A young woman was also expected to be self-controlled. In a short treatise on virtues and vices, Aristotle described self-control as a virtue that disposes people in regard to the pleasures of the body. Its opposite, he wrote, is licentiousness (see *Rhetoric* 1.9.9). The way that the pastor writes about self-control in Titus 2:12 seems to suggest that he considers self-control to be the opposite of slavery to worldly passions (*tas kosmikas epithymias*). A Christian young woman is expected to be free from slavery to worldly passions. It is not only the young woman who was expected to be self-controlled. Young men and old men as well[47] are similarly encouraged to be self-controlled (Titus 2:6); cf.

Philo, *Special Laws* 1.138). Self-control[48] is a quality that one expects to find in a man who would be an overseer in the church (1 Tim. 3:2; Titus 1:8; cf. 2 Tim. 1:7).

The philosophic moralists distinguished the self-control of a man from the self-control of a woman (cf. Aristotle, *Politics* 1.13.9). Self-control (*sōphrosynē*) was considered to be a distinctively feminine virtue (cf. 1 Tim. 2:9, 15). Among the philosophic moralists it was considered to be the most important virtue for a woman, especially a young woman, to have. A young woman's self-control implied that she was modest, well-ordered in her life, chaste in her marriage, and above reproach. A woman's "self-control" was the epitome of her feminine virtue.

That his children are not given over to debauchery (*asōtias*) is an indication that the overseer is a good family man (Titus 1:6; cf. 1 Tim. 3:4). Aristotle speaks of this kind of debauchery in his *Nicomachean Ethics.* "We label as prodigal those who are incontinent and those who become spendthrifts to satisfy their intemperance. That is why prodigals have such a bad reputation; they have several vices all at once" (4.1). The debauched life was one of considerable excess in food, drink, and sex. Hellenistic Jews and Jewish Christians considered debauchery to be a vice of Gentiles (cf. 2 Macc. 6:4; 1 Pet. 4:4). The debauchery that took place in the temple at the time of its profanation by Antiochus Epiphanes was legendary. "The temple was filled with debauchery and reveling by the Gentiles, who dallied with prostitutes and had intercourse with women within the sacred precincts" (2 Macc. 6:4). Debauchery of this or another sort should not exist among the children of a man who aspired to church leadership.

In the exercise of their pastoral ministry, church leaders have responsibilities toward all people, men as well as women, the old as well as the young. The patronymic Paul of the Pastoral Epistles exhorts his disciple Timothy, the paradigm of ministry, to treat old men as fathers and old women as mothers, young men as brothers and young women as sisters (1 Tim. 5:1–2). The church leader, however, is to have a special concern for young women. They are to be treated with absolute purity (*en pasē hagneia*, 1 Tim. 5:2). Despite his presumed youth, Timothy is expected to be a model of purity (*typos . . . en hagneia*, 1 Tim. 4:12) for all believers. The prototypical church leader must be exemplary in regard to his speech and his conduct, his faith and his love, but he should also be a model of purity for the community by his chaste life.[49]

PLEASURE AND PASSION

In his descriptions of the quality of life of various types of individuals within the church, the pastor has made use of classic Hellenistic social terminology and various topoi, such as the household code, the catalogue of virtues (e.g., 1 Tim. 4:12), and the catalogue of vices.[50] Lists of vices are found in all three Pastoral Epistles. In each epistle one catalogue of vices includes some mention of sexual misdirection (1 Tim. 1:9–10; 2 Tim. 3:2–4; Titus 3:3). This list in 2 Tim. 3:2–4 contains two vices that are not mentioned elsewhere in the New Testament. The list cites "profligates" (_akrateis_, literally, "lacking control") and "lovers of pleasure" (_philēdonoi_).[51] A lack of self-control is the antithesis of the self-control that is so often extolled within the Pastorals. The love of pleasure that is characteristic of the evil of the last days is probably not so different from the "slavery to various passions and pleasures" that is cited in the vice list of Titus 3:3.

Titus 3:3 uses a catalogue of vices to describe "then" in a then-now schema of life. The pastor's catalogue includes "slavery to various passions and pleasures" as characteristic of the way of life that his now-Christian flock had once led. As the pastor extols the virtue of self-control for all segments of the population, but particularly for women, he frequently exhorts those for whom he writes to be wary of being enslaved to passion. In two key passages of the epistle, where the author writes about the manifestation of the grace of God (Titus 2:11–14; 3:1–7), "passion" (_epithymia_) is used to describe one's former way of life. That life was one of "impiety and worldly passions" (_tēn asebeian kai tas kosmikas epithymias_, Titus 2:12), a life of "various passions and pleasures" (_epithymiais kai hēdonais poikilais_, Titus 3:3).

Like the philosophic moralists of the day, the pastor had a distrust of the power of passion. Timothy, that prototype of ministry within the church, was urged to flee "youthful passions" (_tas neōterikas epithymias_, 2 Tim. 2:22) so that he might pursue a life of righteousness, faith, love, and peace with a pure heart. With an androcentric bias, the author of 2 Timothy typifies those who are easily led astray by the image of "silly women, overwhelmed by their sins and swayed by all kinds of desires (_agomena epithymiais poikilais_, 2 Tim. 3:6). In their abhorrence of passion, the Pastoral Epistles are on the same wavelength as the writings of the Stoic moralists. In some respects we could hardly expect anything different from the pastor, who expects the people and leaders of the church to lead a life that people of the times would deem to be respectable and upright.

THE EPISTLE OF JAMES

The parenetic tract known as the Epistle of James (see 1:1) can be considered under the rubric of "Revisionist Paul" insofar as its dominant thrust is to assert the validity of moral exhortation in the face of the challenge of the Pauline teaching on faith without works. Its teaching on sexuality includes an important reflection on the seventh commandment, "You shall not commit adultery" (2:11).[52] This commandment is but one of the precepts of the Decalogue. One who lives a Christian life must fulfill all of the demands of the royal law in keeping with the scripture, "You shall love your neighbor as yourself" (Jas. 2:8).

As he dialogues with the Pauline tradition on faith without works, the author of the epistle asks a provocative question, "Was not Rahab the prostitute also justified by works when she welcomed the messengers and sent them out by another road?" (2:25). The rhetorical question is provocative in and of itself;[53] it is even more provocative insofar as the author has juxtaposed Rahab the prostitute with Abraham the patriarch (Jas. 2:21–23) as examples of people who are justified by works and not by faith alone. The author of the Epistle of James does not intend to extol the harlotry of Rahab, whose story is told in Josh. 2:1–21. In Jewish tradition she was known as a proselyte (Josh. 2:11) and esteemed as a model of hospitality.[54] Unlike the author of Hebrews (Heb. 11:31), the author of James does not mention Rahab's faith. He mentions only Rahab's hospitality and her role in ensuring the safety of a pair of Israelite spies.

Jas. 2:11, on adultery, and Jas. 2:25, on Rahab, two isolated verses in the epistle of James that speak of sexual conduct, deserve more than a passing mention in a study on sexual ethics and the New Testament. It is not that they say so much; it is how they say what they do say that is important. The entire epistle with its 108 verses is a treatise of moral exhortation. Yet only two of its verses deal specifically with sexuality. The author's vision clearly considers that one's sexual life is but one aspect of one's moral and Christian life.

In addition, in each of the passages in which the author writes about human sexuality he compares and contrasts sexual conduct with other elements of the moral life. "You shall not commit adultery" is not separable from "You shall not commit murder." Together they are partial negative formulations of the royal law summed up in "You shall love your neighbor as yourself." Harlotry may have been a fact in one woman's life, but hospitality and helpfulness in a time of serious need are works of the righteous person. Sexual ethics are important, but they are not the summit of the moral life.

NOTES

1. The other vice lists in the Pauline pseudepigrapha do not include any vices that come within the purview of the present study. On the other hand, the vice list in 1 Pet. 4:3, an epistle that has been influenced by Paul, includes licentiousness and passions among its six vices.

2. With regard to the dependence of Eph. 4:17–24 on Colossians, see Andrew T. Lincoln, *Ephesians,* WBC 42 (Waco: Word, 1990), 273–74; and Helmut Merklein, "Eph 4,1–5,20 als Rezeption von Kol 3,1–17," in *Kontinuität und Einheit,* ed. P. G. Müller and Werner Stenger (Freiburg: Herder, 1981), 194–210.

3. James D. G. Dunn draws attention to the Jewish character of this list and suggests that the emphasis on sexual transgressions "presumably indicates a considerable concern among the earliest Christian leadership at the continuing attractiveness within their churches of the looser sexual standards for men in Hellenistic society of the time." See Dunn, *The Epistles to the Colossians and to Philemon: A Commentary on the Greek Text,* NIGTC (Grand Rapids: Eerdmans; Carlisle: Paternoster, 1996), 213–14; cf. Peter T. O'Brien, *Colossians, Philemon,* WBC 44 (Waco: Word, 1982), 181. Jean-Noël Aletti, however, opines that the vice list does not so much relate to practices occurring in Colossae as it is a typical list used by Jewish and Christian authors to portray a pagan way of life. See Aletti, *Saint Paul: Épitre aux Colossiens. Introduction, traduction et commentaire,* EBib (Paris: Gabalda, 1993), 224–25.

4. Cf. Pss. 1:6; 16:11; 119:33; Deut. 5:33; 11:22; Josh. 22:5; Prov. 8:13; Jer. 21:8; Zech. 1:4; *Didache* 1–5; *Barn.* 18–20; *Herm. Man.* 6:1; Ign. *Magn.* 5; *2 Clem.* 4.

5. The author uses the Greek verb *paradidōmi,* the same verb that Paul had used three times in Rom. 1:24–32 to describe God's giving idolaters over to various forms of immoral behavior.

6. The noun *koitē,* literally, "the marriage bed" (cf. Luke 11:7; Heb. 13:4) is used euphemistically for sexual intercourse in Rom. 9:10 and 13:13. See M. Silva, "New Lexical Semitisms?" *ZNW* 69 (1978): 253–57, esp. 255.

7. The expression *kata tas epithymias tēs apatēs,* "deluded by its lusts" (NRSV), is one in which lust (*epithymias*) is described as stemming from deception (*apatēs*). "Deception" (*apatē*) is not used by Paul, but it does appear in the Deutero-Pauline Col. 2:8 and 2 Thess. 2:10. It is virtually synonymous with the "error" (*planē*) used by Paul in Rom. 1:27.

8. See R. F. Collins, *Letters That Paul Did Not Write: The Epistle to the*

Hebrews and the Pauline Pseudepigrapha, GNS 28 (Wilmington, Del.: Glazier, 1988), 159–66.

9. See the use of *onomazesthō*, literally, "named" in 5:3.

10. See, however, Eph. 5:8.

11. As a noun or in adjectival form, the vice appears eight times: Mark 7:22; Rom. 1:29; 1 Cor. 5:10; 5:11; 6:10; Eph. 5:3, 5; Col. 3:5. Cf. 2 Pet. 2:14.

12. See, e.g., Mark 7:22; cf. Eph. 4:19; Col. 3:5. See Ceslas Spicq, "*pleonexia,*" *TLNT* 3:117–19, esp. 118–19.

13. See above pp. 104–6.

14. Within the biblical tradition "coveting" where goods were concerned was not merely a matter of "impure thoughts" or a desire to have more. The notion implied the kind of desire that would lead a person to fulfill his wishes insofar as he was capable of doing so. It was an impulse to action. See R. F. Collins, *Christian Morality: Biblical Foundations* (Notre Dame, Ind.: University of Notre Dame Press, 1986), 51, 61–62.

15. In the Deuteronomist's revision of the Decalogue, the wife was removed from the list of a neighbor's possessions and a new commandment was formulated that prohibited a man's coveting his neighbor's wife (Deut. 5:21). This led to an excess of commandments—eleven instead of the traditional ten. The author nonetheless continued to write about the ten words of Yahweh. The Deuteronomist's creation of a new commandment prohibiting the coveting of a neighbor's wife ultimately led to the Christian churches' enumerating the Ten Commandments in different ways.

16. "*Pleonexia,* 'covetousness,'" writes Lincoln (*Ephesians,* 322), "should also be taken as the sort of unrestrained sexual greed whereby a person assumes that others exist for his or her own gratification."

17. See 1 Cor. 5:10; 1 Pet. 4:3; Rev. 21:8; 22:15; cf. Wis. 14:12; *T. Reub.* 4:6; *T. Jud.* 19:1; 23:1.

18. Note the use of the cognate "abusive language" (*aischrologia*) in Col. 3:8. The NRSV adds a footnote to suggest that the noun might connote "filthy language." In fact, the term was used by Xenophon to characterize foul language.

19. The cognate adjective, *eutrapelos,* was used in this sense by Isocrates. P. W. Van der Horst has surveyed much of the extant literary attestation of words with the *eutrapel-* root. He notes that the meaning of the term "cannot now be discerned exactly." Several uses of the root in ancient literature indicate that the term was used of language that Christians might find offensive. These would include insinuations in the direction of shameful things and jokes at another's expense. See P. W. Van der Horst, "Is Wittiness Unchristian? A Note on *eutrapelia* in Eph. v 4," in T. Baarda, W. C. van Unnik, and A. F. J. Klijn, *Miscellanea Neotestamentica* (Leiden: Brill, 1978), 163–77.

20. The author's syndetic construction uses different conjunctions (*kai* and *ē*) to join together the three members of the triad. The first two members are joined by *kai,* forming a sort of hendiadys, "obscene and silly language." Literally, the triad reads "obscene language and silly talk or ribald speech."

21. See Collins, *Letters,* 162–63.

22. Both 1 Cor. 6:9, 10 and Eph. 5:5 speak of inheriting the kingdom of God. The apostle, however, uses the verb "to inherit," whereas the Paulinist uses

the noun "inheritance." The expression "the kingdom of Christ and of God" is unique in the New Testament (cf. Rev. 11:15), but the idea that Christ reigns in the kingdom at the present time is present in 1 Cor. 15:24–28. At "the end," the parousia, Christ will hand over the kingdom to God. That Paul introduces Christ into his moral exhortation is consistent with the overall motivational force of his parenesis. His ethical exhortation has a basis that is both christological and theological.

23. The words "the wrath of God comes on those who are disobedient" are textually the same in Col. 3:6 and Eph. 5:6. The phrase "on those who are disobedient" is, however, absent from Col. 3:6 in P[46], B, and the writings of some fathers of the church.

24. See Wilhelm Pesch, "orgē," EDNT 2:529–30.

25. The full phrase "the wrath of God" (orgē theou) appears, however, only in Rom. 1:18.

26. It is noteworthy that, while 6:1 and Col. 3:20 speak of children's responsibility to obey their parents, 6:4 and Col. 3:21 speak only of a father's responsibility toward his children.

27. 1 Cor. 7:1–7 and 1 Thess. 4:3–5 are the only New Testament texts that explicitly talk about sex in marriage. Cf. Heb. 13:4.

28. On marriage in the New Testament, see R. F. Collins, "Marriage (NT)," ABD 4:569–72.

29. As the English language phrase "be bitter" uses the metaphor of a sour fruit, so the Greek verb pikrainō used in Col. 3:19 is built on the root pikra-, which connotes bitterness to taste.

30. Lest the office of those who held leadership positions in the first Christian generations be too readily equated with office of bishop, presbyter, and deacon in the late twentieth century, I prefer to use a more literal translation of the Greek terms rather than terms that are in use to describe offices within the church today. Similarly, Luke Timothy Johnson, Letters to Paul's Delegates: 1 Timothy, 2 Timothy, Titus, The New Testament in Context (Valley Forge, Pa.: Trinity Press International, 1996), 143.

31. See Jerome D. Quinn, The Letter to Titus, AB 35 (New York: Doubleday, 1990), 88.

32. For a discussion of the various possible meanings of the phrase, see Ceslas Spicq, Saint Paul: Les Épitres pastorales, EBib (Paris: Gabalda, 1969), 1:402, 430–31; Quinn, Titus, 85–87; George W. Knight III, Commentary on The Pastoral Epistles, NIGTC (Grand Rapids: Eerdmans; Carlisle: Paternoster, 1992), 157–59, 223.

33. Similarly, Jouette M. Bassler, 1 Timothy. 2 Timothy. Titus, ANTC (Nashville: Abingdon, 1996), 66.

34. "The pastor" is a convenient epithet to designate the anonymous author of each of the three Pastoral Epistles. The epithet leaves as an open question whether or not one individual is the author of all three texts.

35. See Collins, Letters, 99–100. Some second-century heretical Gnostics were clearly opposed to marriage. These heretics, wrote Irenaeus, "say that marrying and generating come from Satan" (Adversus Haereses 1.24.2).

36. See Johnson, Letters, 139.

37. Bassler says that by linking salvation with childbirth, the author is

making a mockery not only of his Pauline roots but also of his own views concerning the abiding power of divine grace and the efficacy of the gender-neutral virtues of faith and love. See Bassler, *1 Timothy*, 62.

38. Knight's reading of the text seems to be particularly farfetched. He interprets the New Testament *hapax legomenon teknogonia* as "the birth of the Messiah" and reads the inflected form of the verb "she will be saved" as a reference to Eve, the prototypical woman (*Pastoral Epistles*, 144–48). The messianic reading of the text, for which some limited patristic evidence can be cited (e.g., Ign. *Eph.* 19; Justin, *Dialogue* 100), has been rejected also by Stanley E. Porter ("What Does it Mean to be 'Saved by Childbirth'? [1 Timothy 2.15]," *JSNT* 49 [1993] 87–102, esp. 98–102) and Thomas R. Schreiner ("An Interpretation of 1 Timothy 2:9–15: A Dialogue with Scholarship," in *Women in the Church: A Fresh Analysis of 1 Timothy 2:9–15*, ed. Andreas J. Köstenberger, T. R. Schreiner, and H. Scott Baldwin [Grand Rapids: Baker, 1995], 105–54, esp. 146–53).

39. Cf. 1 Tim. 3:15, "the household of God, which is the church of the living God, the pillar and bulwark of the truth."

40. The verb *katastrēniaō* is a *hapax legomenon* in the New Testament. Its root, *strēn-*, is used elsewhere in the New Testament only in Revelation 18. The noun *strēnos* appears in 18:3, where it describes the power of the sexual passion of Babylon the whore. The related verb *strēniaō* is used in Rev. 18:7 and 9 to describe the passion of the whore (v. 7) and her lovers (v. 9). The intensive form of the verb in 1 Tim. 5:11 highlights the intensity of a young woman's sexual desire. The prefix *kata*, however, appears also to control the genitive *tou Christou* (Christ), suggesting, as the NRSV translation implies, that the strength of a young widow's sexual passion somehow alienates her from Christ.

41. See Johnson, *Letters*, 183.

42. Cf. Plutarch, "Aemilius Paulus" 2; *Moralia* 749D; Josephus, *Antiquities* 18.3.4 §66. On the basis of 2 Cor. 11:2, Gottfried Holtz (*Die Pastoralbriefe*, THKNT 13 [Berlin: Evangelische Verlagsanstalt, 1965], 119–20), Spicq (*Épitres pastorales*, 1:535), and Pierre Dornier (*Les Épitres pastorales*, SB [Paris: Gabalda, 1969], 91) think of a young widow as having a kind of spiritual marriage with Christ.

43. See Gordon D. Fee, *1 and 2 Timothy, Titus*, NIBC (rev. ed.; Peabody, Mass.: Hendrickson, 1988), 121. Other options are discussed by Knight, *Pastoral Epistles*, 226–27.

44. See Spicq, "*sōphroneō, ktl.*," TLNT 3:359–65, esp. 362–65.

45. On the meaning of "purity," see below, p. 171.

46. See Quinn, *Titus*, 136–37.

47. The NRSV, however, translates the *sōphronas* of Titus 2:2 as "prudent."

48. *Sōphrona*, "prudent," in the NRSV.

49. That within the four groups of people of 1 Tim. 5:2 it is the young women who are singled out as those to be treated "with purity" is an indication that in 1 Timothy "purity" (from the *hagn-* root) is not simply purity in general, but has the connotation of chaste conduct.

50. See chap. 5 above.

51. The adjective *philēdonos*, "lover of pleasure," is a *hapax legomenon* in the New Testament. It is related to the noun *philēdonia*, "love of pleasure," which Philo identifies as the source of adultery. Cf. Philo, *Decalogue* 122.

52. See above, pp. 54–56.

53. So provocative, in fact, that the verse is virtually the only verse in the epistle that has not been taken over into the liturgical readings of Roman Catholicism.

54. See Josephus, *Antiquities* 5.1.2–7 §§5–30; *b. Meg.* 14b–15a; *Exod. Rab.* 27:4; *Num. Rab.* 3:2; 8:9; 16:1; *Deut. Rab.* 2:26-27; etc.

10

Under the Influence of Paul

I N ADDITION TO THE DEUTERO-PAULINE EPISTLES to the Colossians and
to the Ephesians, the three Pastoral Epistles, and the Epistle of
James, other texts in the New Testament have some relationship
with Paul, albeit a tenuous one.

THE EPISTLE TO THE HEBREWS

The Epistle to the Hebrews is neither a letter, nor was it intended for
Hebrews. Christian tradition has long associated it with the apostle
Paul, but the text itself makes no claim to Pauline authorship.[1] In fact,
the name of the apostle is nowhere cited in the entire text. The so-
called epistle is an anonymous discourse which the author himself
characterizes as a "word of exhortation" (Heb. 13:22). The literary
address consists of a series of pericopes that alternately offer christological exposition and moral exhortation. The one reinforces the other,
and vice versa.

Although the address contains a fair amount of moral exhortation,
there is only one verse that explicitly speaks of human responsibility
with regard to sexual behavior. That single verse appears toward the
end of the tract as the author writes, "Let marriage be held in honor by
all, and let the marriage bed be kept undefiled; for God will judge fornicators and adulterers" (Heb. 13:4).[2]

Hebrews 13 begins with the general exhortation, "Let mutual love
continue" (v. 1). Then the author has a word to say about hospitality to

strangers (v. 2), concern for the well-being of prisoners (v. 3), and marriage (v. 4), before he talks about the love of money (vv. 5–7). In the
parenesis of the philosophic, Jewish, and early Christian moralists, an
exhortation to avoid sexual immorality is frequently paired with the
exhortation to avoid greed.[3] This may be why the author's advice on
the love of money follows immediately upon his two-part exhortation
on chastity. As part of the final parenesis of the address, the exhortation on chastity falls not only under the rubric of "let mutual love continue" (13:1) but also under the rubric of "pursue peace with everyone,
and the holiness without which no one will see the Lord" (12:14). As
did Paul, the author of Hebrews perceives the call to chastity from the
perspective of the Christian's call to be an integral part of God's holy
people.

The exhortation "Let marriage be held in honor by all,[4] and let the
marriage bed be kept undefiled" (13:4) is characterized by antithetical
parallelism. The two parts of the exhortation are essentially synonymous. Hence, the first part of the exhortation must be taken not as an
exhortation directed against those whose ascetic convictions might
lead them to avoid marriage, but against those who might defile
another's marriage bed. The author's language is unusual, at least insofar as the New Testament is concerned. Although "marriage" (*gamos*)
and "marriage bed" (*koitē*) are used elsewhere in the New Testament,
they are infrequent in its epistolary corpus.[5] They are, moreover, used
synonymously in a way that distinguishes their use in Hebrews from
their use in the rest of the New Testament. In Heb. 13:4, both "marriage" and "marriage bed" designate the marital relationship itself.

The point of the exhortation is clear. The call to holiness and love
of neighbor impels a Christian to avoid adultery. The author says so
not once but twice. To further reinforce the point, the author adds a
hortatory warning, "for God will judge fornicators and adulterers
(*pornous . . . moichous*)." The author's terse language, which speaks
of God's judgment, echoes an idea otherwise expressed in the New
Testament. Paul, for example, had affirmed that neither fornicators
nor adulterers would inherit the kingdom of God (1 Cor. 6:9–10). Heb.
13:4's exhortation to avoid adultery is expressed in a manner that is
proper to the preacher himself. It is his way of affirming an element
of sexual parenesis that is deeply rooted within the tradition of the
philosophic and Jewish moralists, not to speak of that of early Christianity.

The Acts of the Apostles

The Acts of the Apostles is another New Testament book that Christian tradition has commonly assumed to have been written under the influence of the apostle Paul. Written by the evangelist Luke—the second part of his composite work, Luke-Acts—the book of Acts presents Paul as the missionary hero who brings the gospel from Jerusalem to the ends of the earth (Acts 1:8). Traditionally Luke has been presented as a disciple and companion of Paul (Col. 4:14), but there is really little evidence to suggest that Luke had any but a passing—if any at all!—personal relationship with the apostle to the Gentiles.[6]

Luke's narrative about the journeys and the arrests of Paul have little to say about human sexuality, with one notable exception. In his efforts to show that there was a place in God's plan of salvation for Gentile Christians, as well as for Jewish Christians, Luke describes the way in which Barnabas and Paul, missionaries to the Gentiles, were welcomed by the church of Jerusalem, with the apostles and elders of the community (Acts 15:4). He then tells about the unexpected but Spirit-inspired results of deliberations undertaken by the apostles and elders on the subject of circumcision.

Under the leadership of Simeon and James, and with the inspiration of the Spirit, the assembly decided that it was not necessary for Gentile Christians to be circumcised. Some minimal conditions were, nonetheless, to be imposed on these Gentiles in order that they may enjoy table fellowship with Jewish Christians. Gentile Christians were to abstain from things polluted by idols and from fornication and from whatever has been strangled and from blood (Acts 15:20). A letter to this effect was to be drafted and brought to the church of Antioch by Paul and Barnabas.[7]

The mention of fornication (*porneia*, 15:20, 29) within this context is a sign of Jewish Christian concern about the sexual mores of Gentiles who would be Christian. The prohibition of fornication appears as the second item on the list (15:20) in the author's narrative account.[8] In the epistolary listing (15:29), abstinence from fornication appears after abstinence from what has been sacrificed to idols, from blood, and from what is strangled. The epistolary order, with fornication as the last item, recurs in the reminiscence of the letter that Luke mentions in 21:25.

Three of the items on the list are dietary taboos, but fornication is not. All four items derive from the Holiness Code in Leviticus 17-18. The code established certain prescriptions not only for the house of Israel but also for aliens who reside among them (Lev. 17:8). The word "fornication," *porneia,* does not appear in the Greek Bible's version of Leviticus 17–18. Illicit marriage within the various forms of kinship identified in Leviticus 18 was known in Jewish tradition as *zĕnût,* a word that is sometimes translated into Greek as *porneia,* "fornication."[9]

Elsewhere in the New Testament *porneia* sometimes designates sexual immorality in general and at other times one or another specific form of sexual immorality.[10] In light of the biblical background of the Jerusalem discussions, there can be little doubt that the "fornication" of which Luke writes in 15:20, 29 and 21:25 is the various forms of incest prohibited by the Holiness Code (Leviticus 18).[11] When he places "fornication" after the three dietary taboos in the apostolic letter (15:29)and its reminiscence (21:25) Luke follows Leviticus 17–18 more closely than he does in the narrative account (15:20). With his triple mention of fornication Luke reminds his readers that a Gentile who wanted to enter into table fellowship with Jewish Christians was to abstain from incest in accordance with the Holiness Code of old.

THE FIRST EPISTLE OF PETER

Although the First Epistle of Peter offers the name of an apostle to the circumcised (Gal. 2:9) rather than that of Paul as its patronym, the epistle remains nonetheless under the influence of the apostle to the Gentiles. It can be argued that the epistle originated in a Pauline school. The epistle contains elements of a household code (2:18–3:7). Lacking the completeness of the household codes found in Ephesians and Colossians, the code in 1 Peter addresses only slaves (2:18–25), wives (3:1–6), and husbands (3:7). Its emphasis clearly lies on the exhortation to slaves and to wives. Slaves are exhorted to accept the authority of their masters; wives are urged to accept the authority of their husbands.

The exhortation to wives is primarily addressed to Christian women married to unbelievers (3:1–2). That the author specifically addresses his exhortation to Christian women involved in a religiously exogamous marriage may derive from the social situation of the times. In Greco-Roman society not only were women expected to be subservient to their husbands; they were also expected to worship the gods of their husbands.[12] Were Christian wives not to follow the accepted social conventions by being obedient to their husbands, they might not only incur the anger of their husbands; they could also be brought before the secular authorities for having violated conventional religious law. This would entail difficulties for the Christian community. So the author encourages Christian wives to accept the authority of their husbands (3:1, 6), gives them the example of Sarah (3:6), and urges them to conduct themselves so as to please their husbands (3:3–5).

From the perspective of the epistle, Christian wives are to remain steadfast in their devotion to God and their following of Christ. The author expects that the Christian wife's behavior, within the parameters of socially normative submission to her husband,[13] will be such as possibly to win over her nonbelieving spouse to the Christian faith. It is specifically the purity of her life (*hagnēn anastrophēn*) that should move the husband to accept the Christian faith. Although she might not preach the gospel to her husband by word of mouth (3:1),[14] the wife's behavior, the purity and reverence of her life, can be a convincing argument in favor of the faith.

The author of 1 Peter may not specifically have had in mind a wife's spousal chastity when he wrote about the quality of the wife's life. The expression "purity of life" may simply refer to an uncompromised lifestyle.[15] The word "pure" (*hagnos*) has, however, been used in the course of history to denote the absence of any impurity, such as incest or sexual intercourse, that could compromise one's ritual purity.[16] This understanding of purity is not to be excluded from the quality of a wife's life that brings her husband to faith in God and his Christ according to the vision expressed in the epistle.

Men, on their part, are exhorted to show respect not only for their wives but also for all women.[17] They are to honor them as the weaker sex, literally, "the weaker vessel" (*asthenesterō skeuei*, 3:7). Although women are not as physically strong as men, they are nonetheless to be honored by Christian men. Despite their relative physical frailty, women enjoy a position of parity with Christian men. They are to be treated with honor and respect. The women about whom the author writes are not only their wives but also all women with whom a Christian man lives, those with whom he shares a common life. Their common life and their common participation in the inheritance of grace, which is life, means that in their interpersonal relationships men and women are equal (cf. Gal. 3:28) despite societal expectation that women should accept the authority of their husbands (3:1).

A Biblical Story

To the extent to which it has adopted the form of an apostolic letter (1–2; 24–25), the Epistle of Jude is indebted to Paul, letter writer par excellence and the first to write an apostolic letter.[18] Jerome Neyrey suggests that the document is a kind of riposte in defense of the honor of Jesus and of Jude within a community under attack from intruders who have perverted God's grace into licentiousness.[19]

To encourage his addressees to be wary of licentiousness (*aselgeian*, v. 4)[20] and the denial of Jesus' lordship which the interlopers would introduce into the community, the author cites three well-known biblical examples. He had announced his intention to use Jewish traditions to support his message when he chose "Jude" as a designation for the epistle's patronym. "Jude" is identified as "the brother of James," that is, the leader of the Jewish Christian community in Jerusalem.

The biblical stories cited by the author are the story of the exodus,[21] the story of the angels,[22] and the story of Sodom and Gomorrah (see Gen. 19:1–26). The author recalls these stories in order to encourage his readers to place the danger of the intrusion clearly before them. As some Israelites of old had been unfaithful, so too are the interlopers unfaithful. As the angels had not respected the position that God had created for them, so the intruders have not respected the positions of either Jesus or Jude. As the inhabitants of Sodom burned with lust, so too have these scoffers been licentious.

Mention of the story of Sodom and Gomorrah places the interlopers' licentiousness within a biblical perspective. The author places it before his readers so as to provide them with an example of divine judgment on sexual immorality. The story of Sodom is told in Gen. 19:1–26. The author of the Epistle of Jude has expanded on the tale of the lust of the people of Sodom by associating Gomorrah and the surrounding cities with the sexual immorality and unnatural lust of the inhabitants of Sodom. The biblical tale has nothing specific to say about the sin of the inhabitants of Gomorrah. It speaks of God's intention to investigate the sin of Sodom and Gomorrah (Gen. 18:20–21) and of the punishment meted out to these and other cities because of their sin (Gen. 19:24–28). The author of the Epistle of Jude probably associated the people of Gomorrah with the sin of Sodom because of the long-standing biblical and extrabiblical tradition that linked the names of these two cities together.

In the book of Genesis the two-part story about Sodom (Gen. 18:22–19:23) is situated between a mention of God's investigation of the sin of Sodom and Gomorrah (18:21) and an account of the retribution of divine justice on the twin cities (19:24–25). Gen. 19:25 extends the punishment visited upon Sodom and Gomorrah to all the plain. Deut. 29:23 attributes a similar fate to Admah and Zeboiim, but this biblical text does not specifically identify the evil for which either of these cities merited the wrath of God. Zoar was another city[23] in the neighborhood of Sodom and Gomorrah. It was exempted from the divine wrath because of Lot's prayer (Gen. 19:20–23). The author of the Epistle of Jude probably had Admah and Zeboiim in mind when he wrote about "the surrounding cities" (Jude 7). By expanding the extent of the sin beyond Sodom to Gomorrah and the other cities, the author of the epistle magnified the evil of which the inhabitants of Sodom had been guilty.

What was the very grave sin committed by the inhabitants of Sodom? The biblical narrator tells a story about Lot, who was sitting by the city gate when he saw two men approach the town. Moved by the oriental spirit of hospitality, Lot invited the strangers to his home. Initially the strangers declined Lot's invitation, but at his insistence they finally decided to take up his offer of hospitality. The reader eventually comes to understand that Lot's guests were messengers of the Lord,[24] but their identity is not immediately clear from the narrative itself. The reader can only assume that the strangers were human.

Before the guests went to bed that evening, Lot's house was surrounded by all of the males[25] in the city of Sodom. The mob demands that Lot bring the visitors out "so that we may know them" (19:5). The male population of the city is not merely interested in making the acquaintance of the visitors. "To know" is a biblical idiom for sexual intercourse, carnal knowledge.[26] Taken aghast by the demand of the unruly townsmen, Lot offers them the use of his two virginal daughters "who have not known a man." Instead of accepting Lot's offer, the men of Sodom tried to force their way into his house, threatening to violate not only the visitors but also Lot himself. At this point, the guests intervened, miraculously inflicting blindness on the members of the mob and offering escape to Lot and his extended family (Gen. 19:10–13).

That Lot would have offered his daughters to be sexually exploited by the men of Sodom is repugnant to a contemporary Western reader of the story. In antiquity, however, a father had virtually absolute authority over his unmarried daughters.[27] As a host, Lot had an obligation to protect his visitors, no matter the cost. The code of honor implied in the oriental custom of hospitality had its demands. Lot's actions, though extreme, illustrate the lengths to which a good host would go to protect his guests.

What then was the sin of the inhabitants of Sodom? A fairly large number of stories that circulated in the ancient Near East indicate that the sin of the Sodomites was primarily a violation of the law of hospitality. These narratives describe the person who offers hospitality as being spared from the punishment meted out by divine vengeance, just as Lot was saved (Gen. 19:20–23).

The Genesis version of the traditional story is such that the sin of the Sodomites appears also to be a violation of a sexual taboo (Lev. 18:22). One must note, however, that this aspect of the violation was not the emphasis of the story. Nor was the sin a matter of consensual homoerotic activity. The sin was the abuse of a male to whom hospitality had been offered. In modern terminology the sexual activity was "homosexual gang rape." Finally, in identifying the malice of the evil perpetrated by the Sodomites, one must take note of their hybris (cf. Ezek. 16:49). They wanted to assert their authority over the visitors. They mocked Lot, the nephew of Abraham, father of Israel, calling him an alien, questioning his wisdom, and threatening to do greater harm to him than to the visitors whom they would rape (Gen. 19:9).

When the story of Sodom is read within the canonical context of the Jewish scriptures, the modern reader must take into consideration not only the cultural context within which the tale had been told—the culture of the times would have placed a very high value on hospitality and assumed a father's almost absolute authority over his nubile daughters—but also the fact that Lot was Abraham's nephew. The salvation of his household was assured because of his relationship to Abraham. From this canonical perspective the story of Sodom illustrates the difference between an Abrahamic ethos and that of the cities of Canaan. The graphic tale of the sin of the Sodomites epitomizes the sins of the Canaanites (cf. Judg. 19:30).

The destruction of Sodom and Gomorrah is the Genesis tale most frequently cited in other Jewish scriptures,[28] not to mention the several references in the Christian scriptures.[29] Biblical prophets interpreted the evil of Sodom in various ways. Isaiah implies that it was a sin of injustice and social oppression (Isa. 1:10; 3:9).[30] Jeremiah speaks of a moral laxity similar to that of the Jerusalem prophets, who were guilty of adultery, lying, and encouraging the malefactor (Jer. 23:14). In Ezekiel we read about a sin of pride and a failure to help the poor (Ezek. 16:49). The Epistle of Jude speaks of sexual immorality and the pursuit of unnatural lust (Jude 7).[31] The Genesis tale itself is a story of God's judgment on human wickedness, illustrated by an ancient legend. In the tradition, as illustrated by both Jewish and Christian scriptures,[32] what serves as an example is the memory of divine retribution on sin.

REREADING THE STORY

In identifying the evil for which everlasting fire served as an expression of divine vengeance, the Epistle of Jude speaks of "sexual immorality" (*ekporneuō*, a verb) and "unnatural lust" (*sarkos heteras*, literally, "alien flesh"). Each of these expressions is unique in the New Testament.[33] The kind of sexual immorality that the author of the epistle ascribes to Sodom and the neighboring cities appears to be a violation of the divine order of created difference. Jewish law prohibited the mixing of things.[34] With regard to sex, difference is to be respected. Men are not to have sex either with animals (Lev. 18:23) or with men (Lev. 18:22; 20:13).

As the legendary characters of old pursued alien flesh, so the interlopers vilified by Jude have "defiled the flesh" (*sarka men miainousin,* Jude 8). Defilement of the flesh is, writes Horst Balz, a reference to general sexual libertinism.[35] Philo associates defilement with adultery (*Allegorical Interpretation* 3.148; *Joseph* 45), licentious passion (*Cherubim* 51), harlotry, and pleasure (*Special Laws* 1.281). Sexual misconduct is, however, not the only evil perpetrated by the intruders into Jude's community. They are also guilty of rejecting authority and slandering angels (Jude 8). Jude 16 fills out the author's description of the evil of the interlopers with a bill of particulars. In addition to their sexual misconduct, their rejection of authority, and their haughty slander, the intruders are also grumblers and malcontents. They indulge their own lusts. They are bombastic in speech and use flattery to their own advantage. The five items are a list of vices. Among them is lust (*epithymia*), a stock item in the ancient catalogues of vices and a matter of great concern for the pastor of the Pastoral Epistles.

The sins of which the interlopers are guilty bring shame upon their perpetrators (Jude 13) and defile the love-feasts (*tais agapais*, Jude 12), the Christian celebration of Eucharist. Divine vengeance will be meted out to them in the same way as it was visited upon Sodom and the neighboring cities. The author of the Epistle of Jude used the traditional motif of the story of Sodom, to characterize the evil of the intruders in the harshest of terms. He also employed traditional motifs to speak of the punishment of these evildoers and slanderers. The judgment of God will be visited on these ungodly persons. This is something about which the legendary Enoch had already spoken:

> See, the Lord is coming with ten thousands of his holy ones, to execute judgment on all, and to convict everyone of all the deeds of ungodliness that they have committed in such an ungodly way, and of all the harsh things that ungodly sinners have spoken against him. (*1 Enoch* 1:9; Jude 14–15)[37]

THE SECOND EPISTLE OF PETER

The Second Epistle of Peter, arguably the last book of the New Testament to be written, is essentially a reworking of the Epistle of Jude.[38] The author of 2 Peter shares with the author of the Epistle of Jude and the author(s) of the Pastorals an abhorrence for lust. His exhortation has been written so that the readers "may escape from the corruption that is in the world because of lust (*epithymia*) and become participants of the divine nature" (1:4). In his view lust has the capacity to corrupt the entire world. Scoffers may revel in their lust (3:3) and entice people with licentious desires of the flesh (2:18), but a day of judgment will come for those who indulge their flesh in depraved lust (2:10). Contrasted with a life ruled by lust is the life of the Christian, which the author illustrates by means of a catalogue of virtues (1:5–7). Among the virtues of the Christian is self-control (*egkrateia*), a virtue that supports knowledge and is strengthened by endurance.[39]

According to 2 Peter, the interlopers are lustful people who will get their just deserts. The author describes them as creatures of instinct whose eyes are full of adultery (*ophthalmous . . . mestous moichalidos*, 2:14).[40] In portraying their maliciousness, he speaks of the allure of licentious desires of the flesh that lead people into slavery (2:18–19). Writing about the licentious desires of the flesh (*en epithymiais sarkos aselgeiais*) as he does, the Petrine author links the licentiousness (*aselgeiais*) of the interlopers to those who are led astray with lust (*epithymiais*) and the corruption of the flesh (*sarkos*).

To make his point that Christians ought not to follow the licentious ways of false prophets, the author of 2 Peter also evokes the story of Sodom and Gomorrah (2:6). The author recasts the story so as to highlight the salvation of Lot (2:8–9)[41] rather than the perversion of the inhabitants of Sodom. The destruction of Sodom and Gomorrah is simply pointed out as an example of what the ungodly are going to receive. Highlighting the salvation of Lot, 2 Peter is more faithful to the Genesis story than is the version of the tradition found in Jude, which does not even mention Lot.[42] In Genesis 19 it is the rescue of Lot from catastrophe, rather than divine retribution on Sodom that occupies the greater part of the chapter and receives the most emphasis in the story.[43] The author of 2 Peter is little concerned with the sin of the Sodomites. He is concerned, rather, with the lustful way of life to which the intruders are enticing the members of his community. In his parenesis the destruction of Sodom and Gomorrah serves as a warning (2:6). The rescue of Lot serves to illustrate the destiny of those who are distressed by the licentiousness of the lawless (2:8–9).

THE BOOK OF REVELATION

The last book in the New Testament is the enigmatic book of Revelation.[44] The presence of the letters to the seven churches in chapters 2 and 3 has led contemporary commentators to speak of a Pauline influence on the book. These "letters"[45] have an epistolary format. They were purportedly written for Christian churches in Asia Minor, an area that the apostle Paul had evangelized.

As an apocalyptic work, the book of Revelation was written to console and encourage its intended addressees at the time of their own difficulties. The readers are reminded that God's judgment will eventually fall on those who do evil, including those who have persecuted them. Readers are encouraged to avoid evil lest God's wrath fall on them as well.

Revelation's words about sexual misdeeds must be understood within this apocalyptic context. Each of the book's three catalogues of vices (9:21; 21:8; 22:15) associates sexual misconduct (*porneia*) with idol worship (*eidolatria*).[46] The wrath of God will descend on those who do such things (9:21; 21:8). They are to be forever excluded from the heavenly Jerusalem (22:15).

One striking feature of the book of Revelation is its imaginative portrayal of Babylon, the whore. The whore, regally clad, is enthroned (17:15). She has committed fornication with the kings of the earth (17:2; 18:3, 9). Her cup is filled with the wine of fornication, from which the inhabitants of the earth have drunk (14:8; 17:2, 4; 18:3). She is the mother of whores and of the earth's abominations (17:5). The wine of fornication symbolizes her enticing power. Seated on the many waters (17:1), she is presented as someone whose evil corrupts the entire world. Babylon, the whore, will get her comeuppance. Once and again the angel proclaims, "Fallen, fallen is Babylon the great" (14:8; 18:2). On her judgment has come (18:10; 19:2). Even the beast will hate her (17:16), while those who have committed fornication with her will only rue her fate (18:9–10).

The imagery of the book of Revelation is such that one ought not attempt to exploit unduly the sexual language used to characterize Babylon, the great whore. In antiquity female figures were used as symbols of cities. In Jewish tradition Babylon was virtually the epitome of evil. It was responsible for the forced deportation in 597 B.C.E., the "Babylonian exile," and the destruction of the Holy City in 586 B.C.E.

Babylon served as a convenient symbol for the evil that late-first-century Christians associated with the Roman Empire. In the biblical tradition and in the Christian scriptures harlotry/sexual immorality/*porneia* was associated with idolatry. The result is the image of Babylon, the great whore, used by an anonymous Christian author to symbolize the evil that Christians of his circle associated with the Roman Empire. As Babylon had fallen, so too Rome will fall. That is the seer's message as he vividly paints an image of the great whore.

Duane Watson has observed:

> As a symbol Babylon embraces more than the empire, city, and culture of Rome. It is the sphere of idolatry and worldliness under the temporary control of Satan, a worldliness in opposition to the people and work of God, a worldliness epitomized first by Babylon and then by Rome. Babylon as the mother of harlots and abominations in opposition to God (17:5) is the antithesis of the Church as the Bride of Christ, the New Jerusalem, and the Kingdom of God.[47]

Her harlotry is much more than mere sexual immorality.

To prepare for the image of the great harlot who epitomizes all that is wrong with humankind, the author of Revelation has shared a vision of the Lamb accompanied by 144,000 who had his name and his Father's name written on their foreheads (14:1–5). In the heavenly liturgy, before the throne of the Lamb, and before the four living creatures and the elders, these 144,000 sing a new song. They are followers of the Lamb who have been redeemed as the firstfruits of all humankind. They are, says the author, those "who have not defiled themselves with women, for they are virgins" (14:4).

As with his presentation of Babylon, the author's language in portraying these virgins is largely symbolic. Philo uses the image of the virgin to speak of those who are detached from worldliness, but "when God begins to consort with the soul, He makes what before was a woman into a virgin again" (*Cherubim* 50). The word "virgin" (*parthenos*) normally evokes a female figure, and it is so used in Philo, but the term was also used of men. In 14:4 the author of Revelation is thinking primarily about men[48] who are virgins. They "have not defiled themselves with women." The author's use of a relative clause in this verse points to the single-mindedness of these 144,000 men.

To appreciate fully the symbolism of the author's metaphorical portrayal of the loyal followers of the Lamb, one must not overlook the context of the heavenly liturgy within which the metaphor appears. Within Israel it was expected that men temporarily abstain from sexual activity before participating in cultic activity.[49] With its many echoes of the biblical tradition, the book of Revelation presupposes that those who approach to worship in the presence of the Lamb be similarly abstinent. The point of the ancient practice is that those who participate in the cult must be singularly devoted to the Lord. The point of the seer's metaphor is that the followers of the Lamb must be undivided in their devotion to the Lamb. In the book of Revelation both "harlotry" and "virginity" are symbols that transcend the sexual imagery that they evoke.

NOTES

1. On Hebrews, see R. F. Collins, *Letters That Paul Did Not Write: The Epistle to the Hebrews and the Pauline Pseudepigrapha*, GNS 28 (Wilmington, Del.: Glazier, 1988), 19–56.

2. On "defilement," see also p. 175.

3. Hence, some interpreters take 1 Thess. 4:3–6 as an exhortation to avoid unchastity (vv. 3–5) and greed (v. 6). See above, p. 105. On "greed," see p. 150.

4. Commentators disagree as to whether *en pasin* means "by all" or "in all respects." The majority of commentators tend to favor the latter interpretation, but the difference in interpretation hardly changes the tenor of the exhortation.

5. That is with the exception of *koitē* in Rom. 9:10 and its plural in Rom. 13:13. See above, pp. 85–86.

6. See the discussion of the relationship between Paul and Luke in Hans Conzelmann, *Acts of the Apostles*, Hermeneia (Philadelphia: Fortress, 1987), xxxix–xl; Joseph A. Fitzmyer, *The Acts of the Apostles*, AB 31 (New York: Doubleday, 1998), 98–103, 124–28; etc.

7. Both the letter and the so-called Council of Jerusalem itself appear to be literary creations of Luke. In terms of strict facticity, they were not historical. Luke's account, however, dramatically tells the story of the interaction between Jewish and Gentile Christians and what it was that Jewish Christians expected of Gentile Christians were the latter to enter into table fellowship with the former. Luke Timothy Johnson speaks of the Apostolic Council as a watershed in the narrative of Acts, but adds that "we are able to engage the author's narrative perspective and thereby engage a quality of narrative 'truth' which is not confined to referential accuracy" (*The Acts of the Apostles*, SacPag 5 [Collegeville, Minn.: Liturgical Press, 1992], 270).

8. The word *porneia* is absent from the text of 15:20 in P[45], the oldest extant manuscript of Acts. The papyrus is fragmentary. It includes neither 15:28–29 nor 21:25.

9. See CD 4:12b–5:14a; see the discussion in Fitzmyer, *Acts*, 557–58.

10. See the discussion above, pp. 80–83.

11. Thus Ernst Haenchen, *The Acts of the Apostles: A Commentary* (Oxford: Basil Blackwell, 1971), 449; Conzelmann, *Acts*, 118–19; and Fitzmyer, *Acts*, 557–58.

12. See Plutarch, "Advice to the Bride and Groom," 19; *Moralia* 140D.

13. See Philo, *Apology for the Jews* 7.3: "Wives must be in servitude to their husbands, a servitude not imposed by violent ill-treatment but promoting obedience in all things." Cf. Philo, *Apology for the Jews* 7.5; Josephus, *Against Apion* 2.25 §201; Juvenal, *Satire* 6; 1 Tim. 2:11–12; Titus 2:5.

14. Some commentators take "without a word" (*aneu logou*) to mean that the wife does not argue with her husband. It seems preferable, however, to take the expression as meaning "in the absence of the word," that is, without a verbal proclamation of the gospel. Thus Paul J. Achtemeier, *1 Peter*, Hermeneia (Philadelphia: Fortress, 1996), 210.

15. Thus J. N. D. Kelly, *The Epistles of Peter and of Jude*, HNTC (New York: Harper & Row, 1969), 128–29; Achtemeier, *1 Peter*, 210.

16. See Horst Balz, "*hagnos, ktl.*," EDNT 1:22–23.

17. Rather than use the noun *gynē*, an adult woman, specifically a wife within contexts that speak of the relationship between husbands and wives, 1 Pet 3:7 uses a substantivized adjective, *gynaikeiō*, a female person. With its translation, "husbands, . . . show consideration for your wives in your life together," the NRSV overlooks the difference between the two words used by

the author in 1 Pet. 3:1–7. See Bo Reicke, *The Epistles of James, Peter, and Jude*, AB 37 (Garden City, N.Y.: Doubleday, 1964), 102, 137–38.

18. See R. F. Collins, *The Birth of the New Testament: The Origin and Development of the First Christian Generation* (New York: Crossroad, 1993), 184–213, esp. 202.

19. See Jerome H. Neyrey, *2 Peter, Jude*, AB 37C (New York: Doubleday, 1993), 52.

20. "Licentiousness" appears in a number of the New Testament's catalogues of vices; see Mark 7:22; Rom. 13:13; 2 Cor. 12:21; Gal. 5:19; 1 Pet. 4:3.

21. As does Paul in 1 Cor. 10:1–13, the author seems to rely principally on the traditions found in the book of Numbers. God's revenge on those who were not faithful to him is described in Num. 14:1–38; 26:64–65.

22. See Gen. 6:1–4, expanded by traditions similar to those found in *1 Enoch* 10:4–6; 12:4–13:1. *1 Enoch* 1:9, a passage that has fortunately been preserved in both a Greek and an Ethiopic version, is cited in Jude 14.

23. Wis. 10:6 refers to the Pentapolis, but historians raise considerable doubts about its historical existence.

24. A telling sign of the messenger's identity is the extraordinary information conveyed to Lot by his guests (Gen. 19:15). With this clue the reader can more fully understand the Yahwist's juxtaposition of the story of Sodom with the tale of the visit of three mysterious (angelic) messengers to Abraham in Genesis 18.

25. Leland J. White, "Does the Bible Speak about Gays or Same-sex Orientation? A Test Case in Biblical Ethics: Part I," *BTB* 25 (1995): 14–23. The Yahwist makes it quite clear that the entire male population of the city is involved. "The men of the city, the men of Sodom, both young and old, all the people to the last man," he writes in 19:4.

26. Ludwig Koehler and Walter Baumgartner's classic *Lexicon in Veteris Testamenti Libros* (Leiden: Brill, 1948–53) offers as a translation of *ydꜥ*, "to know," to "know sexually, lie with" (Gen. 4:1, etc.). The lexicon suggests "paederasty" as the meaning of the verb in Gen. 19:5. The verb *ydꜥ* is used of sexual intercourse by a man in Gen. 4:1, 17, 25 and of a woman's sexual intercourse in Num. 31:18, 35; Judg. 21:12.

27. See the similar story of Gibeah in Judg. 19:22–30. In Judges the host offers his nubile daughter and his guest's concubine to the would-be rapists.

28. Cf. Deut. 29:23; 32:32; Isa. 1:9–10; 13:19; Jer. 23:14; 49:18; 50:40; Amos 4:11; Zeph. 2:9; *4 Esdras* 2:8.

29. There are eight in all: Matt. 10:15; 11:23–24; Luke 10:12; 17:29; Rom. 9:29; 2 Pet. 2:6; Jude 7; Rev. 11:8.

30. Isaiah speaks of Sodom and Gomorrah in 1:10, but only of Sodom in 3:9.

31. One manuscript tradition of the Slavonic *Apocalypse of Enoch*, presumably from the late first century C.E. and therefore more or less contemporary with Jude, speaks of divine retribution being visited upon those "who practice on the earth the sin which is against nature, which is child corruption in the anus in the manner of Sodom" (*2 Enoch* 10:4, MS P).

32. See the references in Claus Westermann, *Genesis 12-36: A Commentary*, Continental Commentaries (Minneapolis: Augsburg, 1985), 298.

33. So too is "example" (*deigma*).

34. In addition to various dietary regulations, see also, e.g., Deut 22:9–11.

35. See Horst Balz, "*miainō*," *EDNT* 2:427; cf. Neyrey, *2 Peter, Jude*, 67–68.

36. "Pleasure" (*philēdonia*) is a noun related to the substantivized adjective *philēdonoi*, "lovers of pleasure," used in 2 Tim. 3:4. See above, p. 160.

37. The citation comes from a section of *1 Enoch* (chapters 1–5) that is a late pre-Christian apocalyptic text. Use of the citation by the author of Jude characterizes the evil of the interlopers as a kind of ungodliness (*asebeia*) that is subject to the eschatological wrath of God.

38. The relationship between 2 Peter 2 and the Epistle of Jude is a minor synoptic problem. At the present time most scholars agree that 2 Peter was dependent on Jude. It is interesting to note that, as the reference to Rahab the harlot (Jas. 2:25) is not used in Roman Catholic liturgy, neither Jude nor 2 Peter 2 is used as a scriptural reading in the Roman Catholic celebration of Eucharist. The exception is Jude 17, 20–25, which has no reference to the sexual excesses of the interlopers. This scripture is used every other year on Saturday of the eighth week in ordinary time.

39. Cf. Gal 5:23. The virtue is frequently mentioned in the writings of Philo and the philosophic moralists, but it is hardly mentioned in the New Testament. What *egkrateia* connotes is human freedom from subjection to various desires, particularly for food, drink, sex, and conversation. Cf. Horst Goldstein, "*egkrateia, ktl.,*" *EDNT* 1:377–78.

40. Cf. Matt. 5:28; 18:9; Mark 9:47, and the comments above, pp. 45–46, 68–69.

41. Lot is described as a just man who was greatly distressed by the licentiousness of the lawless (2 Pet. 2:7).

42. Elsewhere in the New Testament Lot appears only in Luke 17:28–33.

43. See Westermann, *Genesis 12–36*, 297–98. Westermann notes that the story of the judgment on Gibeah in Judges 19–21 is very similar to the Genesis 19 story about Sodom. There is "complete agreement in structure" between the two stories and "much agreement in sentence construction and word usage." In the story in Judges, the emphasis lies on divine vengeance; in Genesis, emphasis lies on divine rescue.

44. The book of Revelation was not, however, the last book to be written. 2 Peter is arguably the last book of the New Testament to have been written.

45. They are, in fact, literary compositions written for the book of Revelation. The formula "These are the words" (*tade legei*, 2:1, 8, 12, 18; 3:1, 7, 14) suggests that the "letters" are oracles rather than pieces of correspondence.

46. See above, pp. 129–41.

47. Duane F. Watson, "Babylon in the NT," *ABD* 1:565–66, esp. 566.

48. John Sweet observes that "their maleness is simply part of the military metaphor; they represent the whole church" (*Revelation*, TPINTC [London: SCM; Philadelphia: Trinity Press International, 1990], 222).

49. Cf. Exod. 19:15; Lev. 15:16–18; 1 Sam. 2:22–24; 21:4–5; etc. Similarly soldiers who go off to war, a "holy war," are to abstain from sexual activity.

11

Sexual Ethics

THIS STUDY OF THE SEXUAL ETHICS of the New Testament has focused on the different books of the New Testament and the varieties of literary genres within which material relevant to a study of sexual ethics is to be found. All but six of the books of the New Testament have something to say that is pertinent to sexual ethics. The exceptions are relatively short New Testament texts, namely, Philippians, 2 Thessalonians, Philemon, and the three Johannine epistles.

Given the diversity of materials found in the twenty-one books of the New Testament that do have something to say about sexual ethics, any attempt to offer a true synthesis would be a foolhardy endeavor. Although the very nature of the material excludes any real synthesis, some elements recur with sufficient force and in various ways as to allow a reader to focus on the principal motifs of the New Testament's sexual ethics.

The dominant motif might well be that the disciple of Jesus is called to live with his or her sexuality in a way that is different from the way that others live with their sexuality. Those who have embraced the gospel of Jesus as adults might be able to contrast the way they live out their sexuality as disciples with their own previous sexual behavior. The sexual mores of the Christian are to be different from the rampant pursuit of sexual pleasure that often characterizes those who are not Christian.

Caricature is often an element of the New Testament authors' portrayal of the sexual mores of those who do not share Christian standards of morality. Overly broad generalizations are part of the caricature. In this respect the New Testament authors are products of the cultures of their times. Hellenistic Jewish writers had little good to say about the sexual mores of Gentiles. The philosophic moralists painted a dismal picture of those whose lack of wisdom and self-control was accompanied by submission to lust and passion. The cultural and ethical biases of the New Testament authors are reflected in the ways in which Paul[1] wrote about the gay and lesbian life of idolaters in Romans 1 and the lustful passion of Gentiles in 1 Thessalonians 4, the way that Matthew wrote about the scribes and Pharisees in the preface to the Sermon on the Mount, and the way that Jude wrote about the lustful sin of Sodom in which the intruders into his community also participated.

That the Christian is to avoid sexual immorality (*porneia*) is certain. The exhortation to shun sexual immorality is a key element of the parenesis that accompanied the preaching of the gospel. Parenesis is, however, a rhetorical form in which the warrant for the appeal is not an explanation of the exhortation. The warrant for the exhortation is the authority to which the speaker or writer appeals. Thus, Christians are simply urged to sin no more (John 8:11) and to shun sexual immorality (1 Cor. 6:18). Rarely is an explanation offered. Recitation of a series of sexual vices, as is often the case in the catalogues of vices, constitutes a more powerful parenetic appeal than does an attempt at explanation.

Paul's use of the powerful symbol of the kingdom of God as a warrant for avoiding sexual immorality in 1 Cor. 6:9–10 and his reflections on the Christian's embodied existence in 1 Cor. 6:12–20 are striking additions to the traditional parenesis. The apostle also offers advice as to how Christians might avoid sexual immorality. He suggests that Christians get married (1 Thess. 4:4) and that, once married, they not get carried away in any ill-advised abstinence from sexual relationships (1 Cor. 7:2–5). Paul is not the only New Testament author to urge that one should not let a misplaced religious or philosophic fervor turn one away from marriage. The Jesus of Matthew's Gospel countered the outburst of his disciples that it is better not to marry with the wise reflection that celibacy for the sake of the kingdom is a gift that only God can give (Matt. 19:10–12). In response to the false teaching of those who taught that marriage was to be avoided, the author of 1 Timothy reminded his addressees of the importance of marriage and children in a Christian woman's virtuous way of life (1 Tim. 2:15).

Paul's realistic attitude toward the strength of the sexual drive, most likely influenced by traditional Jewish lore on the *yēṣer hārāʿ*, is reflected throughout his long treatment of human sexuality in 1 Corinthians 5–7. Although he urges the Corinthians to remain in their current social situation, he counsels widows and widowers to remarry if they are not practicing self-control (1 Cor. 7:9). If a man has strong passions, he should marry (1 Cor. 7:36). Paul's realism in this regard is echoed by the anonymous pastor who was Paul's disciple. The pastor urged young widows with the sensual desires of young people to marry and bear children so as not to discredit the Christian community in the face of outsiders (1 Tim. 5:11–14).

To know that Christians are to shun sexual immorality is one thing; to know what sexual immorality is is another. "Sexual immorality" (*porneia*) is to be avoided, but "sexual immorality" covers a wide range of sexual misconduct. It certainly includes incest, the great sexual taboo. Gentile Christians must avoid incestuous relationships if they are to enter into table fellowship with Jewish Christians (Acts 15:20, 29; 21:25). Paul takes the Christians of Corinth to task because they have failed to deal properly with a particularly egregious form of incest, a man having an affair with his own stepmother (1 Cor. 5:1–8). Within all cultures incest is to be avoided. Despite his Jewish bias, Paul admits that even Gentiles abhor some forms of incest (1 Cor. 5:1). He cites this abhorrence to motivate the Christians of Corinth to do something about the case of incest within their community.

Incest is not, however, the sole sexual offense that can be subsumed under the rubric of sexual immorality. The use of prostitutes was also something to be shunned under the rubric of avoiding sexual immorality. The vice of *porneia* covers other forms of inappropriate sexual behavior as well. The vice lists help the reader to appreciate something of the wide semantic range of "sexual immorality," but it is often difficult to determine precisely what the author had in mind when he mentioned one or another sexual misdeed. Various kinds of sexual misconduct are cited on the vice lists. All told, however, they are but a few among the 110 vices to be avoided by a Christian. Nonetheless, no vice is more frequently cited than "sexual immorality."

In matters of sexual morality, one must look beyond the letter of the law to see what really is at stake. This is perhaps nowhere more evident than it is in Matthew's use of the Jewish catechetical tradition to include within the scope of the seventh commandment, "You shall not commit adultery," not only the prohibition of adultery ("adultery with the feet") but also lustful coveting, masturbation, and divorce. The evangelist's catechesis also includes the classic vice of "sexual immorality" under the traditional rubric of adultery (Matt. 15:19). Unlike other rabbinic authorities, Matthew did not include pederasty in his catechesis on the seventh commandment. He, however, as Mark before him, has preserved the memory of an old tradition that spoke of the evil of child abuse (Matt. 18:6; Mark 9:42).

Adultery is something that the Christian must avoid. The sin is prohibited by the seventh commandment. Adultery appears on several of the vice lists as a form of conduct to be shunned by the Christian. Paul urges the men of Thessalonica not to offend their fellow Christians by committing adultery with their wives (1 Thess. 4:6). The author of the Epistle to the Hebrews squarely faced the possibility of adultery when he addressed to his readers the exhortation, "Let marriage be held in honor by all, and let the marriage bed be kept undefiled for God will judge fornicators and adulterers" (Heb. 13:4). As grievous as is the sin of adultery, it is neither the only sin nor is it an unforgivable sin. Both points are made in the dramatic little story of the woman caught *in flagrante delicto* (John 7:53–8:11). The idea that adultery is not the only sin is reinforced in the catechesis on the Ten Commandments found in all three of the Synoptic Gospels, in Paul's letter to the Romans (13:8–10), and in the Epistle of James (2:8–13).

In the patriarchal society of the New Testament era, the avoidance of adultery was ultimately a matter of not violating the marital and parental rights of a married man. The New Testament authors have added to the traditional respect for another person's marriage the demand of fidelity to one's own marriage. Mark expanded on the traditional teaching of Jesus to remind his addressees that when a man divorces his wife and marries another, he has aggrieved her by committing adultery against her (10:11). The value of fidelity in marriage has prompted the author(s) of the Pastoral Epistles to include "married but once" in the list of qualities that they expect of the leaders of the church as well as of those who are to be enrolled as widows (1 Tim. 3:2, 12; 5:9; Titus 1:6).

The idea of parity within the marriage relationship implied by Mark's addition of "against her" to the traditional logion on divorce (Mark 10:11) is one that Paul fully exploits in his long treatise on sexuality (1 Corinthians 5–7). Men and women are in similar situations with regard to their sexual relationship within marriage.[2] Both men and women have a responsibility to satisfy the sexual needs of their spouses (1 Cor. 7:2–5). Husbands and wives are to be concerned about pleasing their spouses (1 Cor. 7:32–35). Both spouses have a similar responsibility with regard to divorce (1 Cor. 7:10–11). Husbands and wives have similar responsibilities as they live out their call to peace even in a mixed marriage (1 Cor. 7:12–16). The reasons that Paul cites in support of his plea for marital fidelity within an exogamous marriage constitute a short litany of the values of a faithful and permanent marriage. These include the sanctification of the spouses, the welfare of children, and that satisfaction of human needs that biblical tradition has subsumed under the rubric of God's gift of peace.

Paul's extensive parenesis on human sexuality is encompassed within a long letter that focuses on the call addressed to the Christians of Corinth to be God's holy people (1 Cor. 1:2) and to be united as a community (1 Cor. 1:10). The various elements of Paul's parenesis on human sexuality are to be seen in the light of the Christian's call to holiness. This is not so much a matter of piety as it is a matter of living as members of God's holy people. The fashion in which a Christian responds to his or her sexuality is a way in which the Christian responds to his or her call to holiness. In his letter to the Thessalonians, Paul set holiness and sexual immorality in contrast to one another (1 Thess. 4:3–8). The Christian is to shun sexual immorality and pursue holiness. In that pursuit, of which sexual conduct is an integral element, the Christian has not been left to his or her own resources. It is God himself who gives the enabling gift of holiness to his people.

In 1 Cor. 7:7, Paul also speaks of the gift of God with regard to human sexuality. The apostle's language is somewhat different from that of the Synoptic authors. The Synoptists do, however, bring a theological perspective to bear on human sexuality. The Gospel story of the debate over the legitimacy of divorce puts human sexuality within the perspective of God's creative will. "'In the image of God' and 'male and female'" are, says Willem Beuken, "modalities of one single act of creation."[3] Paul also shares this biblical vision. Rather than cite the words of one of the great philosophers as his Hellenistic readers might have expected him to do, Paul introduces into his parenesis on human sexuality (1 Cor 6:16) the words of the book of Genesis, "the two shall be one flesh."

Paul writes of a call to holiness; the Synoptists incorporate "You shall not commit adultery" into the invitation to discipleship and cite the fulfillment of the commandment as a condition for entrance into eternal life (Matt. 19:18; Mark 10:19; Luke 18:20). Paul speaks of a charism (1 Cor. 7:7) and the gift of the Spirit of holiness (1 Thess. 4:8).

In an oblique, yet very real way, Matthew writes of the gift that is given to those who are called to be married and of the gift that is given to those who are called to remain unmarried for the sake of the kingdom (Matt. 19:10–12).

The gift of human sexuality is God's way for humans to exist in the world. The call to holiness is a call to which the Christian responds not as an individual but as a member of God's holy people. Human sexuality is not an isolable gift; it has a relational dimension that is clearly attested in the New Testament scriptures. How the Christian lives out his or her sexual existence is not only a matter of sexual ethics; it is also a matter of Christian morality. The social dimension of human sexuality to which the New Testament scriptures attest is somewhat complex. The sexual relationship can be sanctifying or defiling. How Christians live their sexual lives distinguishes them from those who do not share their faith-filled anthropology. The sexual behavior of Christians also influences the way in which outsiders regard them (cf. 1 Cor. 7:16; 1 Tim. 5:14; 1 Pet. 3:1–2). Accordingly, the Christian community has some responsibility for the sexual conduct of its members (1 Cor. 5:1–13). Sexual immorality is to be banished from its midst.

The Christian community may not be able to do much to reform the sexual mores of outsiders (1 Cor. 5:10), but it can and should do something about the sexual standards that are to be maintained by members of the community. The Christian community may have to tolerate the sexual immorality of those outside the community; it cannot abide sexual immorality within the community. Apart perhaps from 1 Timothy and Titus, none of the books in the New Testament has the literary genre of a legislative text. The New Testament contains nothing similar to the Holiness Code of Leviticus with its precise rules for sexual behavior.

Paul's first letter to the Corinthians, which illustrates for those neophyte Christians the demands of the call to holiness, tells them to shun sexual immorality and offers multiple examples of how that is to be done. In a pastorally oriented treatment of human sexuality (1 Corinthians 5–7), the apostle Paul has relatively little to say about possible sanctions for sexual immorality. Three motifs are, however, cited in passing. The first is the norm of sexual morality in the outside world. Christians must not tolerate forms of sexual behavior that even non-Christians find abhorrent (1 Cor. 5:1). A second notion is that the Christian community must expel those whose sexual conduct is egregiously immoral (1 Cor. 5:4–13). A third idea is that sexually immoral persons will not inherit the kingdom of God (1 Cor. 6:9–10).

The inheritance of the kingdom of God is an eschatological image. The image projects the idea that sexual misconduct has eschatological consequences. The series of graphic images found in the sayings of Mark 9:42–48 sharply contrast entrance into life[4] and the kingdom of God with the hellfires of Gehenna (Matt. 18:6–9; Jude 7). Pedophiles, masturbators, adulterers, and those who debase women will not enter the kingdom. The apostle Paul and the evangelist Mark use the motif of God's ruling as king to urge their readers to avoid sexual misconduct. God's rule does not abide sexual misconduct. In 1 Cor. 5:13 Paul uses the motif of God as judge to reinforce his argument. In Rom. 1:26–28 the apostle exploits that motif to the full[5] in a graphic portrayal of sexual misconduct as the consequence of human rejection of God's rule.

God is judge and God will judge sexual misconduct. The author of the Epistle of James reminds us that mercy triumphs over judgment (Jas. 2:13). Although inserted late into the New Testament, the story of the woman caught in adultery (John 7:53–8:11) serves as a dramatic reminder that even the prototype of sexual sin is forgivable.

The New Testament Christian learned something about sexual ethics from those who were not Christian. Matthew used rabbinic lore to illustrate what the prohibition of adultery was to mean for the members of a Jewish Christian community. Writing for Gentiles, Paul and other New Testament authors used catalogues of vices to illustrate inappropriate sexual behavior. Catalogues of virtues, on the other hand, were used to exemplify an acceptable attitude toward human sexuality. The Christian's call to holiness and the demand that the Christian live in right relationship with God and with others bring a Christian nuance to New Testament sexual ethics.

Even the way one speaks with regard to sexuality, the author of the Epistle to the Ephesians reminded his readers, must be examined when one considers how a member of the church is to live. Elements of the classic household code were used to show that with regard to their sexual lives Christians, and especially Christian leaders, were expected to measure up to accepted standards of sexual conduct. Christian leaders are expected to be a model in that regard (Titus 2:6–7). Indeed, how the Christian is to live as a sexual being in the world is something that must be passed on from one generation to the next (Titus 2:3–5).

FOOD FOR THOUGHT

As the contemporary reader of the New Testament looks at what the New Testament authors have said about human sexuality and attempts to gather some insight for a comprehensive Christian and human sexual ethics, he or she must bring a responsibly critical mind to bear on the interpretation of the ancient texts.

1. First of all the reader must remember that the texts were written in Greek. Any and every translation of the text is an interpretation. Translation is an attempt, more or less successful, to interpret the ancient text. The modern translation will never be perfectly synonymous with the ancient text. At best, it is anachronistic to read into the ancient text the meaning of the words found in a modern translation.

2. Several of the key New Testament terms that pertain to sexuality are difficult to translate. Among these are *porneia* ("sexual immorality"), *koitai* ("debauchery"), *malakoi* ("male prostitutes"), *arsenokoitai* ("sodomites"), and *eutrapelia* ("vulgar talk"). "Sexual immorality" is a term with a wide range of connotations. "Debauchery," "male prostitutes," "sodomites," and "vulgar talk" are terms that are used so infrequently that it is virtually impossible to determine their precise connotation. That they appear in lists of vices where the sheer multiplication of vices—and not the distinction of one vice from another—is the most striking feature makes it all the more difficult to determine what Paul and his disciple had in mind when they used these particular terms.

3. The New Testament is not a homogeneous book. Within its several books is to be found material with different literary genres. All of what the New Testament has to say about sexual ethics must be interpreted with full attention paid to the particular literary genre of the individual texts. Catechetical exposition is one genre. The vice list is another. Each has its own purpose.

4. Each of the New Testament books was written at a particular time and in a particular place. Each was written to respond to the needs of a local church. What the New Testament authors wrote with regard to human sexuality is a response to a particular situation. In his first letter to the Corinthians, Paul has specifically mentioned two situations with which the community had to deal (1 Cor. 5:1; 7:1). That community and others had to cope with various situations. Among them were the issues of whether and to what extent Jewish sexual

mores were to be imposed upon Gentile Christians. Another was the need of the church to be accepted in the world. All of the New Testament texts must be understood within their proper historical contexts.

5. Men of their own times and culture, the New Testament authors were not graced with the insights into human sexuality provided by modern science. Sexual orientation is a notion with which the ancient authors were unfamiliar. The Stoics had their idea of nature and of activity that was contrary to nature. Jewish tradition had the key notion of the God who had created everything, including men and women. In its development of norms of conduct, Jewish tradition capitalized on the distinctiveness of what God had created. The distinction between clean and unclean animals and many of Judaism's dietary laws were tributary to this idea of separation. With regard to sexuality, Jewish tradition was well aware of the bodily distinction between male and female. Its moral code focused on acts. The multiple insights into the complexities of the reality of human sexuality that have been provided by twentieth-century science were not available to first-century Christians, their Stoic contemporaries and their Jewish forebears.

6. Finally, the sage reader of the New Testament must remember that the texts provide a witness to the sexual ethics and expectations with regard to human sexuality of their several authors. They do not offer a comprehensive and systematic sexual ethics. How ethicists deal with this witness and how the churches incorporate it into their teaching are complex matters with which ethicists and churches alike must deal in the way that is appropriate to their own mission.

Foundations of a New Testament Sexual Ethics

A Christian sexual ethics that is based on the texts of the New Testament must incorporate the catechetical and parenetic witness of these early Christian texts. It must also adequately consider why the New Testament authors wrote as they did about human sexuality. Sexual ethics based on the New Testament should not consist of a series of texts pulled out of and away from their biblical context. Beyond the texts is the inspired context to which they belong. The context includes many elements that should be integrated into a New Testament-based sexual ethics. Among these many elements are three that deserve particular mention. The full-length monograph that each of them deserves is precluded by the scope of the present study but they must be at least cited since they are integral to an understanding of the sexual ethics of the New Testament.

One can begin with Paul's notion of embodied human existence. This key element of Pauline anthropology is foundational for his understanding of the Christian's attitude toward human sexuality. Human beings do not have bodies; human beings are embodied. Embodied existence is the human way of being in the world. Humans have been created with embodied existence. Embodied existence with gender difference is God's creative plan for humankind. As embodied existence humans relate to and are in solidarity with one another. Embodied humans are not only capable of the "two in one flesh" of which the biblical tradition speaks; they are also members of the body of Christ. Embodied humans have a transcendental destiny summed up in the creedal notion of the resurrection of the body. Embodied humans are given the gift of the Spirit. This powerful and sanctifying Spirit enables Christians, called to holiness, to be the instruments of God in building up the body of Christ.

One cannot immediately induce from Paul's notion of embodied human existence a set of rules for sexual conduct, nor should one attempt to do so. Paul's vision of embodied existence does, however, provide the reader with a foundational element of Christian anthropology within which human sexuality cannot be separated from the human person. Human sexual responsibility cannot be a matter of individualized ethics, since humans are created as sexual beings as part of the corporate body. Human sexuality cannot be separated from the call to holiness since it is as sexual beings that men and women are one in Christ.

A second element of anthropology that must be incorporated into a New Testament sexual ethics is its understanding of women. The baptismal formula of Gal. 3:28, with its echo of Gen. 1:27, "There is no longer male and female;[6] for all of you are one in Christ Jesus," rejects any superiority of male over female. Paul's extensive treatment of human sexuality in 1 Corinthians 5-7, especially in chapter 7, constantly echoes the theme that with regard to human sexuality men and women have similar rights and responsibilities. That women are not to be treated by men as sexual objects is echoed in such traditions as the Markan saying on divorce (Mark 10:11), the catechetical saying on looking at women with desire (Matt. 5:28), and Paul's exhortation on marriage in 1 Thess. 4:4–6.

The New Testament texts were written for Christians living in a patriarchal society. Some of the later texts show evidence of an accommodation to that patriarchal society. Elements of the classic household code urging the social subordination of women to their husbands are echoed in Ephesians, Colossians, 1 Timothy, and 1 Peter. 1 Timothy 2:15 draws attention to the unique social role accorded to women because of their gender. These texts reflect the efforts of the churches to accommodate a Christian vision of woman to a world in which the church must necessarily live. The vision is not fully realized because the kingdom has not yet fully come. In some respects the baptismal formula of Gal. 3:28 is a promise of things yet to come. Its echo remains as a challenge to the Christian. The vision is that there is no longer Jew or Greek, no longer slave or free, no longer male and female. As long as ethnic, social, and gender discrimination and exploitation continues to exist, there is sin in the world and the kingdom has not yet fully come.

A final element in an adequate New Testament sexual ethics must certainly be the love command. On the two-pronged law of love, says Matthew, "hang all the law and the prophets" (Matt. 22:40). Dependent on the law of love are not only the prescriptions of the Torah but also Matthew's catechesis on adultery. It is the law of love that motivates the Christian to reject pederasty, adultery, masturbation, divorce, and the reduction of woman to being an object of sexual desire.

The New Testament's Johannine tradition has relatively little to say about human sexuality.[7] Its new commandment, however, says it all. The Johannine Jesus left a legacy for his disciples. "I give you a new commandment," he said, "that you love one another. Just as I have loved you, you also should love one another. By this everyone will know that you are my disciples, if you have love for one another" (John 13:34–35; cf. 15:12; 2 John 5). This is no romantic vision of love; nor is it a vision of a love that possesses the object of one's love. It is, if one can borrow a page from the Synoptics (see Matt. 22:39; Mark 12:31; Luke 10:27), a vision of a love that loves the other as the self and of a love that has the sacrificial love of Jesus as its sole model.

In the New Testament, love (*agapē*) is not merely an ethical command; nor is it merely an element of parenesis. Love is also a gift. "God's love," writes Paul, "has been poured into our hearts through the Holy Spirit that has been given to us" (Rom. 5:5). In the very depths of their being, Christians have become the instruments of God's love through the powerful gift of the Spirit of holiness. With this as his vision, it is little wonder that the apostle Paul concluded his first exhortation on sexual ethics (1 Thess. 4:3–8), the oldest such exhortation in the New Testament, with a reminder that Christians have been called to holiness and that they have been given the empowering gift of the Spirit of holiness. It is this Spirit that enables a Christian to live as a human being who is both sexual and saintly.

NOTES

1. Cf. Wolfgang Stegeman, "Paul and the Sexual Morality of His World," *BTB* 23 (1993): 161–66.

2. See also 1 Cor. 7:8–9, where a similar call is addressed to widowers and widows along with a cautious statement of sexual realism.

3. Willem A. M. Beuken, "The Human Person in the Vision of Genesis 1-2: A Synthesis of Contemporary Insights," *LS* 24 (1999): 3–20, esp. 9.

4. The story of the "rich young man" cites the avoidance of adultery as a condition for entrance into eternal life. See Matt. 19:16–19; Mark 10:17–19; Luke 18:18–20.

5. Echoes of the motif of God as judge of human sexual behavior are found in 1 Cor. 5:5; Heb. 13:4; Jas. 2:8–13; Jude 7, 14–16.

6. The use of the connective "and" (*kai*) rather than the disjunctive "or" (*oute*) between male and female harks back to the Genesis text.

7. See above, pp. 1–10, 177–79.

Index

Names

Achtemeier, Paul J., 180n. 14
Aland, Kurt, 16n. 29
Aletti, Jean-Noël, 162n. 3

Balz, Horst, 175, 180n. 16, 182n. 35
Bassler, Jouette M., 164nn. 33, 37
Bauernfeind, Otto, 97n. 39
Baumgärtel, Friedrich, 145n. 37
Becker, J. Christiaan, 52–53, 60n. 45
Becker, Ulrich, 16n. 29, 17n. 35
Betlyon, John W., 21n. 62
Beuken, Willem A. M., 194n. 3
Beyer, Klaus, 70n. 4
Blidstein, Gerald, 59n. 38
Botha, J. Eugene, 21n. 64
Boyarin, Daniel, 98n. 58
Brenner, Athalya, 98n. 58
Brooks, Roger, 59n. 36
Brooten, Bernadette J., 146n. 47
Brown, Raymond E., 16n. 24, 95n. 24, 99n. 79, 146n. 48
Bultmann, Rudolf, 145n. 37
Burchard, Christoph, 56n. 6
Burge, Gary M., 16n. 29

Cameron, Ron, 18n. 41
Caragounis, Chrys, 126n. 27
Clements, Ronald E., 72n. 18
Collins, Adela Yarbro, 125n. 5
Collins, R. F., 19n. 52, 21n. 66, 38nn. 2, 12; 39nn. 25–28; 40nn. 33–35, 38, 42; 41n. 44; 56nn. 2, 3; 57nn. 15, 17, 18; 58nn. 21, 24; 59n. 31; 60nn. 42, 43; 61n. 60, 72n. 18, 95n. 24, 96nn. 26, 32; 106nn. 1, 2;

107n. 4, 108nn. 12, 15; 125n. 8, 127n. 39, 162n. 8, 163nn. 14, 21; 164nn. 28, 35; 179n. 1, 181n. 18
Colombo, G., 17n. 29
Conzelmann, Hans, 180nn. 6, 11

Day, John, 143n. 10
Deidun, T. J., 107n. 5
Delobel, Joël, 20nn. 55, 58
Deming, Will, 70n. 5, 71n. 8, 127n. 42
Derrett, J. D. M., 19n. 49, 71n. 13
DeYoung, James B., 144n. 30
Dibelius, Martin, 61nn. 58, 62
Dornier, Pierre, 165n. 42
Dunn, James D. G., 143n. 14, 162n. 3
Dupont, Jacques, 56n. 5

Ehrman, Bart D., 18nn. 40, 44
Ellis, E. Earle, 19n. 49, 20n. 55
Epstein, Louis M., 71n. 10
Evans, C. F., 20n. 54

Fee, Gordon D., 165n. 43
Fitzmyer, Joseph A., 19n. 54, 60n. 47, 96n. 33, 146n. 43, 180nn. 6, 9, 11

Goldstein, Horst, 97n. 39, 182n. 39
Gordis, Robert, 15n. 14
Gordon, Cyrus H., 15n. 14
Gourgues, Michel, 17n. 35
Greenberg, Moshe, 58n. 27, 59nn. 32, 37; 60n. 41
Grundmann, Walter, 20n. 55
Gundry, Robert H., 70n. 5, 72n. 20

Haenchen, Ernst, 21n. 65, 180n. 11

Hagner, Donald A., 56n. 5, 57nn. 9, 13;
Harrington, Daniel J., 57n. 8
Hauck, Frederick, 97n. 38
Hays, Richard B., 144n. 22, 146n. 48
Healey, Joseph P., 143n. 10
Heil, John P., 17n. 29
Holtz, Gottfried, 165n. 42
Hultgren, Arland J., 38n. 3

Jensen, Joseph, 96n. 34
Jeremias, Joachim, 19n. 49
Jewett, Robert, 145n. 37
Johnson, Luke Timothy, 60n. 51, 61n. 62, 157; 164nn. 30, 36; 165n. 41, 180n. 7

Kadosh, David, 59n. 37
Kamlah, Erhard, 95n. 20
Kelly, J. N. D., 180n. 15
Kingsbury, Jack Dean, 18n. 46
Knight, George W., III, 164n. 32, 165nn. 38, 43
Koester, Helmut, 145n. 32
Kramer, Johannes, 16n. 26
Krebber, Bärbel, 16n. 26
Kroll, Wilhelm, 144n. 23

Lazure, Noël, 38n. 1
Leaney, A. R. C., 19n. 52
Lee, D. A., 21n. 67
Licht, Hans, 144n. 23
Lincoln, Andrew T., 162n. 2, 163n. 16
Lindars, Barnabas, 38n. 15
Luz, Ulrich, 56n. 5, 57n. 9

Malick, David E., 98n. 59
Malina, Bruce, 71n. 8, 96n. 34
Marshall, I. Howard, 19n. 49
Martin, Dale, 89, 99n. 67, 125nn. 5, 13

195

Ancient Sources